WITHD

UTSA

D1022114

Congress

AND THE

Environment

Edited by
RICHARD A. COOLEY
GEOFFREY WANDESFORDE-SMITH

Seattle and London
UNIVERSITY OF WASHINGTON PRESS

Copyright © 1970 by the University of Washington Press
Second printing, 1970
Third printing, 1971
Library of Congress Catalog Card Number 76–103295
Printed in the United States of America

LIBRARY
University of Texas
At San Antonio

Acknowledgments

Since the idea of this book was first aired, we have had the generous support of the individual contributors. The value of the book stems principally from the quality of their essays, and it has been our pleasure to edit the work of a very thoughtful and patient group of people. We are especially grateful to Professor Grant McConnell of the University of California at Santa Cruz and to Professor Lynton K. Caldwell of Indiana University, who agreed to provide, respectively, the prologue and the epilogue. Both these men visited the University of Washington during the time this book was in its formative stages and the challenge of their thinking is reflected in the pages that follow. We are indebted to several typists and should like to thank particularly Mrs. Susan Barwell and Miss Marie Kvarnberg of the Department of Geography at the University of Washington, and the secretarial staff of the Institute of Social, Economic, and Government Research at the University of Alaska. We gratefully acknowledge the helpful criticisms of numerous people in government and academic circles who have assisted the individual contributors. We should like to thank also professors Robert Warren and John Sherman for their unfailing generosity in a number of ways.

It is our belief that this book provides a necessary and timely perspective on public policy issues concerning the American environment. We think that it will be of interest and value to a wide variety of readers in government, the universities, and the general public. The chapters of the book point repeatedly to serious weaknesses in the capacity of government, and particularly the United States Congress, to respond to environmental problems now facing the nation. In a sense the prognosis offered by the book as a whole is depressing: the economic and political forces pressing for further degradation of the environment seem to be unshakeably entrenched. Nevertheless, a clearer understanding of the nature of the issues and of the opposing forces is a prerequisite for a more sane and balanced discussion of environmental policies that are in the public interest.

RICHARD A. COOLEY
GEOFFREY WANDESFORDE-SMITH

College, Alaska
August, 1969

Contents

FIGURES

Introduction: Politics, Technology, and the Environment

RICHARD A. COOLEY

The conservation challenge of today is essentially one of quality. Technology holds the key to survival for years to come, if we are to believe the scientists. But what kind of survival? Glassed-in-air-conditioned boxes with elbow-to-elbow barbeque pits and wall-to-wall frustrations hardly add up to quality, even though the pits are replete with beef steaks and the arm-chair table sports a box of chocolate creams.[1]

THESE words from former Secretary of the Interior Stewart Udall raise one of the major issues of public policy facing this nation in the last third of the twentieth century. Despite the high and continuously increasing levels of material affluence which have made this nation and its cornucopian, consumer-oriented economy the envy of most of the rest of the world, there has been a steady deterioration in the quality of the human environment. The problem stems in large measure from man's increasing mastery of science and technology which has given him unprecedented powers to alter and manipulate the biophysical environment. While this has produced much that is good in modern society, it has also brought unanticipated consequences in the form of smog, malodorous rivers, noise, atomic radiation, filthy streets, littered highways, junkyards full of rusty auto bodies, loss of

RICHARD A. COOLEY is associate professor of geography at the University of Washington. He has been director of the Alaska Natural Resources Center in Juneau and has published articles and books on conservation issues, including *Politics and Conservation: The Decline of the Alaska Salmon* and *Alaska: A Challenge in Conservation*. He is currently working on a study of the international management of polar bear.

[1] U.S., Department of the Interior, *Conservation Yearbook No. 2* (Washington, D.C.: Government Printing Office, 1966), p. 4.

recreational opportunities, landscapes scarred by freeways and open-pit mines, urban and rural blight, deterioration of fish and wildlife populations, and a myriad other affronts to the quality of life. A continent that was once virgin and beautiful has been relentlessly and in too many cases recklessly degraded.

This man-made pollution is bad enough in itself, but it reflects something even worse: a dangerous illusion that technological man can build bigger and better industrial societies with little regard for the long-term cumulative impact of his actions upon the natural environment. As Dr. Roger Revelle of Harvard University recently put it, "Man is using his dominance of the earth to produce the most far-reaching, sudden and drastic upset of natural conditions the world has ever seen." [2] Adds Dr. Barry Commoner in his book, *Science and Survival*, "Like the sorcerer's apprentice, we are acting on dangerously incomplete knowledge. We are, in effect, conducting a huge experiment on ourselves." [3] That the problem does not respect political boundaries is attested to by the recent remarks of the eminent Soviet physicist, Dr. Andrei Sokharov, who writes of the "senseless despoliation of the Soviet Union caused by bureaucratic and egotistical interests and sometimes simply by questions of bureaucratic prestige." He concludes:

> The problem of geohygiene [earth hygiene] is highly complex and closely tied to economic and social problems. This problem cannot therefore be solved on a national or local basis. The salvation of our environment requires that we overcome our divisions and the pressure of temporary local interests. Otherwise, the Soviet Union will poison the United States with its wastes, and vice versa.[4]

I

There is nothing new about apprehensions and warnings of possible environmental disaster. Paul B. Sear's *Deserts on the March*, William Vogt's *Road to Survival*, Fairfield Osborn's *Limits of the Earth*, Samuel Ordway's *Resources and the American Dream*, and Rachel Car-

---

[2] U.S., Congress, Senate, Committee on Interior and Insular Affairs, *Hearings, Ecological Research and Surveys*, 89th Cong., 2d sess., 1966, p. 142. Quoted in *A Report on Environmental Issues*, Conservation Foundation Letter, February 23, 1968, p. 2.

[3] Barry Commoner, *Science and Survival* (New York: Viking Press, 1963), p. 67.

[4] *New York Times*, July 22, 1968, pp. 14–16.

son's *Silent Spring* are representative of a large number of books published in the last few decades aimed at arousing the concern of thoughtful people—a literature of protest that actually reaches back to more than a century ago when George Perkins Marsh expounded his influential thesis about how man was abusing his powers to alter nature in his classic work, *Man and Nature: or, Physical Geography as Modified by Human Action.* Most of these were denigrated as polemical "scare books" from the pens of unduly sensitive or naïve authors, for few were inclined, scholars included, to see these threats as anything to be taken very seriously. Technology and continued economic growth would surely solve these problems.

What *is* new, however, is that around the beginning of the 1960's complacency started to give way to awareness. The metamorphosis has been rapid, and as the evidence of environmental deterioration has compounded, complacency has become the hallmark of only those few who cannot comprehend the obvious. This has been reflected in the tremendous outpouring of books, magazine and newspaper articles, television specials, and other pronouncements through the mass media raising the question of why ugliness, disorder, and a mutilated environment must necessarily be the price of material progress. Belatedly, but no less significantly, natural scientists, economists, political scientists, lawyers, psychologists, geographers, urban planners, and other scholars and professionals for the first time have begun to dig into the fundamental problems of man's critical relations to his environment in the twentieth century; and this has resulted in a plethora of scholarly publications almost as great in volume as the popular literature on the subject.[5]

The nation's scientific community has demonstrated its genuine concern. At the 1968 annual meeting of the prestigious American Association for the Advancement of Science, a series of heavily attended symposia were devoted to vigorous discussions of unanticipated environmental hazards resulting from technological intrusions, and to the global effects of environmental pollution. The association's board of directors also created a permanent Committee on Environmental Alterations to conduct a continuous review and evaluation of the intrusions man makes into the environment on which life depends.

[5] A good discussion of recent literature can be found in Ian Burton, "The Quality of the Environment: A Review," *Geographical Review,* LVIII (July, 1968), 472–81.

The board issued the following statement in announcing establishment of the new environmental committee:

> With dams, pesticides, bulldozers, cities, chemical fertilizers, noise, defoliants, power plants, garbage dumps, automobiles, huge construction projects, and other means, man changes the land, the waters, and the atmosphere, in ways he intends and often in ways he does not intend. Widespread realization that man's intrusion into the environment sometimes brings results that are clearly undesirable and often bring results that are not understood has led a number of recent committees, commissions, and planning groups to consider the problems of improving the quality of life and of protecting our planet from the ravages of man. It is not because no other group is actively studying these problems that the Board of Directors decided to create the new AAAS committee, but rather because the problems are of such widespread importance that many groups *must* be involved.[6]

In the political sphere this awakening in the 1960's has given birth to what has become known as "the new conservation." Some have termed it "the third wave" of a conservation movement which first took root in the mid-nineteenth century and was given fresh impetus and new goals at the beginning of the twentieth century under the leadership of President Theodore Roosevelt. But if the new conservation is related historically to these earlier waves, it is by no means a replica. The familiar theme of the old conservation was scarcity, the fear of running out of basic natural resources which were the prime ingredients for economic growth. But by the 1960's, the idea of protecting the environment for its nonmaterial values began to challenge this utilitarian view as the central purpose of conservation policy. In large measure, this shift in emphasis came about because continuing improvements in technology had eased the fears of resource exhaustion, even among the most obdurate economists. At the same time, Americans were beginning to realize that an environment conducive to material survival—even affluence—was not enough.[7] As President Johnson expressed it in his historic message to Congress on natural beauty in 1965, in which he called for massive public efforts to rescue the cities and the countryside from blight:

[6] Editorial by Dael Wolfe, "The Only Earth We Have," *Science*, CLXIX (January 12, 1968), 155.

[7] Roderick Nash, *The American Environment: Readings in the History of Conservation* (Reading, Mass.: Addison-Wesley Publishing Company, 1968), contains excellent material on the history of the conservation movement.

Our conservation must not be just the classic conservation of protection and development, but a creative conservation of restoration and innovation. Its concern is not with nature alone, but with the total relation between man and the world around him. Its object is not just man's welfare but the dignity of his spirit.[8]

Like questions of poverty and civil rights, questions of environmental quality raise perplexing ethical and moral issues which cut deep at the core of existing economic and political institutions, and it is this more than anything else that distinguishes the old from the new conservation.

II

It is not possible to pinpoint when the new conservation began to become a major political force. Neither President Truman nor President Eisenhower evinced much interest in environmental issues, though during the 1950's a movement began to develop in Congress for wilderness preservation, water pollution control, the protection of the integrity of the National Park System, and the effort to save public access to shorelines on the oceans and the Great Lakes. In 1958, Congress also created the Outdoor Recreation Resources Review Commission, which took a hard look at America's outdoor recreation needs. However, presidential initiative on environmental policy did not become evident until the administration of John F. Kennedy. In May, 1962, President Kennedy called a White House Conference on Conservation in which over five hundred delegates and observers from across the country came to Washington, D.C., to discuss the future of American conservation policy. The conference heard and discussed the thoughts of the President and his cabinet, members of Congress, and the governors of states. The major concern was not natural resource management in the older sense of wise and efficient use but the deteriorating quality of the environment and the necessity to find means to prevent the continuing foreclosure of opportunities for choice and variety in the environments of the future.

President Kennedy's influence over Congress proved to be weak and only a few major pieces of conservation legislation were enacted prior to his assassination; but he accomplished much in drawing public

[8] "The White House Message on Natural Beauty to the Congress of the United States, February 8, 1965" (mimeographed release of the text of the message), p. 1.

attention to the changing nature of environmental issues and in laying the groundwork for future governmental action. His appointment of Stewart L. Udall as Secretary of the Interior in 1961 was another significant factor in stimulating the new conservation. Secretary Udall chose to direct the Department of the Interior not as a loose federation of bureaus whose primary purpose was to promote resource development in the West, but as an arm of government that should encompass the environmental needs of all the nation. A glance through the series of Conservation Yearbooks which replaced the staid annual reports of the department gives ample evidence of the change. Their titles alone are indicative: *The Quest for Quality; The Population Challenge—What It Means to America; The Third Wave—America's New Conservation; Man—An Endangered Species?* The continuity of Udall's leadership throughout the Johnson administration was a significant factor in the emergence of environmental quality as a major public policy issue in the United States.

Political action to implement the concepts of the new conservation rose to a peak in the Johnson administration, with both Congress and the executive branch strongly committed to change. Lyndon Johnson knew a political issue when he saw one. As the political scientist Lynton K. Caldwell analyzed it:

His Great Society address on May 22, 1964, spoke directly to the values of the post World War II generation that would shortly determine the direction of American politics. His espousal of natural beauty and environmental quality issues surprised and gratified conservationists who had not looked for this type of commitment from a professional politician from western Texas. The depth of the Johnson commitment was open to question. But regardless of the president's sincerity, the fact that he had publicly identified himself with the quality of the environment issue strengthened its position in American life. It added status and dignity to the efforts of those who sought to better the public environment and who had characteristically been dismissed by practical politicians as ineffectual nature lovers and utopians.[9]

Shortly after his inauguration, President Johnson called for a White House Conference on Natural Beauty to produce new ideas and

[9] Lynton K. Caldwell, "Natural Beauty—and the Politics of Environmental Quality" (unpublished manuscript), 1966, p. 17. This contains an excellent analysis of the political developments during the last two decades. Professor Caldwell's numerous papers on environmental administration have also been drawn upon. See the Bibliography for specific citations.

approaches for enhancing the American environment. The conference, held in the spring of 1965, stimulated great new efforts by public agencies and private organizations in a coordinated attack on some of the more obvious and immediate problems of environmental deterioration.

In the ensuing years, Congress considered and passed a record volume of conservation legislation. Early in the decade Congress established a new Bureau of Outdoor Recreation, and enacted the Land and Water Conservation Fund Act in an attempt to provide revenues to meet the nation's growing recreation demands. In rapid succession came the Wilderness Act; the Open Space and Green Span programs; the Federal Water Project Recreation Act; the Water Resources Research Act; the Water Resources Planning Act; the Solid Waste Disposal Act; the enactment of several measures to control air, water, and oil pollution; the establishment of the Public Land Review Commission; far-reaching fish and wildlife conservation measures; the Multiple Use Sustained Yield Act; measures to authorize studies and regulation of pesticide use; the Highway Beautification Act; to name only a few of the more important ones. Congress also acted to set aside and preserve for future generations portions of land, mountains, beaches, and lakes in unprecedented amounts. In 1961, for example, there was only one national seashore but by 1968 five more had been created. A system of national lakeshores was started, and the nation acquired its first six national recreation areas between 1964 and 1968. Since 1958, Congress has also established four national monuments, five national memorials, four national historic parks, and thirteen national historic sites. For two years in a row in the late 1960's, Congress actually set aside more land for parks, refuges, and recreational uses than were consumed by asphalt, cement, and bulldozers.[10]

Late in 1968, in the last few weeks of the Ninetieth Congress, additional historic legislation was approved aimed at checking environmental deterioration. Congress strengthened the Land and Water Conservation Fund, created the Redwoods and North Cascades national parks, established a National Wild and Scenic Rivers System and a National Trails System, added several areas to the Wilderness

[10] Senator Henry M. Jackson, "Environmental Quality—Progress and Prospect," Address to the National Council of State Garden Clubs, Biloxi, Mississippi, April 3, 1968 (mimeograph release).

System, authorized an inventory and study of the nation's estuaries, created a National Water Commission to review the nation's water resource problems, and passed the first Federal legislation on noise pollution. These and other measures came in response to a steadily growing public concern about the quality of the environment.

III

There is no question that Congress has responded admirably in the last few years, and senators and representatives have been quick to impress upon their constituents the volume of legislation that has been passed. But the mere volume of legislation leaves open the question of whether the quality of the congressional response is in keeping with the nature, magnitude, and complexity of environmental issues facing the nation. Just how successful have these past efforts been? Has Congress really come to grips with the ethical questions raised by the modern conservation movement? Are recent acts of Congress likely to create conditions which will enable the people of the United States to enrich the quality of their lives? Have policies been formulated that will direct science and technology toward a future wherein man will find satisfaction in sharing life rather than in destroying it? If the recent achievements of Congress are the best that Congress can produce, is the best good enough?

And what about the future? There is some indication that the close of the Ninetieth Congress late in 1968 may mark the end of this remarkable period in the history of conservation politics in the United States. Some members of Congress, as well as of the new Republican administration, have suggested that we are reaching the end of a long wave of significant and highly visible progress, and that the widely hailed "environmental crisis" has, in a certain sense, passed the peak of critical national interest and public concern. This theme was taken up by the new Secretary of the Interior when testifying before the Senate Interior and Insular Affairs Committee in connection with his confirmation hearing early in 1969. He suggested that in the future the Federal government should be occupied increasingly with reviewing, amending, and making adjustments in existing environmental programs. Said Mr. Hickel:

Now I believe it should be the duty and responsibility of the new Secretary of the Interior to continue these programs established by Congress. I believe we should devote a period of time to the consolidation of the gains that have been made and to a reassessment of our long range objectives.[11]

It appears from this and other recent pronouncements from the new administration that the emphasis may be shifting from enlarging the role of the Federal government in enhancing and protecting environmental quality to "making existing programs work." There is the suggestion here that in the foreseeable future environmental issues will lack the drama and conflict over basic principles evident in the fight to preserve the Redwoods, the North Cascades, or the Grand Canyon; that the urgent environmental needs have been met and the crisis has passed.

But there are some haunting doubts and apprehensions. Can the United States afford to pause in its efforts to stem the tide of environmental deterioration, a tide that according to some authorities is incompletely understood but may threaten the very existence of man on this planet? Does the volume of recent environmental legislation provide the kind of sound basis for future public policy which Congress and the administration need now only review and refine? Is the great American middle class which President Nixon rightly regards as his basic constituency now properly pacified?

IV

These questions were raised recently in a graduate seminar held in the Department of Geography at the University of Washington. The seminar was based on the realization that it is much easier to raise questions in the detached atmosphere of a university than it is to provide answers in the American political system. It was based also on the assumption that much could be learned from an attempt to relate the two worlds of academic reflection and political action. Drawing upon the literature from a wide variety of academic disciplines, the participants in the seminar attempted to reach a clear understanding of the public policy issues inherent in the effort to improve the quality of the environment. Simultaneously, each seminar participant undertook a case study of a recent piece of legislation to determine how Congress has handled a particular environmental problem. The participants came from a variety of academic backgrounds: political sci-

[11] U.S., Congress, Senate, Committee on Interior and Insular Affairs, *Hearings, Interior Nomination*, 91st Cong., 1st sess., 1969, p. 7.

ence, geography, economics, public administration, urban planning, psychology, and the natural sciences. Each case study was organized around five general questions. What was the environmental problem that gave rise to the need for governmental action? How did legislation come to be introduced in Congress and what did it propose to do? How was the legislation influenced and modified as it moved through the various steps of the congressional decision-making process? What are the strengths and weaknesses of the final legislative product? And finally, what can be said in a broader sense about the ability of Congress to respond to environmental issues?

A number of the case studies prepared for the seminar were selected for inclusion in this book. Each was chosen to illustrate a particular environmental issue which is likely to present Congress with a challenge for many years to come. How are the costs of a quality environment to be met and how are these costs to be distributed? How can intangible aesthetic values be weighed against tangible dollar values? What adjustments may be needed in the American federal system to realize a closer relationship between the jurisdictions of existing governmental units and the areal scale of environmental problems? What can be done to eliminate or control conflicts among Federal departments and agencies with responsibility for programs affecting the environment? To what extent must private property rights be constrained for the good of society as a whole? Can institutional arrangements be devised to handle international conservation issues? Each essay attempts to plumb the depths of a recent political experience relevant to these and other questions, and to examine the implications for Congress.

A recent editorial in *Science* magazine admonished the American university for not paying more attention to balancing its responsibilities to society. There are those among the public at large, the editorial pointed out, who resent the fact that the university is a haven for dissent, for criticism, for the free examination of assumptions and practices, and they imagine the chief role of the university should be to endorse the *status quo*. On the other hand, there are some within the university community who seem to want to cut all ties with the rest of society and to persuade students to choose the life of detachment and dissent. They do not like the way society is run, but they are not inclined to prepare young people to run it better; and they communicate to their students a moral snobbism toward those who live with the ethical dilemmas of responsible action. The editorial concluded:

Our society must have the wisdom to reflect *and* the fortitude to act. It must provide the creative soil for new ideas *and* the skill and patience and the hardihood to put those ideas into action. . . . And no institution in our society can do more to keep that interaction vital and productive than the university. . . .[12]

The seminar that resulted in these papers was one attempt to meet this situation; to get as close as possible to the ethical dilemmas of responsible political action without sacrificing legitimate academic criticism. It is not expected that this book will represent the last word on the subject of Congress and the environment. It does, however, provide a fresh and useful perspective into the complex political problems involved in the making of environmental policy in this country; and it points to serious limitations in our existing political institutions. It is appropriate and salutary that the perspective comes from the younger generation, for it is they that must live in the environment now being shaped.

[12] *Science*, CLIV (November 18, 1966), 849. The editorial was adapted from remarks delivered by John W. Gardiner at the California Institute of Technology at the 75th Anniversary Convocation.

Congress and the Environment

1. Prologue: Environment and the Quality of Political Life

GRANT McCONNELL

RECENTLY one of the scholarly journals carried the observation that the conservation movement "has come of age." In its implicit recognition of the growing effectiveness of conservation, this is a statement in which all of us must take much interest. This paper glances back over some of the history of conservation and looks at some of the reasons why it is possible to say that conservation has come of age.

In 1954, which is really not so very long ago, I made an assessment of the conservation movement, being curious about the meaning of conservation and what it amounted to as a political movement. Here is a bit of what I wrote then, a statement that has unfortunately recently found its way into a textbook: "Today we see a conservation movement that is both different in content and weaker than that which was for a time the most conspicuous political movement alive."[1] In my own defense I hasten to say that the 1954 article was justified on the evidence before us at that time; I think it was correct. But in less than a decade and a half the situation is completely changed.

GRANT MC CONNELL is professor of politics and academic assistant to the chancellor at the University of California at Santa Cruz. Until 1969 he taught at the University of Chicago, where he was chairman of the political science department. He has been director of both the National Parks Association and the North Cascades Conservation Council. Among his published works are *Private Power and American Democracy*, *Steel and the Presidency*, and *The Decline of Agrarian Democracy*.

[1] Grant McConnell, "The Conservation Movement—Past and Present," *Western Political Quarterly* VII (September, 1954), 463–78. This article has been reprinted in Ian Burton and Robert W. Kates, eds., *Readings in Resource Management and Conservation* (Chicago: University of Chicago Press, 1965).

3

I

What has been the nature of the conservation movement in recent years, and in what ways has it changed? Consider what the situation was in 1954. The drive for the Upper Colorado Storage Project was in high gear, and the fate of Dinosaur National Monument and with it the sanctity of the entire National Park System was all but sealed. Conservation representatives were valiantly testifying before hostile senators from Utah and other Rocky Mountain states. Senator Watkins, for example, attempted with all the advantages of his official position to break the dignity and courage of David Brower, who was dramatically demonstrating the technical possibility of an alternative plan that would leave Echo Park untouched. One of the facts that Senator Watkins extracted was that the Sierra Club was an organization of a mere eight thousand members. In the Northwest, the Olympic Park had just been subjected to another of its periodic attacks. And in the Northwest, also just a year later, it became apparent that the North Cascades were marked for the sort of "intensive management" by the Forest Service that could only spell destruction of their unique values of wilderness and beauty. A handful of people met in a living room in Auburn, Washington, to discuss the problem; it was a very glum occasion.

Contrast this situation with that of the first decade of this century. The conservation movement was apparently the strongest political force in the country. It was led by an unusually gifted politician, Gifford Pinchot, a man who not only had a very firm idea of what he was about but also had the ear of a very sympathetic President. He was largely responsible for the act establishing the Forest Service and for creating the administrative doctrine by which the agency has been run since. In 1908 he and his chief held a conference of the governors of the United States, justices of the Supreme Court, members of Congress and representatives of some sixty-eight national societies, and other distinguished individuals. The subject was conservation— conservation of forests, minerals, soils, and water. There was a spate of similar conferences around the country, and "conservation" must have been a word of greater currency then than any other of its length in the English language. And it was in 1908 that the term, "conservation movement," was invented—once again the work of Pinchot and his associates.

On comparing these two times—take the dates of 1908 and 1954—it would seem that after a remarkable beginning there had been a grievous decline and failure. We might even leap to the conclusion that in 1954 there were only shattered remnants left of a one-time crusade. It is true that the term "conservation movement" dates from 1908. It is also true that there was an enormous lot of talk about conservation in the early years of the century. It is also true that in 1954 conservation groups were fighting a steep uphill battle. But there the list stops. Conservation as a cause much antedates the efforts of Pinchot, important as these were. The prodigality and heedless destructiveness of Americans with their natural environment aroused thoughtful men long before the beginning of this century. Perhaps we should begin with Jefferson, who had a keen sensitivity to the soil and the need for its protection. But probably a more reasonable point of beginnings is the publication of a still-great book, *Man and Nature,* by George Perkins Marsh, in 1864. This was a work of science, but it was also something much more, an appeal for morality. Let me quote one passage:

Man has too long forgotten that the earth was given to him for usufruct alone, not for consumption, still less for profligate waste. Nature has provided against the absolute destruction of any of the elementary material of her works, the thunderbolt and the tornado, the most convulsive throes of even the volcano and earthquake being only the phenomena of decomposition and recomposition. But she has left it within the power of man irreparably to derange the combinations of inorganic matter and of organic life, which through the night of aeons she had been proportioning and balancing, to prepare the earth for his habitation, when in the fullness of time, his Creator should call him forth to enter into its possession.[2]

During the second half of the nineteenth century there was a succession of men of science who turned their efforts to the problem of protecting the natural environment against the dangers which were menacing it. Much as we are inclined to think of American science as influential only in the last few decades, one of its times of glory was the latter part of the nineteenth century. There was the achievement of men such as John Wesley Powell, who personally traced the course of the Colorado River and profoundly affected the development of the U.S. Geological Survey. There were the warning memorials passed by

[2] George Perkins Marsh, *Man and Nature* (New York: Charles Scribner and Company, 1864), p. 35.

the American Association for the Advancement of Science in 1873 and 1890, which culminated in the establishment of a bureau of forestry in the Department of Agriculture. There was the push given the idea of national forests by the National Academy of Sciences in 1897. And there were other groups and other individuals who got their messages to the ears of the mighty, and together achieved a series of significant checks upon the destructiveness of Americans on their land. Gifford Pinchot, whose own personal passion was the science of forestry, stood in a culminating point of a long line of American scientists. He was less a scientist than some of his predecessors, but he had much greater talent as a politician than any of them, and this was the essential talent. He gained the nearly unqualified support of a strong President at a moment when much hung in the balance.

There are several features which deserve particular attention in this early period. The first is that conservation was hardly a popular movement. The achievements were made by the fortunate influence of a handful of thoughtful men upon a few receptive presidents. The setting aside of the national forests in the first place was anything but the response of government to a great national outcry. On several occasions, in fact, the way land was thus set aside was almost conspiratorial. In substance, the early conservation achievements were the work of an elite—of a few peculiarly well-placed and influential individuals and small groups. In time, of course, the wisdom of these elites has been vindicated by great popular support, but it is clear that this support came considerably later, and it came because the case that the scientists had made was a good one and because they stood firmly on principle. Perhaps it cannot be claimed that true morality always wins, but without the moral stance exemplified by that passage from George Perkins Marsh, what was won would not have endured to become the object of a popular cause.

In the years between 1905 and 1910, Gifford Pinchot put forth mighty efforts to make conservation a popular cause. Not only did he invent a name, coin slogans, and hold meetings—he wrote and spoke endlessly. To him we can be grateful for the fact that nobody today will admit he opposes conservation—to do that would be equivalent to spitting on the flag or decrying motherhood. It is a great advantage. But we should not lose sight of the fact that in hard political terms, he got his real results by virtue of his close personal association with

Theodore Roosevelt. When Roosevelt left office and took off for his African safari, the influence of Pinchot quickly faded, and, with it, that of the conservation movement he had invented.

The national forests were firmly established, however, and the gain was solid. But the job of going beyond, to gain for the American people protection of some of those values of which Marsh had spoken during the Civil War, the path of achievement had to continue to be what it had been before—dedicated effort by a small handful of gifted individuals and a few small groups influencing the mighty, trusting always that in time popular support would follow to make achievement secure and lasting. This, in general, is what has happened with the development of the National Park System. With the work of John Muir and a quite small group of his followers, many critical areas of the nation's most magnificent scenery have been set aside. At each moment it has largely been true that few Americans were aware of their stake. But, within a short time after the establishment of each park, the general support has appeared, and we can say that America has, to this date, a good record of preserving its parks.

One other feature of the first part of the century calls for special note. The effort to make conservation a popular movement at that time involved a very particular political philosophy. This was the doctrine of Progressivism. This was undoubtedly inevitable, since conservation was dependent on a particular group of national leaders who were committed to that doctrine. It was not a very sophisticated doctrine, indeed to call it a political philosophy is to dignify it unduly. It is worth noting briefly several of the tenets of Progressivism. In the first place, Progressivism dwelt particularly, in Pinchot's words, on "the greatest good of the greatest number in the long run." That this slogan was a very slightly amended bit of plagiarism seems never to have been appreciated by Pinchot. He was not an intellectually sophisticated man, and all the evidence indicates that he thought he had invented a scientific formula that would lead inevitably to certain and unquestionable results. The fact, of course, was that this formula, minus the bit about the long run, was the invention of an eighteenth-century English philosopher, Jeremy Bentham, and that it was ridden with ambiguity. Specifically, what *kind* of good, and for which people? Are all "goods" equal in nature? And are all desires to be placed on the same plane? Such questions never entered into Pinchot's reflections, at least insofar as we are able to determine from his autobiography, his speeches, or his teachings to his agency. He was a supremely self-assured individual.

These abstract questions would be unimportant were he a mere political philosopher. But, on the contrary, he was a powerful agency head, with something like an eighth of the surface of the United States under his command and with the formation of a whole doctrine under his pen. What this all meant in practice was that the question about the *kind* of good was answered—all goods were equal. It was simply a matter of adding them up. Ultimately, it meant that those which could be measured were to be regarded as the only values that were hard and real. It is not surprising in the American context of the highly materialistic period of the early twentieth century that the dollar proved to be the best unit of measurement. And, at a later date, it has not been surprising to find that a sort of head count (as in the number of people using a bit of wilderness) should be a major test by Pinchot's agency as to whether it was justified in setting aside the area to be unimpaired. Both tests flew in the face of the experience and history that has just been traced. The dollar test was hopelessly biased in favor of material returns—sawlogs, jobs, and so on. The head count test necessarily produced the result that wilderness was less satisfying of the greatest good than a network of logging roads paid for by the logs taken out but providing an abundance of picnic tables in however devastated a landscape. If there is any doubt about this outcome from his outlook—after all, Pinchot was a logical man—consider this authoritative statement: "The object of our forest policy is not to preserve the forests because they are beautiful . . . or because they are refuges for the wild creatures of the wilderness . . . but . . . the making of prosperous homes. . . . Every other consideration becomes secondary." [3] He was an out-and-out materialist, and, not surprisingly, his child, the United States Forest Service, has had great difficulty in surmounting the limitations which he set for it.

This test of the greatest good, moreover, implied something else which has had great importance in the shaping of American public policy. It implied some quasi-mathematical criterion and a kind of scientism in the process of decision making. Professor Samuel P. Hays has characterized conservation in the period of Pinchot and in the

[3] Quoted in Samuel P. Hays, *Conservation and the Gospel of Efficiency* (Cambridge, Mass.: Harvard University Press, 1959), p. 41.

tradition that followed him as "the gospel of efficiency."⁴ Standing in the tradition briefly outlined above, Pinchot's doctrine implied that when it came down to choices as to which values should be preferred in the use of National Forest land, experts should have the say and the decision. In choosing, for example, between logging and wilderness, the Forest Service should be allowed to make the determination in the light of its peculiar expertise. This might be well and good if the decisions were merely whether logs could be economically taken out at a given moment, but there is no scientific expertise that can say whether logs are better than wilderness at *any* time. The claim to the power to decide was a claim to an extreme of discretion. This claim was all the more serious for being made in the presence of a material- istic bias of which Pinchot and his followers were unquestioning, and, perhaps, unaware. This characteristic of scientism, at any rate, under- lines the degree to which the "conservation movement" started by Pinchot in the early part of the century was less than a popular movement. In a quite ultimate sense it was nondemocratic, although it had pretensions as a democratic movement. But this was democratic in the sense that experts would determine what was the greatest good. Whether by the test of popular support or by that of philosophic intent, conservation in the early period of this century was not a democratic movement.

II

What we see today, what goes by the old tag of conservation movement, is a different kind of animal. We now behold a movement with a strong popular base. It is not the sort of thing that progressiv- ism fostered, a gathering up of material demands upon the natural resources of the environment, with all demands having equal standing except as they were made by more or fewer people as measured by an elite of experts. We have, rather, a body of belief firmly grounded on a set of principles cherished by a substantial and growing segment of the public. This is a fact of the first political magnitude, one that requires explanation.

In 1954 this was not evident. That period looked, at the time, like one of decline from the period just after the turn of the century. From today's prospect, however, it was a critical moment in a new develop- ment. Senator Watkins did not win that argument with David Brower,

⁴ *Ibid.*

and Echo Park has not been buried in mud. That little group of eight thousand in the Sierra Club has grown to over seventy thousand. The dismal little group in Auburn worrying about the North Cascades has become the North Cascades Conservation Council, which led the fight for a park in the Cascades through to success. A park has been created in the redwoods. A Wild Rivers System and a National Trail System have been established. All this certainly does not mean that there is now a mighty conservation movement rolling on to inevitable victory everywhere. We cannot forget that the Upper Colorado Project destroyed the grandeur of Glen Canyon and that politicians have deleted significant parts of the North Cascades from the Park Act or that the Redwoods Park is small. What is significant is that today there is a conservation *movement* and that it is grounded firmly in *both* popular support and in principle. It is no longer a matter of a handful of scientists and other enlightened individuals quietly influencing key statesmen to slip actions through which will have genuine public support only at a later time. This is the sense in which it is appropriate to agree that conservation "has come of age."

What accounts for this development?

A full explanation would be complex. On the face of things it might seem that the values of great numbers of Americans have changed over the years. In the sense that values are really testable only by choices actually given effect, this is plainly true. But this is to say very little. There is a genuine possibility that recent generations have wanted different things than their predecessors, but in view of the possibility that the political system may have had a bias in validating some preferences instead of others, casting aspersions on our ancestors as a wholly materialist lot is not justified. If current Americans show more signs of caring for the nonmaterial aspects of their environment, it may well be because the political order has evolved sufficiently to allow such concern to have occasional effect.

There are good grounds for believing that this is the case. Very briefly, the United States is much more of a nation than it has been in the past. It is knit together with roads, airlines, telephones, television, and magazines to a degree difficult to foresee even a relatively few decades ago. The horizons of the average American have vastly expanded so that the inhabitants of Sauk Center and all its real counterparts now share a national culture as never before. Inevitably, this has been reflected in the workings of the political system. Many decisions that were formerly within the exclusive provinces of states and localities are now made in larger arenas, arenas in which an inevitably greater diversity of citizens participate.

Formerly, choices on the allocation of values, as for example between natural beauty and resource exploitation, was largely in the hands of localities and, in fact, was regarded as mainly a private matter. Insofar as the choice lay in the hands of a lumber or a mining company, the choice for exploitation was preordained. But the situation was more complex than this suggests. If the choice were in the hands—as it usually has been—of a locality or a state in which the lumbering or mining industry bulked particularly large, the support of the community or state would flow to the narrow interests of such industry. Some local citizens would be aggrieved at the costs in natural beauty and wilderness but their voices would be so weak in face of the seemingly monolithic determination of their neighbors as to be beneath the threshold of hearing. Indeed, the feeling of powerlessness would generally lead them not to speak at all, given the inevitability of failure and the necessity of living with those neighbors.

Thus, it has generally been true that fights for conservation have taken on an aspect of outsiders against locals. The appearance has been false in that almost any locality contains some individuals concerned for conservation. Nevertheless, these individuals could only be heard in chorus with like-minded fellows drawn from a larger constituency. The exploiters of commodities, understanding the situation at least intuitively, have persistently appealed to the strong American tradition of decentralization as a supposedly democratic principle and have sought to retain the power of decision in local hands. There have been contests in which localities have lined up for conservation, establishment of the Gila Wilderness, for example, but these have been rare. Conservation, and conservation of wilderness and scenic values especially, have depended on creation of larger constituencies. Thus it is not difficult to imagine what would have happened to the Grand Canyon if its future had been left to Arizona to decide instead of the nation; the American people as a whole have a far smaller per capita money stake in damming the canyon's potential kilowatts than do the people of Arizona. It is also understandable why officials of Humboldt County resisted creation of a Redwoods National Park, while a strong drive for the park came from San Francisco, and why opposition to the North Cascades Park was loudest in Bellingham and Wenatchee and weakest in Seattle.

The change that has come about is far from total. It is in degree only. It is, moreover, a change of some complexity. It involves a new awareness and knowledge of people in New England, the Midwest, and California about the North Cascades, many miles distant from their homes. It involves the increasing urbanization of Americans and the drift of political power to city dwellers. It involves the changing economic base of cities like Seattle, with the relative decline and position of the lumber industry. Thus, it is not inconceivable that the success of the Boeing Company may have been the essential factor in preserving the North Cascades. The change also involves the development of national conservation organizations. All of these have converged in the creation of a larger and more diverse constituency, with a consequently growing power supporting wilderness, scenic values, and environmental protection.[5]

III

Second, a deep and general change has occurred in our national political life. This is now a rich and prosperous nation. We now have a large generation of youth that has no memory of depression. At long last, we are generally free of the incubus of fear that tomorrow the economy will collapse. This has a very profound meaning—that the substance of political and moral life is no longer almost wholly economic. Economic matters have, in the past, been highly preoccupying, simply because hitherto we have never been out of the shadow of potential famine or other economic disaster. It is highly unlikely that men have ever really believed that economic affairs are the most important department of life, but it is true that we have always so far had to give first thought to that department simply because it has had a prior urgency. As a result, our political system has been formulated to adjust economic claims, and it has worked peculiarly well. The reason for this is that economic claims are bargainable; it is almost always possible to split the difference somewhere in an economic contest so that each side is reasonably satisfied. When we respond to the injunction, "Come, let us reason together," it is to bargain and to split differences.

[5] Regarding the general principle involved, see my *Private Power and American Democracy* (New York: Alfred A. Knopf, 1966), chap. iv.

As the nation has become richer, however, economic values have lost their old urgency and other more important matters have emerged and taken the foreground. The values of natural beauty and wilderness are critical examples here. But these are really not bargainable. The sort of "reasoning" which has been characteristic of politics on the economic model does not apply. It is faintly conceivable, for example, that by offering a sufficiently high price to the National Museum in Amsterdam to acquire its treasure, *The Night Watch,* one could get that great painting away from the Dutch; but it is absolutely inconceivable that one could make a deal to get a two-foot square cut out of the lower left-hand quadrant of the picture for *any* price. This is just not a possible bargain.

So it is with supposed bargains offered on natural beauty and wilderness. To bargain over the Grand Canyon, the redwoods, the North Cascades, may seem eminently sensible if you are interested in kilowatts, lumber, or copper, but it is nonetheless immoral if your concern is with scenic beauty and wilderness. Such a bargain might be possible if the value of scenic beauty and wilderness could be stated in the same dollar measure as kilowatts, lumber, and copper. It would, alternatively, be bargainable if the economic developers were able to offer a new Grand Canyon, some new two-thousand-year-old redwoods, or some new North Cascades in the exchange. Unfortunately, however, this alternative has practical difficulties. The fact of the matter is that any such bargain is completely one-sided—to take away more or less of the Grand Canyon, the redwoods, or the North Cascades. The brute power of the opposition may conceivably win, but such an outcome will not be a bargain in the sense of being mutually acceptable.

This fundamental characteristic of the politics of conservation is deeply involved in what has occurred with the conservation movement. There is much evidence that Americans today have moved beyond the conception that everything of meaning in life can be stated in either dollar or head-count terms. It is evident, for example, that many Americans are willing to go to extreme lengths in their principled opposition to the Viet Nam War. It is plain that many individuals are willing to lay their lives on the line for simple human dignity. And many of our best young people are going to extremes to assert their rejection of the material calculus. Both moral and aesthetic principles are emerging everywhere as the fundamental material of politics and common life. In this setting, increasing numbers of individuals are declaring themselves for what they really believe in. It is hardly surprising that many are declaring the values of scenic beauty and wilderness; there are hardly any values less uncertain and ambiguous than these. Formerly, the sort of ridicule offered by spokesmen for firms such as the Kennecott Copper Corporation, that concern for these values is "sentimental," was effective. We were once half persuaded that such concern was soft-headed, and that these values were inferior. It is beginning to emerge that the really soft-headed sentimentalism is that attaching to money.

IV

The striking evidence of growth in the conservation movement since 1954 is directly related to the clarity with which the conservation leaders of today have perceived the strategic nature of conservation issues. A telling incident on this score is one related to the Echo Park controversy. When the Upper Colorado Project was put forward, nearly everyone believed Echo Park was necessarily doomed. But a small group of individuals got together and decided that the principle involved was simply wrong and that they should say so. This was to be a gesture, but the declaration struck such a chord of public response that ultimately it became possible to save Echo Park by sheer mass support.

The style of the conservation movement is intransigent. It is often shrill and strident. It gives rise to internal controversies of much intensity. However distressing those controversies may be, they are themselves strong evidence of the movement's vitality. They are a measure of the degree to which participants regard their cause as serious. By the same token, today's movement is principled. This very feature is responsible for the great current growth of the conservation movement, and, in fact, is why there is a genuine movement today where there was none before. To the degree that it stands by its principles, it will continue to grow and frequently to succeed. To the degree that it seeks to compromise and make deals, it will fail and wither.

The leaders of the modern conservation movement must expect to be told that they are unreasonable. They must expect continued demands to enter into "bargains" in which they can only lose and never gain. They may be told that they should go back to the old reliable way of quietly finessing things through men of influence. But those days are gone, and with all gratitude to the notable men who managed those coups of influence, their coups cannot now be emulated. Henceforth, the conservation movement will have to succeed as a movement, enduring all the committee meetings, the endless work of organization, and, most of all, hammering out the principles and applications of those principles.

2. Indiana Dunes National Lakeshore:
The Battle for the Dunes

JAMES J. KYLE

WHEN President Johnson signed the Indiana Dunes National Lakeshore Act, a controversy extending over fifty years appeared to be resolved. Since the establishment of such a park was first suggested in 1916, two competing uses of Indiana's Lake Michigan coast have been on a collision course. As nearby cities increased in population and area, more people used the dunes for periodic retreats from urban life. Meanwhile, the land-consuming steel industry had spread from Chicago to other sites along the lakeshore, expanding to meet the needs of a burgeoning national economy. As it occupied picturesque beaches, the industry acquired a Jekyll and Hyde reputation. To some people, the building of a steel mill signified new jobs, a boost for the economy, and more solvent local government. To others, the industry was an unwelcome intruder threatening to destroy the countryside.

The battle for the dunes illustrates at least two significant and recurring problems of democratic government. In the first place, the dunes are located in Indiana, while the homes of a majority of the people using them for recreation are located in Illinois, primarily in the Chicago vicinity. The issue has a built-in regional conflict of interests with roots in the American Federal system. In the second place, the history of this conflict underlines the advantage private industry frequently holds over Congress when there is disagreement over land use. A flick of the wrist will start a powerful bulldozer, but Congress usually meditates for years when questions of natural environment preservation are at hand.

JAMES J. KYLE is a graduate student in geography at the University of Washington.

I

It has taken centuries of waves, currents, and wind action to build the magnificent dunes along Lake Michigan's coastline. As sand is swept onto the beach, prevailing westerlies push it farther inland. Vegetation partially stabilized the wandering hills of sand. Streams were dammed, creating numerous permanent lakes and marshes. The resulting variations in soil types, moisture content, and sun exposures have produced a remarkably diverse plant and animal population. The unique ecology of the dunes has long been prized by scientists.[1] A more popular reason for the preservation of the dunes, however, is the recreational needs of the seven and one-half million people who live within one hour's drive. The beaches are excellent. Comparable recreational choices, for Chicagoans at least, do not exist.

By the same token, "the southern end of Lake Michigan is ideally suited for steel production,"[2] and regional demand for steel remains ahead of production. The transportation network for moving raw materials and finished products includes the inland waterway system, the Great Lakes, and the St. Lawrence Seaway. Location of plant facilities on the lakeshore gives two other advantages: water for production and lakefront property for possible filling and lakeward expansion. But construction of steel mills is incompatible with recreational land use, as large areas of land are required and sand dunes must be leveled. Confrontation of industrial and recreational interests was inevitable, and indications of this appeared many years ago.

The scenic, scientific, and recreational values of the dunes were recognized by Stephen Mather, the first director of the National Park Service, who called for establishment of a national Indiana dunes park in 1916. Attention was centered on world events for the next few years, and Congress did not respond to Mather's request. However, the Indiana Legislature passed a law in 1923 creating the Indiana Dunes State Park, setting aside four miles of the thirty-five-mile Indiana shoreline. The beaches near the state park remained undeveloped. Conservationists sought extended protection, but were opposed not only by those who favored industrial development of the shoreline

[1] Cowles Bog, part of the national lakeshore, is reputed to be the birthplace of American ecology.

[2] Harold M. Mayer, "Politics and Land Use: The Indiana Shoreline of Lake Michigan," *Annals of the Association of American Geographers*, LIV, No. 4 (December, 1964), 512.

but also by many scientists, who feared that additional visitors to the dunes would damage the delicate ecology.[3]

Encroachments by industry continued, and by 1950 the twenty-seven-mile beach between the harbors of Chicago and Gary, Indiana, had become completely industrialized. By mid-century, the largest remaining underdeveloped shore was the ten-mile stretch between U.S. Steel's Gary works and the state park to the east; but industrial expansion into that area was imminent, and this prospect renewed the concern of both the public and the scientific profession. The Indiana dunes controversy focused on this short and magnificent stretch of beach (see fig. 1). The Midwest Steel Company had purchased a small tract of land in the heart of this area in 1929. The land straddled

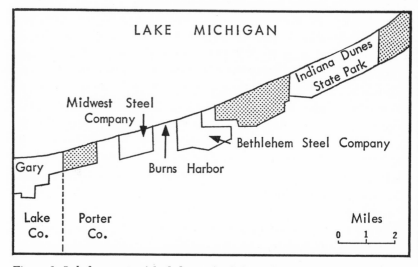

Figure 1. Lakefront units (shaded areas) of the Indiana Dunes National Lakeshore and intervening industrial and port complex (After Harold M. Mayer)

Burns Ditch, a small, shallow waterway which the company coveted as a potential harbor. Throughout the controversy, the Burns Ditch Harbor proposal was the center of attention. Hoosier politicians, notably Charles Halleck, had worked for years to promote "development" of the area.

The construction of the harbor would be expensive, requiring an extensive dredge and landfill operation. Soon after it purchased the land, Midwest Steel began seeking Federal aid for the port construc-

[3] Personal letter from Senator Paul H. Douglas, June 12, 1968.

tion. For two decades the Army Corps of Engineers resisted these efforts, pointing out that other harbor facilities in the region were adequate, and that any Federal aid for Burns Ditch Harbor would represent a subsidy to one company. Since U.S. Steel had financed its own harbors on Lake Michigan, Federal aid for the Burns port would constitute discrimination.

A change of viewpoint came in 1949 when the district office of the corps recommended that further consideration be given to the Burns Harbor proposal. Several factors contributed to this policy change. Demands on the lakeshore's harbor facilities had increased. Administrators in Indiana's state government supported the development with increasing enthusiasm, and the corps was becoming more aggressive in support of public works projects in general. A private feasibility study began, and the port proposal slowly gained respect. Anticipating Federal aid for the port, Bethlehem Steel purchased land adjacent to the Midwest tract in 1956. The sale was promoted by Indiana political and financial interests. The opening of the St. Lawrence Seaway in 1959 increased the demand for harbor facilities, and the same year Midwest began construction of a steel finishing plant adjacent to Burns Ditch. Both companies pushed strongly for the construction of a harbor which would allow them to build fully integrated steel mills. The Indiana state government established the Indiana Port Commission, whose primary mission was to promote Federal participation in harbor construction.

Northern Indiana property owners and conservationists—especially from the Chicago area—formed the Save-the-Dunes Council in 1952 and set out to enlist the aid of their state government and congressional delegation. After five years of frustration, the council turned to Senator Paul Douglas of Illinois for assistance, tapping for the first time the favorable sentiment for their cause that existed in the Chicago area. Beginning in 1958, Senator Douglas introduced and promoted national lakeshore legislation in each session of Congress. His bills, as well as numerous others, met the same fate in both chambers: referral to the respective Committees on Interior and Insular Affairs, and then stagnation. The strongest opposition came from the Indiana congressional delegation, which unanimously favored the Burns port proposal and the protection of Bethlehem's property. Senator Douglas' lakeshore bills would have taken property otherwise available for both Bethlehem's mill and the port.

Senate hearings on the port proposal revealed that no alternatives to the Burns Ditch site had been considered, and a request was made for the study of all possible sites on the Indiana lakeshore before any Federal action was taken. Indiana's governor countered by claiming that the Burns port would be built with or without Federal assistance. With this reassurance, Bethlehem committed itself to build a finishing mill. Leveling of the dunes began in September, 1963, and continued despite angry protests from Senator Douglas and his supporters. The Corps of Engineers, disregarding the objections of conservationists, the U.S. Public Health Service, and the Department of Interior, gave Bethlehem permission to build a three-hundred-acre landfill over the lake. In anticipation of the mill, the Northern Indiana Public Service Company had already constructed a generating plant for electrical power in the heart of the area. It was alleged by conservationists that the company deliberately destroyed as much of the natural area on its own land as possible in order to weaken the argument for saving the dunes. Bethlehem stood on unquestionable legal grounds and declined suggestions to delay excavation until Congress could decide whether or not to include the construction site in a national lakeshore. Consequently, the land surrounding the site of the proposed harbor was ruined for preservation purposes, and opposition to Federal aid for the Burns Ditch port diminished. By the same token, those who had opposed the national lakeshore in order to protect the harbor proposal could now support lakeshore legislation. A representative of President Kennedy served as mediator, and the two sides reached agreement. The Federal administration confirmed its long-standing support for the lakeshore proposal, while also agreeing to back the financing of the port as well. The Senate Interior Committee held extensive hearings on Senator Douglas' lakeshore bill in early 1964. The Senate passed the bill, but it died in the House Interior Committee at the close of the Eighty-eighth Congress.

A delicate situation followed in the Eighty-ninth Congress. There was general agreement that both the port and the lakeshore should be approved, but both sides were fearful of being out-maneuvered. Action first occurred in the Senate Public Works Committee, where the port was under consideration. Senator Douglas persuaded the Committee to incorporate into the omnibus rivers and harbors bill, which included the Burns project, a contingency provision to prevent the harbor from being funded until the lakeshore bill had been approved.

But the House Public Works Committee inserted language in the House version of the omnibus rivers and harbors bill which divorced the port and lakeshore, making it possible for the harbor to be approved with no strings attached. However, the basic agreement that both the lakeshore and the harbor should be approved was renego- tiated by Senator Birch Bayh of Indiana, and the wording of the final omnibus bill as passed by both chambers made the appropriation of funds for the harbor contingent upon both chambers having a chance to vote on a dunes preservation bill before the end of the Eighty-ninth Congress.

The Senate again passed a national lakeshore bill, and the effects of the contingency provision attached to the Burns Harbor approval were soon apparent. Indiana's Democratic delegation to the House petitioned Representative Wayne Aspinall, Chairman of the Interior Committee, urging him to report an Indiana Dunes bill out of commit- tee in 1966. The primary interest of the Indiana Democrats was still the Burns Harbor approval, but the contingency provision accompa- nying the port approval forced them to encourage the progress of the lakeshore bill rather than oppose it. Representative Aspinall's commit- tee held extensive hearings at both Valparaiso, Indiana, and Washing- ton, D.C., and issued a favorable report to the House in July, 1966.[4] The House voted its approval, and the Indiana Dunes National Lake- shore Act (PL 89–761) was signed by President Johnson in November, 1966.

Included in the national lakeshore were three lakefront units and several noncontiguous inland tracts (see fig. 1). Most of the land was privately owned. Appropriations for land purchases were authorized and the right of condemnation was granted to the Secretary of the Interior to force a transaction upon unwilling landowners. However, the power of condemnation was suspended with respect to land already being used for residential purposes, with a three-acre maxi- mum placed on the area a homeowner could protect. The Secretary of the Interior was directed to oversee the use of land remaining in private hands by enforcing standards designed to guide county and municipal zoning commissions. Certain standards were specified by the act, including the banning of commercial activities incompatible with planned objectives and preservation of the natural environment.

---

[4] U.S., Congress, House, *Indiana Dunes National Lakeshore*, 89th Cong., 2d sess., H. Rept. 900, 1966.

Proposed administration of the lakeshore would attempt to reconcile past development with recreational and preservational objectives. Several small towns, along with appropriate commercial activities, continued to function as before. The primary objective of the act was to maintain the *status quo* with respect to the physical environment within the lakeshore boundaries.

II

Indiana's governor, Harold Handley, and the president of the National Steel Company (subsidiary of Midwest) shared a shovel in 1959 to turn the first sand for construction of a steel mill near Burns Ditch. This alliance proved to be a powerful factor in the battle for the dunes. Encouraged by the state, Bethlehem's strategic excavation of 1963 completed the job of protecting the Burns Ditch area from national lakeshore legislation. It is understandable that state and steel would share a concern for industrial development. Industry creates jobs and economic growth, votes for politicians, and profits for stockholders. These are significant private and social benefits.

Most labor organizations in northern Indiana gave enthusiastic support to the state-steel position, although the United States Steel Workers officially supported the lakeshore. Joined by many owners of property in the dunes area, the opposition to lakeshore legislation used arguments other than simply the need for economic development. It was claimed that the state park already provided adequate facilities, and that any future park needs should be handled by the state. Several senators feared the "patchwork" lakeshore would set a dangerous precedent and might later allow the government to "take the best part of a landowner's holdings and leave him with only the scraps." [5] Landowners objected to the limitations on their property rights. Most of these arguments were basically concerned with the increasing authority of the Federal government.

There was disagreement among affected landowners. On the one hand, those who opposed the lakeshore maintained that land would be taken off the tax rolls while demand for municipal services, such as law enforcement and road maintenance, would continue to expand, necessitating tax increases. They further argued that the option of profitable sale of land to industry would be lost and employment

[5] U.S., Congress, Senate, *Providing for the Establishment of the Indiana Dunes National Lakeshore,* 88th Cong., 2d sess., S. Rept. 1362, p. 10.

opportunities would be limited. On the other hand, some landowners who favored the lakeshore were willing to make personal sacrifices for the public interest. They accepted the possibility of high property taxes, and one landowner actually refused to sell his land to Bethlehem at a substantial profit, instead offering it to the Department of Interior at a much lower price.[6] These lakeshore proponents feared industrial expansion into residential districts. They were confident that national lakeshore status, as compared to local zoning ordinances, would give them more lasting protection against this intrusion. These disagreements among property owners were reflected in the varied positions taken by the town governments. As a result, the voice of local residents in the dunes controversy tended to be neutralized.

Senator Douglas' long-standing interest in conservation was reinforced by his urban constituency. Most Chicagoans, including steelworkers, supported lakeshore legislation. The Save-the-Dunes Council and the Izaak Walton League expressed strongly the traditional conservationist sentiments, and many scientists familiar with the dunes' ecological values backed the national lakeshore. The Department of Interior supported preservation of the area after Senator Douglas took Secretary Udall and other officials on a hike through the dunes in 1962. Following this, the National Park Service began assuming a more active political role and providing pertinent information on the proposal to the legislative committees.[7]

The over-all outcome of these different forces and pressures was that preservationists gained a national lakeshore at the expense of having a very unaesthetic industrial complex bisect its lakefront. The State of Indiana gained two large steel mills and a federally subsidized port, but lost control over much land considered valuable for further industrial development. The steel industry was perhaps the biggest winner. One company (Inland) was threatened with the loss of much of its remaining unoccupied land on the lakeshore, but the

---

[6] U.S., *Congressional Record,* 88th Cong., 1st sess., CIX (1963), 1677.

[7] This raises an interesting question concerning the propriety of various types of lobbying by executive agencies. Rep. Thomas B. Curtis (R., Mo.) has commented: "[Executive agencies] . . . have a forum . . . in the Congressional Committees, and they should use it. They also have the ability to communicate directly with the people, as the President does on TV time. . . . So let's have a cessation of . . . Executive officials [and] cabinet officers coming into Congressmen's offices." *Legislators and the Lobbyists* (Washington, D.C.: Congressional Quarterly Service, 1965), p. 17.

two largest concerns, Bethlehem and Midwest, retained their property rights and gained Federal subsidization in the form of the Burns Ditch harbor.

The industrial complex undoubtedly will be harmful to the lakeshore. Psychic damage is obvious, and serious pollution is a possibility.[8] This raises the question of whether economic gains from the steel mills and the port outweigh the resulting social losses. The ethics of the state-steel alliance have been questioned. In its overt form, the coalition resulted from a natural sharing of interests and was acceptable. It has been alleged, however, that important state officials had financial interests in the Burns Ditch tract, and this may explain in part why state administrators resisted the examination of alternative port locations.[9] This failure to consider alternatives to the Burns Ditch harbor makes the wisdom of the outcome of the controversy subject to reasonable doubt.

III

In a paper on the environmental effects of economic development, John Krutilla has argued that "there are reasons to fear that additional and unnecessary degradation of the natural environments may continue. This is due partly to the imperfection in the economic organization of production, and partly to the imperfection with which governmental processes work."[10] Neither votes nor dollars accurately appraise the value of natural environments to mankind. A free enterprise economic philosophy gives the market place the first chance to make necessary resource allocation decisions; and political institutions generally come into play only when the failure of the market system is obvious. There is a strong tradition of decentralized authority in

[8] "The Federal Water Pollution Control Administration has not detected unacceptable environmental contamination from the Burns Ditch steel complex during either the construction or operational phase." Personal letter from J. E. N. Jensen, Associate Director, National Park Service, April 9, 1969.

[9] "Governor [Matthew] Welsh is so committed to the Burns Ditch site that he rejects out of hand any suggestion that alternative sites can be considered, and he is extremely sensitive to references to land speculation and ties between public officials and industrial interests working for the Burns Ditch port." William Peeples, "Indiana Dunes and Pressure Politics," *Atlantic Monthly*, February, 1963, p. 87.

[10] John V. Krutilla, "Environmental Effects of Economic Development," *Daedalus*, XCVI (Fall, 1967), 1063.

American government which demands that initial land-use zoning responsibility rest with local government. Higher levels of government generally take action only when it is determined that local authorities have in some way failed. There exists, in effect, a hierarchy of appeal courts with respect to decisions about land use. These are, in order of ascending authority: (1) the free market system, (2) the local zoning authorities, (3) the state governments, (4) the Federal government. The Indiana dunes controversy involved all of these levels of decision making.

The limitations of the market system can be suggested by posing the following question: If facilities for outdoor recreation were in such high demand, why did not the Bethlehem Steel Company consider using its land as a privately owned and operated park, instead of deciding to build a steel mill? The answer to this question is obvious. Recreational demand is a difficult thing for an entrepreneur to turn into profit, and any privately owned park in the Indiana dunes would have to compete with free or nominally priced public park facilities. More generally, when a natural environment is preserved, society retains options which otherwise may be lost. These options are in the form of social goods that cannot be bought and sold in the market place.[11] Social goods relating to land use have been given priority over private rights by the courts, and land-use zoning has long been considered a constitutionally acceptable regulation of the free market system.[12]

In the Indiana dunes controversy, the reaction of the local zoning authorities and of the state government can usefully be considered together. In the first place, both levels of government opposed establishment of a large national lakeshore on the grounds that it would limit industrial expansion and prevent the increase in land prices. Second, a different and perhaps more rational solution of the controversy was frustrated by the limitations placed on both local and state governments by existing political jurisdictions (see fig. 2). For example, officials of Porter County, which contains most of the dunes area, were reluctant to take into account the recreational needs of adjacent, urbanized Lake County. Similarly, state officials in Indiana showed

[11] For a more detailed explanation, see John V. Krutilla, "Conservation Reconsidered," *American Economic Review*, September, 1967.
[12] See F. Fraser Darling and John P. Milton, eds., *Future Environments of North America* (New York: Natural History Press, 1966), p. 674.

little concern over the recreational problems of large urban areas in adjacent Illinois. In short, the spatial jurisdiction of the officials of both Porter County and the State of Indiana was insufficient to allow them to exercise control over the larger political arena involved in the problem.

This raises an important question about the ability of existing political units to handle the external regional effects of public policy issues. How, for example, can the needs of large urban centers be met when the necessary resources lie in adjacent but politically separate

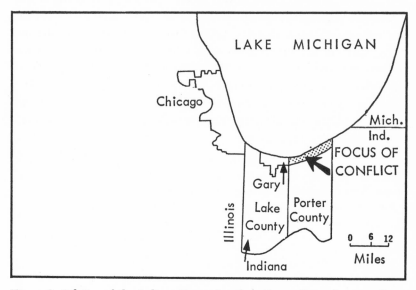

Figure 2. Relation of the Indiana Dunes (northern Porter County) to significant cities and political boundaries (After Harold M. Mayer)

cities, counties, or states? Zoning authority in the United States is lodged mainly with the counties, and the objectives of most counties are dominated by the notion of economic growth indefinitely extended.[13] Rural county zoning commissions perform what is essentially an urbanizing rather than an urban-serving function. This is partly explained by what Lynton Caldwell has called the "subversion" of county planning commissions by real estate interests.[14] Both the local and state governments involved in the conflict over the Indiana dunes

[13] Robert E. Dickinson, "The Process of Urbanization," in *ibid.*, p. 497.
[14] *Ibid*, "General Discussion," p. 592.

provide an illustration of this subversion. The testimony from officials of Porter County in the hearings on the lakeshore proposal exemplifies the reluctance of counties to have land removed from the tax rolls, which often is merely a subterfuge argument to permit land speculation.

It is true that rural county governments must provide services within the limits of a narrow tax base, and public acquisition of land for a national lakeshore could indeed aggravate county fiscal problems. There is, in fact, little or no incentive for rural county zoning commissions to serve urban needs. In the absense of such incentives, rural counties naturally prefer development within their own boundaries to the much more uncertain prospect of some form of cost-sharing on the part of the urban areas with needs to be served. Everyone appears to recognize the necessity for natural environment preservation as long as it does not happen in his particular county or state. The following verbal exchange between Representative Morris Udall and an Indiana labor official during the House hearings on the lakeshore proposal illustrates this point:

UDALL. The people who have the greatest stake are people like your [labor union] members who work for a living and can't afford to go long distances [for recreation in a natural environment].

BOCANEGRA. We are willing to go to Michigan, 165 miles away, if you give us a job and don't . . .

UDALL. I am not so sure the Michigan people will welcome you any more than the Indiana people welcome the Chicago people.

BOCANEGRA. We do welcome them, but not at the expense of our jobs and our tax potential.[15]

The United States does not have urban-oriented land-use planning and as long as the counties retain their zoning and taxing powers without alterations the situation is unlikely to improve. In some case the interests of cities in rural land-use matters are protected by raising the problem to the state level, but in the dunes controversy the interests of the State of Indiana happened to parallel those of its rural Porter County. Consequently, the urban needs of Chicago's millions could be expressed only by raising the issue to the congressional level in Washington, D.C.

Congress tends to be a conservative body, unable to respond to

[15] U.S., Congress, House, Committee on Interior and Insular Affairs, *Hearings, Indiana Dunes National Lakeshore*, 89th Cong., 1st sess., 1966, pt. 2, p. 506.

many issues unless of crisis proportions. The committee system, the independence of committee chairmen, and the dual chamber structure all provide opportunities for delaying or killing a bill, even though a majority of congressmen may support the measure. This is especially true with respect to national park and wilderness preservation issues. Congressional inertia permits the infliction of permanent demage in a natural environment even while its future is being debated. There is at least a possibility, for example, that Congress might have included the Bethlehem Steel tract in the national lakeshore had it been able to respond sooner. Bethlehem acted in a rational (from the company's point of view) and legal manner to further the interests of its stockholders by excavating the Burns Ditch site. In so doing, however, the steel company made a decision which would have been made by the representatives of the people, had they not been hampered by the structural inertia of Congress. Since sweeping congressional reform is unlikely, private industry will continue to possess the legal right and the technological ability to destroy natural ecosystems while Congress ponders their preservation.

Does the executive branch offer an alternative source of action? The office of the modern Presidency contains an impressive array of informal powers—the kind exercised, for example, by President Kennedy in the steel price crisis of 1963. Could these informal powers of the Presidency be used to restrain private enterprise from leveling sand dunes or felling redwoods while Congress deliberates? A particular President may, of course, oppose this kind of restraining action for personal reasons, but the main constraint upon presidential intervention is the relatively low priority given to issues. Compared to international political problems, a single issue such as the Indiana dunes controversy is insignificant. The President simply does not have time to study specific conservation issues in the detailed way required to plan effective national strategy. Stewart Udall, after discussing various conservation problems with President Kennedy in late 1963, exclaimed, "He is imprisoned by Berlin." [16]

At least two relatively simple steps can be suggested to protect the preservation alternatives open to Congress and the nation. First, Congress could provide the President with the authority to invoke a freeze on further development at any site being considered for preservation,

[16] Arthur M. Schlesinger, Jr., *A Thousand Days* (Greenwich, Conn.: Fawcett Publications, 1965), p. 363.

though the constitutionality of such action might be open to question. A second and perhaps politically more acceptable step would be to establish in the Executive Office of the President a council of ecological or environmental advisors to oversee government and private activity in relation to the outstanding natural environments of the country. The council would keep the President informed about ecological and environmental change and advise him on suitable courses of action. This suggestion is currently before Congress and is discussed in Chapter 14 of this volume. Either of these steps could help to reduce the number of irreversible decisions that are destroying our few remaining natural environments. A national policy for land use must be developed if these conflicts are to be settled in a more rational manner in keeping with the needs of the people in the last third of the twentieth century.

The attractiveness of the Presidency as a means of counteracting the present ill effects of congressional inertia is increased by the fact that the constituency of the President is essentially urban. The need for Federal intervention on land-use decisions would, of course, be decreased if urban-oriented zoning and planning authorities are created. However, if the present predominance of the counties in matters of zoning is perpetuated, the existence of an effective alternative mechanism for intervention by the Federal government becomes all the more important.

IV

All levels of government face increasing complexity in preservation and conservation issues. The variety of demands that can be made upon an environment and the conflicts that these demands engender are clearly illustrated in the battle for the Indiana dunes. Steel mills and harbor facilities perform vital economic functions but preclude other uses. Good bathing beaches are suitable for intensive recreation, but naturalists and other scientists are interested in areas where the level of use leaves the natural ecology undisturbed. The conflicting and competing interest groups involved in the Indiana dunes controversy tended to confuse and, perhaps inevitably, to oversimplify the solution to the problems. Each faction asserted that the issue could be resolved fairly only if its own particular values were accepted by all. Senator Douglas' comments on this problem are highly revealing:

If it had not been for Congress in this matter, the Dunes would have been completely destroyed long ago. Under the prodding of some of us, Congress stepped in and saved the remnants. The previous head of the National Park Service, Conrad Wirth, turned tail and ran before a Congressional Committee which he believed to be hostile. The National Planning Association refused to object to the coming of the steel mills and the harbor, and indeed opposed a Lakeshore Park. Northwestern University gladly joined in by despoiling the lakefront so that they might erect a building devoted to the natural environment.

In short, the common people and a few of us politicians saved the remainder of the Dunes. . . . This has been done, if all goes well, over the objections of (1) the big industrial interests, (2) the Republican leaders of Indiana and Illinois, and (3) without the help of many who we had hoped would assist.[17]

Congress frequently turns to the academic community for advice and assistance, and Senator Douglas has expressed deep disappointment with the response. He observes, "Many scientists seem to think the world is a preserve which only they should enjoy."[18] He adds that the scientific community should make up its mind about what it wants to happen to America's natural environment. "If you remain neutral or hostile because having poor people swim and walk will significantly damage the ecology and aesthetics of the area, then I want to suggest that 'science' of this type is a deterrent rather than an aid to mankind."[19] There is, of course, a need for protection of certain unique natural environments from mass recreational use. Douglas' point is that the needs of natural scientists and naturalists are in competition with the needs of urban areas. All competing needs are to some extent social needs and each solution offers a different mix of social benefits. It is a task for social scientists to suggest ways of comparing the potential social benefits of different land-use policies, but here too the academic community has failed to measure up to the need.

Was the Indiana Dunes National Lakeshore Act an acceptable and final allocation of this unique land resource? The act's acceptability has been doubted, and it has no pretensions to finality. Opponents of the lakeshore have introduced a bill in Congress which would drastically reduce the size of the protected area. Its passage is unlikely, but other intrusions threaten. A jet airport is planned nearby with a

[17] Personal letter from Senator Paul H. Douglas, June 12, 1968.
[18] *Ibid.*
[19] *Ibid.*

land approach directly over the protected zone of the shoreline so that even the most isolated retreats would be subject to frequent over-flights. A railroad marshaling yard and a four-lane freeway may be constructed within lakeshore boundaries. Land acquisitions by the National Park Service are proceeding slowly because, in part, necessary appropriations have been fought by lakeshore opponents.[20] The authority of the Secretary of the Interior to condemn land within lakeshore boundaries is seldom used because of the need to maintain workable relations with local citizens and units of government. The secretary's authority to issue standards for zoning is similarly hampered by lack of cooperation from local zoning commissions. Congress' initial action creating the lakeshore was called a compromise; now it seems possible that the Indiana dunes will be compromised into oblivion.

The controversy over the Indiana dunes draws attention to the absence of a national land-use policy and the antiquity of the political structure. Will American democracy evolve more efficient institutions for dealing with land-use questions? The answer must be sought in underlying trends of American politics. Perhaps the confrontation between value systems over the Indiana dunes is not as critical as other more prominent social crises, but within the particular context of conservation politics in the United States the Indiana dunes controversy gives cause for alarm. If our physical environment and our political institutions are to be protected and enhanced, the lessons of this confrontation must be widely understood.

[20] "The Act of Congress authorizing the establishment of the national lakeshore provided for the appropriation of not more than $27,900,000 for the acquisition of land. To date eight and a half million dollars has been appropriated." Personal letter from J. E. N. Jensen, Associate Director, National Park Service, April 9, 1969.

3. Presidential Proposal and Congressional Disposal:
The Highway Beautification Act

EARL HALE, JR.

THE tremendous quantity of goods and services produced in the United States has yielded an affluent society which is becoming aware of some negative aspects of this unparalleled production. An example of this awareness is the increased concern for the qualitative aspects of man's environment. This concern is being reflected in the political arena, and, more specifically, in legislation dealing with such problems as air and water pollution and others which are discussed elsewhere in this volume. In 1965, President Johnson's legislative program included an omnibus proposal to improve another segment of our environment—the highway system. The Highway Beautification Act of 1965 (PL 89–285) was the eventual product of this presidential initiative. In his letter of transmittal on May 26, 1965, President Johnson said:

The economy, and the roads that serve it, are not ends in themselves. They are meant to serve the real needs of the people of this country. And those needs include the opportunity to touch nature and see beauty, as well as rising income and swifter travel.

Therefore, we must make sure that the massive resources we now devote to roads also serve to improve and broaden the quality of American life.[1]

The act sought to provide for these goals in three ways: controls on outdoor advertising, controls on placement and shielding of junk

EARL HALE, JR.; was a research associate for a study of the Community Action Program in Spokane, Washington, before entering the armed forces. He has an M.P.A. degree from the University of Washington.

[1] U.S., Congress, House, Committee on Public Works, *Highway Beautification*, 89th Cong., 1st sess., H. Doc. 191, 1965.

yards, and increased efforts for landscaping and other scenic enhancements.

The act directed that 10 per cent of the federal-aid highway funds payable to the states annually under an earlier act be withheld after January 1, 1968, from those states that had not passed legislation to control advertising signs and displays within 660 feet of the nearest edge of the right-of-way of interstate and primary highways. The Secretary of Commerce was allowed to make the determination and to suspend enforcement in specific cases if he deemed it in the public interest. Under terms of the act, outdoor advertising would be limited to directional and other official signs and notices; those signs advertising the sale or lease of property on lands in which they were located; those advertising activities conducted on the property on which they were located; and those within areas zoned commercial or industrial, or in unzoned areas, the latter to be determined by agreement between the secretary and the states.

The act also provided that advertisers would not have to remove unlawful signs for a five-year period, and that just compensation would be paid to the owners, with the Federal share amounting to 75 per cent. These provisions were obviously designed to reduce the economic impact of the act upon private advertisers. They also served to delay implementation of the act. Another section which provided opportunity for delay, but which was entirely consistent with American concepts of justice, was the provision requiring judicial review of appeals from those states that contested action taken by the secretary. Finally, the act authorized appropriations to be determined after the act had been in effect for two years.

Efforts to control the placement of junk yards were to be supported by the withholding of federal-aid highway funds in a similar manner. Control was specified to mean that junk yards must be screened by natural objects, plantings, or fences or other appropriate means, so as not to be visible from the interstate and primary highway systems. Exceptions included junk yards in areas zoned industrial, or in areas not zoned but used for industrial activity as determined by the secretary. The impact upon the junk-yard owners was again delayed and reduced by provision of just compensation (Federal share was 75 per cent) and specification of July 1, 1970, as the date for removal of yards which could not be adequately screened, in the secretary's judgment. An appropriation of twenty million dollars was authorized for each of the fiscal years 1966 and 1967 to implement junk-yard control.

To strengthen Federal efforts for "scenic enhancement," the act authorized the secretary to include the cost of landscaping and road-side developments as part of federal-aid highway construction costs borne by the Federal government. It also allowed the states to spend 3 per cent of their Federal highway funds for landscaping and roadside development within the right-of-way, and for acquisition and im-provements of strips of land necessary to enhance scenic beauty adjacent to the highway. An appropriation of $120 million was author-ized for each of the fiscal years 1966 and 1967 to carry out these purposes.

A general provision directed the Secretary of Commerce in coopera-tion with the states to prepare and submit to Congress a detailed estimate of the cost of implementing the act, and to conduct a compre-hensive study of the economic impact of the highway beautification program on affected individuals and commercial and industrial enter-prises, together with an examination of the effectiveness of the pro-gram and alternate methods of accomplishing the act's objectives. This provision reflects the desire of members of Congress to have all costs measured in dollar values, and, implicity, to evaluate the pro-gram's effectiveness in economic terms. In part, this was contrary to the President's emphasis upon qualitative aspects of the environment, but was consistent with attitudes and values of many of the "publics" with which the congressmen were in contact.

President Johnson remarked at the signing of the Act that:

. . . this bill does more than control advertising and junkyards along the billions of highways that people have built with their money—public money, not private money. It does more than give us the tools just to landscape some of those highways. This bill will bring the wonders of nature back into our daily lives. This bill will enrich our spirits and restore a small measure of our national greatness. . . . It does not represent what we need . . . but it is a first step.[2]

Did the bill represent a significant first step, or, as many critics contend, did its exposure to numerous pressures in the legislative process eliminate its effectiveness in light of the goals mentioned above? Consideration of this question requires examination of the political development of highway beautification efforts.

II

Questions of environmental quality have traditionally received harsh treatment in the formal political arena of the United States. Many public efforts take the form of isolated *ad hoc* reactions to specific crises, and are marked by a minimal effort. Why does our government—by and for the people—respond in such a manner? Dennis McElrath argues that the political culture presents serious obstacles to comprehensive programs of environmental improvement. In addition to certain organizational difficulties, he argues that principles and bases for action are not widely shared, or they are constrained by strong norms which run counter to the establishment of such programs.[3] Indeed, it is often impossible to find a generally agreed-upon concept of the public interest in environmental questions, for there is no widely shared general image of the good environment or of our relation to it.

This was the situation in the political debate surrounding the highway beautification efforts. No congressmen or interest groups were opposed in principle to beautiful highways, but many were opposed when attempts were made to implement the concept in the form of legislation; no agreement could be reached as to what constituted the public interest. An example is the remark with which Representative William C. Cramer of Florida, a leading opponent of the bill, prefaced his argument in the House floor debate. "I am for beauty," he said. "Nobody can say I'm not for beauty and no one can say I'm not for beautification of highways."[4] Then he proceeded to rip the bill to shreds.

One could argue that our relativistic republican form of government would be appropriate to the task of offering public answers to general but ill-defined problems. A central assumption underlining our form of government is the inherent worth of an open political system which allows the interplay of interests and alternative policies. This interplay, which Justice Holmes described as "the free trade in ideas," involves a struggle among a multiplicity of groups which yields a working definition of the public interest, and which, as a requisite for

[3] Dennis C. McElrath, "Public Response to Environmental Problems," *Environmental Studies*, ed. Lynton K. Caldwell (2 vols.; Bloomington: Institute of Public Administration, Indiana University, 1967), I, 2.

[4] U.S., *Congressional Record*, 89th Cong., 1st sess., CXI (1965), 26252.

survival in the political arena, includes general rather than particular interests. This ideal type, which, obviously, has great relevance in certain areas of public concern, has, however, tended to yield *ad hoc*, segmented, "lowest common denominator" efforts in the field of environmental problems. Cultural and organizational factors have contributed to the development of a body of weak or segmented public policies marked by log-rolling or manipulation to retain a facsimile of the *status quo*.

Traditionally, the state legislatures have presented a relatively unsympathetic ear to pleas for positive action to control the quality of the environment. Conservationist appeals based upon such noneconomic values as aesthetics and future recreational needs have often been unsuccessful when confronted by opposing economic considerations. In light of the intense interstate competition for industry, it is obvious why generalized arguments appealing to "the public" rather than to specialized economic "publics" have been unsuccessful. The dominance of personality factors in state elections, the low level of public interest and understanding of local and state government, and the low quality of the legislative and administrative officials in many states have contributed to a political environment which is unresponsive to qualitative issues such as highway beautification. With a few exceptions, the states have been reluctant to issue strict regulations of billboards or junk yards, and aesthetic values have, traditionally, been neglected or subordinated to economic and engineering considerations when highway routes are initially selected.

In recognition of this situation, some commentators have suggested "the carrot and stick" approach.[5] This involves the Federal government's offering economic incentives for some type of state action. This *quid pro quo* tactic was tried for seven years in an attempt to encourage state efforts to beautify the federally aided highway system. In 1958, a billboard law provided for a bonus in highway funds for states which agreed to enforce standards similar to those later inserted into the 1965 act. When the law expired on June 30, 1965, only ten states had received a bonus. The Federal incentives were not sufficient to overcome local opposition to the controls. This situation provided the legislative background for the 1965 attempt at the Federal level to enact mandatory highway beautification legislation.

[5] Daniel R. Grant, "Carrots, Sticks and Political Consensus," *Environmental Studies*, I (1966), 36.

At the national level, attitudes concerning some types of public policies often split along structural lines between the executive and legislative branches. This has encouraged an active presidential role in legislative politics, summed up by Woodrow Wilson in these words:

Some of our Presidents have felt the need which unquestionably exists in our system for some spokesman of the nation as a whole, in matters of legislation no less than in other matters, and have tried to supply Congress with the leadership of suggestion, backed by argument and by iteration and by every legitimate appeal to public opinion.[6]

Wilson touched upon a central motivating factor in the recurring differences between Congress and the President: the differing constituencies of the two branches of government. Congress represents the pluralistic aspect of American society. Because, by definition, the congressman represents a specified geographic area and a small segment of the total population, specific interests have a larger voice in the congressional decision-making process than in the presidential decision-making process. The President's constituency is the entire population and special interests are relatively small fish in a bigger pond. The conflicting constituencies are aggravated by the seniority system in Congress and by the electoral college system.

The differing constituencies, and resulting differing perspectives on national policy issues, contributed to the active legislative leadership role by President Johnson in the highway beautification issue. The national character of the issue, combined with the attractiveness of the general concepts of beauty to the apathetic majority, made the cause much more attractive to the President than to the pluralistic Congress.

On February 1, 1965, in his Natural Beauty Message, the President first mentioned the need for beautification of the highway system. He followed this by sponsoring the White House Conference on Natural Beauty in May, 1965. The eight hundred delegates represented most of the interested parties in the beautification issue. The conference staff had prepared reports which did not represent the thinking of many of the conferees. A struggle ensued, centering primarily upon such aspects of billboard control as zoning exemptions, but the staff reports prevailed as the basis for the legislation drafted by the administration and submitted to Congress on May 26. The controversial

[6] Woodrow Wilson, *Constitutional Government in the United States* (New York: Columbia University Press, 1961 edition), pp. 72–73.

nature of the conference set the tone for later developments. In the
Senate, the legislation took the form of an omnibus bill (S. 2084), but
in the House, four bills embodying the administration's views were
introduced.

The President's support, both personal and institutional, was instrumental in the degree of success the legislation had. Presidential influence varied. Mrs. Johnson, who took a personal interest in the issue,
traveled about the country drumming up support for the bill, and,
aside from the personal impact, the publicity surrounding this rather
unusual activity for a First Lady was effective in stimulating indirect
pressure on congressmen in the form of letters from home. President
Johnson must be given credit for an effective tactic in the use of the
key word beauty. As Henry Diamond, the co-director of the White
House Conference on Natural Beauty observed, the word beauty
struck a much more responsive chord both with the public at large
and among congressmen than has much of the jargon normally used
by conservationist pressure groups.[7] Johnson relied heavily upon
spokesmen from the upper levels of the Department of Commerce,
including the Secretary of Commerce, and from the Bureau of Public
Roads. These spokesmen provided most of the public governmental
testimony on behalf of the bill. The President restrained his personal
efforts to behind-the-scenes telephone calls to key legislators and to
efforts at "eye-ball" persuasion at his normal Tuesday morning breakfast with congressional leaders. Most of his specific efforts were
shielded from the public eye, but his desire to push through a bill, and
the public outcries of "arm twisting" by Representative Gerald Ford
of Michigan and other opponents, give evidence of the presence of
persuasive presidential efforts.

Many of the interests opposed to the beautification efforts were
vocal in the committee testimony, and this was reflected in the floor
debate on the bill. Examination of the positions of the interest groups
not only reveals the political pluralism of our society, but also the
differing concepts of the public interest, as distinct from private
economic interests. Representatives of the American Association of
State Highways officials and the National Association of Counties, as
well as several state governors, opposed the administration's provision
for financing the beautification programs from the Highway Trust
Fund, which is parcelled out to the states for construction. This

[7] *New York Times,* September 9, 1965, p. 25.

revealed a priority of values which favored continued rapid construction of the highway system over beautification efforts. Conflict over the scarce resource—money—may not have been entirely the result of private economic considerations, but it is highly possible that these state and local officials were influenced by private interest groups throughout the country whose economic well-being is tied closely to the Federal highway construction program. Opposition to this provision also included such prominent organizations as the American Road Builders Association and the Associated General Contractors of America, Inc. This reaction proved so strong that the administration accepted an amendment providing for separate financing of the program through an additional congressional appropriation.

The billboard provisions proved to be the most controversial. Such private groups as the American Motor Hotel Association and the Roadside Business Association asserted at the committee hearings that beautification should be a local and state responsibility, perhaps because, as noted above, lower levels of government are generally more vulnerable to private pressures. It should be noted, however, that the largest advertising lobby, the Outdoor Advertising Association, supported the billboard provisions, primarily because its major objection was satisfied by the administration's provision to exempt commercial and industrial zones, where most of its activities are conducted. This had been a primary bone of contention at the White House Conference, which indicates that this lobby's political influence was acknowledged before the bill was ever submitted to Congress. The billboard industry does a $500 million per year business, a strong argument to confront those based on aesthetic values in the eyes of most congressmen.

The junk-yard provisions were opposed by the Institute of Scrap Iron and Steel, the National Association of Secondary Material Industries, and the National Auto and Truck Wreckers Association. Their opposition centered on the zoning provisions and the compensation provisions. Substantial amendments were won in both of these areas.

Interest groups supporting the bill, or stronger measures, included the Garden Clubs of America, the National Wildlife Federation, and the Izaak Walton League. Their arguments were usually based upon aesthetic and other noneconomic values. Because of the pluralistic segmented character of Congress, especially the House, these arguments often fell on unsympathetic ears. Although public attitudes concerning beauty and the environment are becoming more favorable, in 1965 this change did not manifest itself in a strong, effective lobby on behalf of the bill. It is probable that without the President's strong support no bill would have been enacted by the Eighty-ninth Congress.

The Senate Public Works Committee (Public Roads Subcommittee) completed hearings on S. 2084 on August 13, 1965, and reported the bill favorably on September 14, with several key amendments. First, the control provisions exempted junk yards in industrial areas, a change sought by the Institute of Scrap Iron and Steel primarily on the grounds that the billboard industry had similar exemptions. In a concession to billboard interests, a second amendment specified that existing signs which violated the control requirements could not be required to be removed before July 1, 1970, or until the end of the fifth year after they became nonconforming, whichever was later. The administration bill had specified that billboard and junk-yard controls extended to 1,000 feet from the nearest edge of the pavement, but in a third amendment the committee amended this to read "within 660 feet of the nearest edge of the right-of-way." The committee provided for direct funding out of the Treasury instead of the originally proposed plan to earmark allotments out of the highway fund. Funds for landscaping were increased, but a proposal to construct scenic roads with Federal funds was dropped.

The enforcement provisions were severely weakened by the elimination of the use of the police power, a move which had serious implications for several state efforts. Congressman Thomas Pelly (R., Wash.) noted that several states (twenty-three in all, with Washington as an example) had beautification legislation which relied upon zoning laws and police enforcement. However, he argued, the Federal legislation, in effect, would eliminate these efforts because the resulting discriminatory application of police powers to advertising interests could never stand a court test. The administration bill would have relied on state police powers to control billboards and junk yards first, and then, if this proved ineffective, would have allowed use of Federal funds for partial compensation. The amended version required Federal funds for compensation in all cases, eliminating altogether the use of state police powers. This change reflected a congressional value judgment that the cost of removal—the external costs to society for certain advertising and junk-yard practices—should not be borne by the industries but rather by the government. This position has been sharply criticized in many quarters. One of the most influential and articulate came in a *New York Times* editorial:

Secretary of Commerce John Conner has estimated that it would cost one hundred and eighty million dollars to buy the advertising rights on land adjacent to the Interstate and primary road systems. . . . It is scandalous that the Federal Government should have to pay this large sum to purchase a "private right" that had not existed before the Government built the road.[8]

In a letter to bill manager Jennings Randolph (D., W.Va.) on September 16, President Johnson accepted the Public Works Committee amendments and said, "The bill which the Senate is acting upon today, together with the amendments I understand you have worked out with Administration officials, is a far-reaching and acceptable step toward achieving the purposes of this program." This analysis considerably stretched the meaning of "far-reaching." The Senate passed S. 2084 by a roll-call vote of 63–14 on September 16 after two days of floor debate. The major enforcement tool available to the Federal government was drastically reduced when, as a price for several governors' support, a floor amendment reduced from 100 per cent to 10 per cent the amount of funds that could be cut off from the states which did not comply with the billboard and junk-yard controls.

The Roads Subcommittee of the House Public Works Committee had concluded hearings on the four White House bills on September 7, but did not hold hearings on S. 2084. Instead, because of pressure from the White House, the entire House Public Works Committee met in executive session on September 20 and agreed to report it out the next day. This pressure was accentuated by the hasty preparation of the report, which was completed the night of September 22. The House Rules Committee granted the bill a rule on September 30 by a 7–6 vote.

Opposition began to develop along party lines, perhaps as a result of the active White House role, and this led to acrimonious debate on the floor of the House. On the afternoon of October 7, word was received that the White House wanted passage of the bill that night. Republicans charged that it was to be a present to Ladybird at a party planned for that evening. The House was kept in session late into the night, largely because of the opposition's delaying tactics of requesting time-consuming teller votes on the amendments. It was finally

[8] *Ibid.*, September 14, 1965, p. 38.

passed at 12:51 A.M., October 8, 1965, by a vote of 245–138. The
Senate agreed to the House version of S. 2084 by a voice vote on
October 13, the House amendments were uncontroversial in nature,
and the President signed the bill into law on October 22, 1965.

III

The impact of the act has been reduced by several recent developments. Examination of the control provisions reveals that much depends upon the judgments made by the Secretary of Commerce in the
administration of the act. These judgments have since taken the
partial form of standards and regulations issued by the Bureau of
Public Roads relating to the definition of unzoned commercial and
industrial areas—size, spacing, and lighting of signs—and national
standards for outdoor advertising on public lands. Using testimony
received at fifty-two public hearings held in compliance with provisions of the act, the bureau developed standards and criteria which
reflected the varied pressures of the political environment, and which,
unfortunately, represented a compromise of the position of many
supporters who had favored strict interpretation of the controls.[9] This
may perhaps be explained by the position of Secretary of Transportation Alan Boyd. (Responsibility for administration of the act was
shifted to the Department of Transportation under an administrative
reorganization in 1966.) Secretary Boyd accepted the states as equal
partners in the formulation of the regulations. As noted earlier, the
position of the various state governments is likely to diverge from that
of the Federal government on questions of environmental quality, and
this basic conflict has had a major impact.

The standards also came under fire from the advertising industry.
They were criticized both for being too strict and for creating a
minimum acceptable level which the states could not alter through
negotiation. These criticisms were also voiced by Congressman Cramer and by Congressman Klycynski, Chairman of the Subcommittee
on Roads. By the spring of 1967, the act was under fire both from
supporters and opponents of strong beautification efforts, and this
tended to erode congressional support for the act. This was strikingly
revealed when the highway beautification program failed to receive
reauthorization for fiscal 1968; the programs expired for lack of fund-

[9] U.S., Congress, Senate, *1967 Highway Beautification Program*, 90th
Cong., 1st sess., Senate Doc. 6, 1967, p. 45.

ing on June 30, 1967. The fierce competition for nondefense funds and the budget cuts accompanying the recent tax surcharge cast doubt on possible funding of the act for fiscal 1969.

Lack of support for the act has also been revealed in the record of state cooperation. As of June, 1968, only eleven states had signed agreements with the Secretary of Transportation to regulate billboards pursuant to the act. In recognition of this lack of support, the Secretary has not enforced the 10 per cent penalty for noncompliance, which, in effect, has rendered the act voluntary. Some states, however, have continued or initiated programs independent of the Federal program. A key feature of most of the state programs has been the reliance upon police power for enforcement. Contrary to the arguments presented during the passage of the act, most courts have upheld the use of police power by the states to enforce billboard control provisions. For example, the Washington Highway Advertising Control Act of 1961 was upheld by the State Supreme Court in *Markham Advertising Co., Inc., et al.* v. *The State of Washington.*[10] The majority opinion stated, "The intrusive quality of highway outdoor advertising, coupled with the hazard it poses to traffic safety and its purely commercial nature, all persuade us [that the law is a reasonable regulation]."

IV

This review of the development of the Highway Beautification Act and its administration by the Department of Transportation has revealed the very limited impact of the legislation upon the goals cited by the President in his letter of transmittal. Was the act, whatever its impact, the strongest measure possible at the time? President Johnson accepted the bill as such, and, though acknowledging that it was weak, felt that it was a "first step." This position was entirely consistent with his concept that "politics is the art of the possible." Many have disagreed with this strategy in view of the political forces present in 1965. For example, the *New York Times* editorially argued that he should have waited until the second session of the Eighty-ninth Congress when he could have organized much stronger political pressure for enactment of a much stronger bill. The *Times* likened the act to the junk-yard provision: "It hides the problem—it does not solve it." [11]

[10] 73 2d *Washington Documents*, p. 413.
[11] *New York Times*, October 8, 1965, p. 4.

Any judgment concerning the best political strategy must be highly intuitive, for it is difficult to determine in any kind of precise form the changing attitudes of the public concerning questions of environmental quality in general or highway beautification in particular. It is obvious that without strong presidential support no bill would have passed the Eighty-ninth Congress, for a change in public attitudes concerning questions of beauty certainly did not manifest itself in a strong, effective lobby on behalf of the bill. Given the strengths and priorities of other demands upon the nation's resources (the urban crisis and the Viet Nam War, for example), it was improbable that a strong bill could have passed the second session. The President simply had too many other pressing priorities, and he would not have risked his waning influence with Congress over a bill which would probably not have been a key element of his 1966 program. It can be argued that the act was indicative of a general, longer-term change in public attitudes toward a quality environment. Indeed, before 1958 there were no major beautification efforts at the national level, and before 1965 only an incentive program existed. Viewed in this context, and to the extent that Congress is representative of public sentiment, the 1965 act marked a shift in public sentiment in favor of positive governmental action.

This case study reveals the harsh treatment highway beautification efforts have received in the political arena at both the state *and* national levels. There are major weaknesses in the Federal legislation, both in the approach it takes to the problem and in specific provisions concerning zoning exemptions and enforcement powers. The approach to highway beautification centered on the altering of existing roadsides. This cosmetic approach ignores a real problem—that of an emphasis on economic and engineering considerations at the expense of aesthetic values when initial routes are selected. These selections are crucial to highway beauty and therefore should have been given attention in this legislation. The zoning exemptions of the billboard and junk-yard control sections are also major loopholes in attempts to provide meaningful contributions to a quality environment. These provisions are actually worse than no control in that they encourage the creation of billboard "alleys" in the exempted areas which all too frequently are the highway approaches to the urban areas.

A provision banning off-premise advertising, combined with stricter spacing and size limitations, would have strengthened this section.

Off-premise advertising bans already exist in some states, including Vermont and Hawaii. The compensation arrangements represent another major weakness of the act. A major reduction in the percentage provided by the Federal and state governments from the current 100 per cent to 25 per cent would represent a more equitable private-public distribution of the external costs of the advertising and junk-yard businesses. Why should the government subsidize blight?

The last major weakness is revealed in the administration of the act. The lack of enforcement of the 2 per cent penalty for noncompliance removes the major enforcement tool and leaves the control provisions virtually useless. The lack of enforcement resulted from the "agreement" provisions specifying Federal and state negotiation of advertising controls. Increased authority for the Secretary of Transportation would make it easier to reconcile the divergent views of the states and the Department of Transportation in the public interest.

V

Final judgment concerning the over-all value of the act to society involves some form of identification of the public interest in questions of environmental quality. Obviously, the highways serve many functions, and one must always keep this central fact in mind. J. B. Jackson, the editor of *Landscape*, has argued that there are varying types of "customers" for the nation's highways, and that only a small fraction are using them for pleasure. He noted that highway signs serve a definite function by providing directions and information to motorists and this must not be forgotten in efforts to beautify the nation's roads.[12] However, the Department of Transportation has noted that a recent study revealed that a majority of motorists indicated no difficulty in finding highway services where billboards had been restricted.[13] Clearly informational needs and aesthetic values are not in irreconcilable conflict.

The Highway Beautification Act of 1965 supplemented by refinements in the areas suggested would make a significant contribution to the public interest, a public interest which includes aesthetic values as well as economic interests. However, if it is Congress that proposes the next step in highway beautification rather than the President, then

[12] J. B. Jackson, "Abolish Highways!" *The National Review*, XVIII (November 29, 1966), 1213.
[13] Senate, *1967 Highway Beautification Program*, p. 23.

it is reasonable to expect that the already inadequate provisions of the Highway Beautification Act will not be significantly strengthened.

The fact is that Congress is ill-equipped to handle environmental issues in which aesthetics and ethics are involved. The kinds of changes needed to move beyond a cosmetic approach to highway beautification are changes that involve a greater political risk for Congress than for the President. Alterations in the Federal highway program to induce state highway departments to include aesthetic considerations at the highway planning stage can be expected to meet resistance, especially if the allocation of Federal funds is made dependent upon the inclusion of these considerations. Congress is much more vulnerable than the President to the political pressures that might follow such a change. In the same way, groups such as the Outdoor Advertising Association and the American Roadbuilders Association are likely to be much more influential in the election of a congressman than in the election of a president. A congressman is likely to obtain a greater political advantage from an expensive but ugly addition to the highway system of his state or district than from his vigorous support of aesthetically pleasing highways in the country as a whole.

Phrases such as "natural beauty" and "highway beautification" have a low priority on the list of phrases from which congressmen can generate political capital. This situation is changing as environmental issues demand increasing attention from government and become a source of genuine concern among the general public and the people who represent them. The passage of the Highway Beautification Act illustrates quite clearly the more general point that environmental issues cannot be given the attention they deserve without the political support of an agency that can force Congress to rise above the specialized and localized interests which it finds politically attractive. The history of the act also demonstrates that there are limits to what a President can achieve, even if environmental issues had a higher priority on the list of national policy goals than they do now. The implication here is that structural changes in the Federal government are required to improve the ability of the President to provide the kind of environmental policy initiatives which Congress seems unable or unwilling to propose in furtherance of the public interest.

4. The Wilderness Act:

A Product of Congressional Compromise

DELBERT V. MERCURE, JR., and WILLIAM M. ROSS

WILDERNESS is the basic ingredient from which American civilization has grown. American history can be regarded as a continuous struggle to vanquish a seemingly hostile wilderness in the name of social progress. The earliest settlers perceived wilderness primarily as a physical resource to be conquered, to be transformed by man's initiative and technology for use in furthering man's economic and material well-being. A large proportion of the natural environment was thus destroyed to provide the raw materials with which to build and maintain American economic strength. Pleas from men such as Henry Thoreau, George Marsh, and John Muir for a more humane treatment of wilderness and the environment were largely ignored by successive Congresses, which pursued policies designed primarily to encourage the economic development of all unsettled lands. It has been only in recent decades that wilderness has come to be regarded much more highly for its spiritual, aesthetic, and scientific qualities; and it was not until 1964 that Congress provided statutory protection to preserve a small part of the remaining wild landscape in more-or-less its natural state through passage of the Wilderness Act.

America's conception of her wilderness has been a compound of attraction and repulsion in which the extremes of opposing views have

DELBERT V. MERCURE, JR., was a graduate student in geography at the University of Washington before entering the armed forces. His experience includes work on the improvement of regional parks for the Los Angeles County Parks and Recreation Department.

WILLIAM M. ROSS is a teaching assistant in geography at the University of Washington, where he is currently completing work for his doctorate.

been uncompromising and at times dogmatic. Arguments presented in the early 1960's by supporters and opponents of wilderness legislation reflect this basic dichotomy in American thinking about wilderness, a dichotomy often present to some degree in every individual. Preservationists have pointed with horror to the adverse environmental impact of rapid population increases and sprawling urban growth. Business interests interpret the rapid transformation of the natural landscape as a necessary and even desirable concomitant of economic growth. The existence of these contradictions in man's perception of his environment has made it difficult to formulate a common set of working assumptions within which discussion and compromise can occur. Both wilderness preservation and economic growth may be regarded as desirable objectives and the passage of an act giving statutory protection to wilderness necessarily required a compromise between them. It will be helpful in analyzing passage of the Wilderness Act to examine in general terms the two dominant schools of thought on wilderness preservation.

I

The backers of a strong wilderness bill considered man to be the guardian of the earth's natural resources, and they felt a strong commitment to preserve as much of the landscape as possible for future generations. Their arguments have found expression in the past largely through the writings of poets and philosophers. A recent statement by Paul Oesher captures the spirit of this thinking. Wilderness, he writes, is something people seek "not to be less human but to be more human, to simplify their lives in order to see life's purpose more clearly, to be able to return to society freed of the haze and uncertainty that obscured their vision, to identify themselves with a part of all that ever was, is, or will be in the universe." [1] Preservationists contended that there is only a limited amount of wilderness which, if we allow it to be exploited, can never be replaced. Sentiments such as these have found a growing number of adherents in the highly mechanized and urbanized United States of the last several decades. Roderick Nash eloquently describes this change in American thinking in his book, *Wilderness and the American Mind.*[2]

[1] Paul H. Oesher, "A Footnote to the Philosophy of Wilderness," *The Living Wilderness*, No. 86 (Spring-Summer, 1964), p. 5.
[2] Roderick Nash, *Wilderness and the American Mind* (New Haven, Conn.: Yale University Press, 1967).

But supporters of wilderness legislation are relatively few in number and it would be misleading to assume that wilderness is universally regarded as the highest use of all the nation's remaining primeval lands. The dominant voice in American society still belongs to those who see wilderness as something to be transformed into the continuing flow of resources needed to sustain industry and economic growth. What may be called the economic argument considers man to be the master of the planet and regards the natural environment as a vast storehouse from which man may extract goods to satisfy his material needs. The economic argument is highly anthropocentric, stressing the importance of material growth driven on by increasingly higher levels of technology. To the supporters of this position wilderness must be viewed as only one of several potential uses that can be made of the remaining Federal wildlands; and many actually equate use of the land for wilderness as a form of nonuse. Since nature is to serve man, multiple use of the land, with the emphasis on extraction tempered only by a need to sustain yields, is held to be the best way to maximize resource output. A Chamber of Commerce spokesman succinctly stated the industry view: "We have long supported the multiple use of our National Forests and Wildlands, and feel that such progressive steps as the Multiple Use Act of 1960, which included wilderness areas as a responsibility of the Forest Service . . . will, in time, resolve the question of further dealings with wilderness areas."[3] These consumption-oriented forces consider it irrational to "lock up" areas of public land merely to preserve intangible wilderness qualities.

The often dogmatic positions of the advocates and the opponents of wilderness protection stemmed not only from their differing philosophical and emotional attitudes toward nature, but also from their interpretations of the ability of wilderness to survive under existing administrative machinery. Proponents of a wilderness system protected by statute maintained that the management of wildlands by both the United States Forest Service and the National Park Service had reached a crisis point. The Forest Service could classify and declassify wilderness lands by administrative directive, while the National Park Service treated all decisions for new roads or more intensive recreational development on park lands as internal matters and

[3] U.S., Congress, Senate, Committee on Interior and Insular Affairs, *Hearings, National Wilderness Preservation Act*, 88th Cong., 1st sess., 1963, pp. 388–89.

did not subject them to public review. Interest groups such as the Wilderness Society and the Sierra Club were disturbed by the Forest Service's declassification of existing primeval lands to the benefit of commodity interest, as well as by the National Park Service's favoring of mass recreation demands in its master plans. If further intrusions into wilderness areas were allowed solely by administrative decision, America could find itself with no areas left to preserve. They maintained that the nation had reached a point in time when wilderness, a nonrenewable natural resource, could no longer be viewed as something only to be conquered and transformed. If Congress failed to act there would be no chance to reconsider later, for once a wilderness area is destroyed it can never be replaced.

By asking Congress to implement a bill giving wilderness statutory protection, proponents challenged Federal agencies to consider wilderness as a legitimate and necessary use of some of the nation's remaining wildlands, and sought to open the problem of wilderness preservation to more intensive public scrutiny and discussion at the national level. Opponents of wilderness legislation, on the other hand, argued that the preservationists were alarmists who would commit the nation to economic stagnation with an ill-advised program. Before any action was taken to preserve wilderness, the opponents of preservation insisted that at the very least there must be comprehensive study and evaluation of the natural resources and unique qualities of each area, followed by a sober projection of future demands for wilderness as a source of recreation.[4]

Also subject to vehement controversy was the question of the actual extent of the demand for wilderness as a recreational land use. That the recreational taste of the American people has become increasingly outdoor oriented in recent years is a fact well substantiated by numerous government and private studies. But what about wilderness, *per se?* As preservationists have noted, the National Park Service has been forced in the face of an unrelenting demand for mass recreation to allow large-scale development of some of the most wild and beautiful parts of the park system; and they contended that as more people become familiar with the benefits of camping and hiking, a substantial proportion will shun lodges and trailer areas and demand more primi-

[4] U.S., Congress, House, Committee on Interior and Insular Affairs, *Hearings, Wilderness Preservation System*, 88th Cong., 2d sess., 1964, p. 81.

tive forms of recreation.[5] Fearing the invasion by large numbers of people of the few remaining remote areas, they argued that only immediate and massive action could save some traces of our wilderness beginnings from the dual pressures of commercial interests and mass recreationists. In answering this argument, the opposing forces agreed that there is a rapidly growing demand for outdoor recreation but seriously doubted that more than 1 or 2 per cent of the population would ever use these areas. They argued instead that many more roads and developed campsites were needed to open up the National Parks and National Forests to allow more people to enjoy nature with a minimum of effort. This point of view was expressed tersely by an industry lobbyist in his presentation before a House committee: "Let's be realistic," he said. "Today the American masses of people travel on wheels and wings, be it for business or pleasure, and not on foot or horseback. Thus this proposed legislation defeats the very purpose sought by making vast areas of the public domain inaccessible to all but the wealthy few who are financially able to hire horses and guides to enjoy such wilderness areas." [6]

Given these highly polarized views, there is some justification for arguing that the advocates and opponents of the Wilderness Act can be given meaningful though perhaps highly generalized political labels. Preservationists' arguments have a decidedly national orientation. In the congressional hearings on the bill, some of the strongest proponents could be labeled also as members of a liberal-urban establishment which has been pressing for a more active commitment by the Federal government to improve the social and physical environment of Americans. They favored strong executive action based on a national constituency. Forces opposing the Wilderness Act may be characterized as taking a somewhat more local or regional view. The key opposition was led by western legislators from states with economies tied closely to extractive industries. To many of these men it was of critical importance that employment in local mines and mills could be endangered by blanket protection for large wilderness areas. In contrast to the "liberal-urban" group, the forces opposed to the bill

[5] Senate, Interior and Insular Affairs Committee, *Hearings, National Wilderness Preservation Act*, p. 174.

[6] House, Interior and Insular Affairs Committee, *Hearings, Wilderness Preservation System*, p. 328.

may be thought of as "conservative and western." Some of the most forceful arguments against the legislation charged that Congress was surrendering its constitutional authority over the public lands. Finally, it is worth noting that despite the wide divergence in views between the preservationists and their opponents, all generally thought of themselves as solid conservationists.

II

Passage of the Wilderness Act was a slow, agonizing process extending over a period of many years. Perhaps the first governmental efforts to protect wilderness came with the establishment of the National Park System. However, no systematic effort was ever made by the Park Service to designate wilderness areas, as such, to be kept roadless; and as park planning intensified over the years, wilderness merely became the residuum. It was the U.S. Forest Service in the 1920's and 1930's that took the first positive steps to set aside areas for the specific purpose of protecting wilderness. Within the ranks of Forest Service personnel, men such as Aldo Leopold, Burton Silcox, and Robert Marshall took the lead in introducing and pressing the concept, and by the early 1940's, several million acres of wilderness, wild and primitive areas, had been established within the national forests by administrative directive. But the move in this direction by the Forest Service was also a defensive and bureaucratic one aimed at preventing the continued take-over of choice scenic and recreation lands by the Park Service for the establishment of new national parks.

Following World War II, national wilderness preservation organizations found themselves engaged in a series of conflicts over proposed developments in wilderness areas in both the national forests and national parks. Among these threats to wilderness values were proposed acreage deletions for logging purposes from Olympic National Park; a dam in Glacier National Park; a reservoir in the Bob Marshall Wilderness Area; dams in Kings Canyon National Park; mining in Joshua Tree National Monument; tramways in Mount Rainier National Park and in the San Jacinto Primitive Area; and, the most controversial of all, the proposed Echo Park Dam in Dinosaur National Monument. The heated battle over the latter proposal extended over several years. The preservationists, led by Howard Zahniser of the Wilderness Society, waged a nation-wide publicity campaign against the dam. By 1956, they not only had won this battle but had succeeded in bringing the larger issue of wilderness protection before the American public for the first time.

As early as 1947, Howard Zahniser and other preservationists had begun to advocate the establishment of a national system of wilderness protected by the statute, and in 1949 the Sierra Club held the first of a continuing series of biennial wilderness conferences which served to bring the various national and regional preservation organizations into closer bond on the issue.[7] However, it was not until after the Dinosaur victory that preservationists were sufficiently emboldened to ask Congress to put an end to the continual conflicts over wilderness preservation by providing clear statutory authority for the designation, maintenance, and protection of wilderness areas. Under Zahniser's leadership and in cooperation with the Sierra Club, the National Parks Association, the National Wildlife Federation, and the Wildlife Management Institute, a draft bill was prepared. Senator Hubert Humphrey of Minnesota became interested in the proposal, and on June 7, 1956, he introduced the first wilderness bill. An identical bill was also introduced in the House. As Michael McCloskey has pointed out in his admirable analysis of the legislation:

> These bills were initially opposed by both the Forest Service and the National Park Service and were bitterly resisted to the end by lumber, mining, power and irrigation interests. Nine years of deliberation were needed before enactment could be secured. Some sixty-five bills were introduced in the course of that time. . . . Eighteen hearings were held, six in Washington, D.C., and twelve in the field. Thousands of pages of transcript were compiled, and congressional mail ran as heavy as on any natural resource issue of modern times.[8]

As originally introduced, the bill proposed to protect wilderness by removing the authority of the Forest Service either to decrease wilderness acreage or to declassify wilderness and primitive areas; by protecting forest wilderness areas against intrusion of mining and water development interests; and by requiring the designation of selected additional wilderness areas within the National Park System, Federal wildlife refuges, and Indian reservations.

As noted, the original bill was vigorously opposed by both the Forest Service and Park Service, and much of the early congressional

[7] Jack M. Hession, "The Legislative History of the Wilderness Act" (unpublished Master's thesis, San Diego State College, 1967), pp. 5–13.

[8] Michael McCloskey, "The Wilderness Act of 1964: Its Background and Meaning," *Oregon Law Review*, XLV (June, 1966), 288–321.

consideration of the wilderness legislation was devoted to drafting amendments in an effort to make the bill acceptable to them. In early 1960, some four years after the wilderness bill had been introduced, the executive branch finally gave its approval. To satisfy the executive branch, the bill was amended to remove any reference to Indian reservations; and the Forest Service succeeded in securing various amendments, including those to eliminate a proposed advisory council and to allow mining and water development on wilderness lands upon findings by the President that such action was in the national interest.

Although the Forest Service finally approved the draft bill, it also encouraged passage of the Multiple Use Act of 1960 as an attempt to counter the growing support for wilderness in the Congress. The act confirmed multiple use and sustained yield as continuing objectives in the administration of national forest lands. Advocates of the multiple use legislation claimed that it would protect national forests from "over-utilization" as a result of pressures from "single interest groups." In effect, the Forest Service sought statutory protection for its existing management practices in an attempt to render unnecessary or meaningless the passage by Congress of a separate wilderness bill. Supporters of a wilderness bill were alarmed. Perhaps the most classic expression of preservationists' distaste for multiple use insofar as it overrode wilderness values was Harvey Manning's pithy definition: "No logging will be permitted above timberline." [9] Preservationists waged a difficult but successful battle to secure an amendment to the Multiple Use Act which provided that the establishment and maintenance of wilderness areas were consistent with the purposes of the act. As a result, the Multiple Use Act had little effect on the wilderness issue, and the battle over the wilderness bill raged on.

With the endorsement of the wilderness bill by President Kennedy in 1961, the idea of statutory protection for wilderness areas received an important political boost. Opponents relied heavily on Representative Wayne Aspinall of Colorado to secure the weakest possible bill. Aspinall is of particular importance in the debate over wilderness legislation. As chairman of the House Interior and Insular Affairs Committee, he held the power to call hearings on the wilderness bill after it had been referred to his committee, which is dominated by western legislators from states where mining, timber produc-

[9] Hession, "Legislative History of the Wilderness Act," p. 64.

tion, and grazing on public lands are held to be essential for economic growth. His past voting record has consistently favored commodity interests, especially where those interests clashed with legislation seeking to enhance the quality of the environment. Much of the delay over the wilderness bill centered on Aspinall's tactics to prevent or at least severely weaken any wilderness legislation.

Several points of contention were aired in the congressional debate, but the three most critical problems centered on who would have authority to add lands to the wilderness system; the status of mining and other economic endeavors in wilderness areas; and the amount of land that was to be originally included in the system.

The question of delegating authority to add lands to the system prompted considerably more controversy in Congress than among the general public. Congressmen who desired a strong executive acting in the national interest favored the wilderness bill introduced in April, 1963, by Senator Clinton P. Anderson of New Mexico during the Eighty-eighth Congress. The bill directed the Secretary of the Interior to study additional areas to determine which were suitable for inclusion in the system. Following the study, the President was to submit recommendations to Congress for the inclusion of additional areas. The President's recommendations would go into effect automatically *unless* either chamber passed a resolution of disapproval. Thus, the President would have the initiative and the Congress a veto. This system was defended as being in line with the Reorganization Act of 1949. It was also thought that the specialized staff of the executive was more qualified to study the various proposed additions, and that Congress would be spared the task of dealing with a long list of similar bills. However, the more conservative legislators saw the provisions of this bill as another step toward the erosion of congressional authority. It was forcefully argued that the Constitution clearly gave ultimate authority over the public lands to Congress and that only an affirmative act by Congress could establish a new wilderness area. Representative Aspinall took a particularly vocal and uncompromising stand on the issue, arguing that each new area would have to be evaluated by Congress before separate legislation would be passed. By requiring affirmative congressional action, Aspinall was in effect seeking to capitalize on his own powerful position as chairman of the House Interior and Insular Affairs Committee. Other congressmen held that public agencies were too easily influenced by outside pressures and that Congress was in a better position to judge objectively the need for more wilderness.

A second problem concerned the degree to which multiple use would be compatible with wilderness. Preservationists contended that mining, grazing, and lumbering must be curtailed in wilderness areas. If commercial exploitation were permitted, the idea of wilderness would be virtually meaningless. While some minor resources may be left untapped, the preservationists claimed that it was more economical to intensify use of established and more accessible regions, or to import more ore. It was further argued that if at some future time the national security demanded the use of the resources in the wilderness areas, the President could, of course, open up the areas to exploitation. The question of continued mining in the wilderness areas was one of the truly critical considerations for the opponents of the Wilderness Act. It was said that the preservationists could endanger the growth of the national economy by refusing the mining industry access to new sources of ore. The issue of national security was introduced into the debate when Howard Gray, who represented the American Mining Congress, spoke on the mineral needs of America in his testimony opposing the wilderness bill: "The position of the mining industry is not arbitrary, nor does it stem from self interest. It is based upon the fact that our standard of living, our national defense and welfare, and our strength in international affairs requires and in fact demands adequate availability of mineral resources. Access to these resources must be unobstructed." [10] The mining industry considered that an immediate termination of existing mineral policy in wilderness areas would be an economic disaster. They argued that the industry had invested huge sums in fixed assets, and that much of it would be lost if they could not explore and exploit new areas. On a local scale, it was pointed out that immediate suspension of new claims could destroy some communities and put thousands of men out of work. At a minimum, it was felt that a twenty-five-year period should be allowed before any limitation on mining went into effect. Herders and lumbermen, for similar economic reasons, also criticized restrictions on access to public lands. Herders were particularly concerned about the impact of the bill on their grazing rights on Federal lands and sought to maintain these historic claims. Lumbermen focused on wilderness

[10] Senate, Interior and Insular Affairs Committee, *Hearings, National Wilderness Preservation Act,* p. 107.

area boundaries. They fought for individual hearings on each bill creating a new wilderness area with a view to excluding valleys with valuable timber.

The third point of contention concerned how much and which land should be included within the original national wilderness system. The principal disagreement was over the lands classified as "primitive" by the Forest Service.[11] Supporters of strong wilderness legislation urged adoption of Senator Anderson's bill which included some 14.6 million acres, of which approximately 9.1 million acres were classified as wilderness and the remaining 5.5 million acres as primitive. The bill provided for a review of the primitive areas with possible later deletion of some of them. Opponents to the wilderness bill objected vigorously to the inclusion of the primitive lands in the original system and urged that designation of these areas as wilderness should be made only after government and industry had clearly demonstrated that the highest economic use was to leave the areas in their natural state.

III

In 1961, the Senate passed a strong wilderness bill which included the primitive areas; gave the President the affirmative authority to add lands to the system with Congress having only the power of veto; and contained strict limitations on mining and other economic land uses. Led by Senator Anderson, who was at that time Chairman of the Senate Interior and Insular Affairs Committee, the bill easily passed the Senate despite concerted efforts from Senator Gordon Allott of Colorado for a bill more favorable to the mining industry and other economic interests.

Following passage in the Senate, the House Interior and Insular Affairs Committee began consideration of the bill, but there it suffered a harsher fate. After sitting on the bill for several months, the House committee reported the bill in a radically different form, reflecting the majority of industry objections. Congressman Aspinall was personally against the presidential authority clause. The House bill provided

---

[11] As used here, a "primitive area" is one with natural, wild, and undeveloped characteristics in which commercial uses are allowed as long as they are compatible with the original purpose for which the area is designated; while a "wilderness area" is a primitive area set aside and managed to preserve these characteristics, with wilderness as the sole use.

instead that primitive areas, as well as areas within national parks and wildlife refuges, could be added later to the initial wilderness system *only* by affirmative congressional action. Thus, each new area added would require a special act of Congress. The House bill also specified that wilderness was only one of several special and legitimate uses of wildlands. Backed by a group of western congressmen, Aspinall sought to bring the amended measure to the floor of the House for a vote under suspension of the rules, which would have meant no amendments could be offered. Aspinall realized that if amendments were allowed, a strong effort would be made to restore the bill to its earlier Senate form. The Speaker of the House, backed by preservationists and President Kennedy, refused to allow the rule change, making it clear to Aspinall that no bill would be preferable to the watered-down House measure. As a result, the wilderness bill died in the House Interior and Insular Affairs Committee when Congress adjourned for the mid-term elections late in 1962.

In 1963 another strong wilderness bill sailed through the Senate and was again referred to Aspinall's committee in the House. Aspinall maintained there should be no hearings on the wilderness bill pending a general review of policy-making for management of all Federal lands. When this rear-guard action threatened to kill the bill, newspaper comments and public opinion became vitriolic. Representative Aspinall complained about the unfairness of these attacks on the floor of the House and remained adamant on his stand. For some time no action was taken, but in the fall of 1963 it became obvious to the preservationists that time and the realities of congressional power were against them and that it was better to get some protection rather than none at all. It was also recognized that while they had to invest huge amounts of money in an attempt to arouse the public, the opposition had friends of long standing in Congress who could block the measure forever. As a result, the preservation groups agreed to support Aspinall's proposed legislation to create a Public Land Law Review Commission on the condition that he would report out a wilderness bill that could be debated and amended on the House floor where there was greater support for wilderness than in Aspinall's committee. Accordingly, the House Interior Committee reported out the usual watered-down version of the wilderness bill. It required affirmative congressional action to add areas to the wilderness system; allowed mining exploration for twenty-five years after the passage of the bill; and allowed the Forest Service to declassify primitive areas at will by administrative directive.

Although the preservationists were put in a position of accepting half a loaf rather than no bread, they did manage to gain some concessions. On the floor of the House an amendment was accepted to do away with the Forest Service's authority to declassify primitive areas. Representative John Saylor of Pennsylvania also led a successful floor fight to restore the highly controversial San Gorgonio Wilderness Area in southern California, which had been eliminated from the system by the House Interior Committee at the request of commercial interests who sought to open up the area for skiing to meet the huge demand for winter sports in the Los Angeles area. As amended, the bill passed the House by an overwhelming vote of 373–1. In the House-Senate conference committee, the Senate acceded to the insistence of the House to reserve the sole right to Congress to add new areas to the system, while the House agreed to reduce the period in which mining would be allowed from twenty-five to nineteen years (i.e., until 1983).

President Johnson signed the bill on September 3, 1964. The act provides the beginning for a wilderness system. It was born out of conflict between two extremely divergent views on the primary use of the nation's remaining wild areas. Preservationists were able to obtain action only by massive pressure on Congress. They persevered over nearly a decade, slowly gaining public sympathy for their stand. Wilderness groups consistently and repeatedly placed on the record testimony in support of the act. National newspapers such as the *New York Times* and the *Washington Post* also took up the cause. The executive branch and the Senate gave substantially more support to the bill than the House. The willingness of the President and some members of the Senate to take a broader view of wilderness preservation is partly linked to the size of their constituencies. Elected by the whole country, the President can view problems in a national context. Senators serve state needs and are not held as directly accountable for maintenance of local economies as their colleagues in the House. They are freer to debate national issues than representatives, who must pay closer attention to the narrower needs and interests of their constituents if they expect to be re-elected every two years.

The final legislation establishing the National Wilderness System must be considered a compromise; but it may also be said that the economic interests gained rather more than they were forced to give up. Of all the issues compromised in Congress during consideration of the law, the one which may prove the most critical is the rejection of Presidential initiative as the means for adding new areas to the system.

Under the terms of the act, all of the existing national forest wilderness, wild, and canoe areas were automatically placed in the system. These areas totaled 9,108,000 acres in fifty-four separate units. But the act left the thirty-four primitive areas of the national forests, totaling some 5,580,000 acres, to be brought into the system during a ten-year period after public hearings and review by the Secretary of Agriculture. The same procedures apply to wild and roadless portions of over seventy national parks, national monuments, wildlife refuges, and wildlife ranges (areas totaling nearly 60,000,000 acres) which are to be reviewed by the Secretary of the Interior during the same ten-year period. Each area recommended for addition to the system must be introduced in Congress as a separate bill and run the gauntlet of the House and Senate Committees on Interior and Insular Affairs, which are responsible for reporting authorizing bills for additions to the system. Hardly a more tedious, time-consuming, and obstructive method could have been devised. It means that preservationist groups will be working at a heavy disadvantage. They cannot realistically hope to mobilize national opinion behind every attempt to add a new area to the system, especially with powerful mining, grazing, and timber interests pressing Congress to exclude many areas. Such a procedure places heavy reliance on an administration favorable to wilderness and puts great faith in the willingness of Congress to expedite passage of a large number of wilderness bills. In short, the act does not in itself create a diversified wilderness system; it provides statutory protection for a very small area of highly remote and relatively uncontroversial land, and it gives wilderness supporters the "opportunity" to debate the relative merits of each near area in the national legislature. The never-ending conflicts over wilderness preservation which the bill originally expected to correct must still go on despite the legislation.

Given these conditions, it is no surprise to find that the history of the wilderness system since passage of the act has been marked by delays and controversies similar to the fight over the original bill. The Departments of the Interior and Agriculture have been slow in formulating regulations and guidelines to implement the act. Delays in issuing regulations are manifested in a backlog of reviews on primitive areas to be added to the system, and in the slowness in which presidential recommendations are being submitted to Congress. On the basis of the reviews completed by the September, 1967, deadline, President Johnson made thirty favorable recommendations to the Ninetieth Congress; four in 1967 and twenty-six in 1968. By June, 1969, Congress had added only four areas. Three of these had been requested in 1967 and one in 1968. The Senate passed three additional bills which would have added eight additional areas to the wilderness system but the House Interior and Insular Affairs Committee never acted upon them. Aspinall successfully postponed consideration of further additions to the wilderness system in the Ninetieth Congress. He refused to call committee hearings during the summer and then adjourned the committee in early September for the congressional elections.

Despite these problems, the act does, however, represent a significant advance over previous procedures for protecting wilderness. It gives a clear directive to both the Forest Service and the National Park Service to consider wilderness a valid use of Federal land where previously no firm policy existed. The congressional mandate is strong: "To secure for the American people of present and future generations the benefits of an enduring resource of wilderness," these areas "shall be administered . . . in such manner as will leave them unimpaired for future use and enjoyment as wilderness, and so as to provide for the protection of these areas, [and] the preservation of their wilderness character." These are bold words toward which only a beginning has been made.

IV

The position of the natural environment in the total American value system is characterized by some strong paradoxes. For over three centuries American pioneers battled nature in a heroic effort to conquer a vast and hostile continent. As we approach the last third of the twentieth century, the American public has suddenly committed itself to a frantic effort to salvage or restore to its former wilderness state a small but nonetheless significant portion of the nation's remaining public lands. Does the recent passage of the Wilderness Act signify a fundamental shift in national policy and popular thinking, or is it only a tribute to a small but vocal band of purists? Is the Wilderness Act an effective tool to preserve primitive environments, or are basic adjustments needed? What are the prospects for additional legislation to safeguard other qualities in our rapidly changing and deteriorating environment?

The question of why Congress passed wilderness legislation in 1964 when it had steadfastly resisted earlier efforts may be approached from at least two general points of view. Taking a political approach, it can be argued that the Wilderness Act was the culmination of a long and arduous running battle between two well-organized political interest groups. According to this thesis, a preservationist elite, by political juggling, was able to obtain significant concessions from the dominant economic interests. There is much truth to this, but there is also an interpretation which holds that the passage of the Wilderness Act was essentially a result of public, as well as congressional, re-examination of the question of wilderness preservation, and thus marks a major adjustment in our value system. Both points of view have validity. America is experiencing a unique period in its development in which large parts of the working class have attained sufficient affluence, and the more mundane economic needs no longer dominate their outlook. The relative economic security of a large part of American society has significantly shifted public demand from quantitative to qualitative considerations. There are hopeful signs that the United States may be gradually moving away from a social system which stresses only the maximization of economic production. Change is slow, and at times we even regress, but it is possible that the passage of the Wilderness Act represents one of the first attempts to justify a major national policy decision on noneconomic grounds.

Certainly the Wilderness Act of 1964 should not be considered a final step toward the preservation of wilderness, but rather as a commitment to work toward a limited set of objectives. The final act was passed in an atmosphere of crisis after a long and frustrating battle in which enraged public opinion played a major role. The general public is inclined to overlook these important points and to assume that the passage of a congressional act will in itself provide adequate protection. This complacent attitude is dangerous, for it makes it difficult to rally public opinion behind needed additions and alterations to the general law. Nor does the simple existence of the present wilderness system ensure that land-use restrictions will be adhered to, or that the system will continue to grow. It can be assumed that the mining industry will expand its operations to the legal limit and will pressure Congress for variances to expand into closed areas.

While mining and other exploitive economic interests were in the forefront in the fight against wilderness legislation, there are other less obvious and perhaps more dangerous opponents of wilderness. Comprehensively planned mass recreation is a powerful and deadly enemy of wilderness. Any beautiful natural setting can be used in a variety of ways. It would be comforting to think that as more and more people turn to outdoor recreation the public will respect the ecological balance of nature; but there is massive evidence to the contrary. A pale gray cloud of smoke is continuously suspended over the Yosemite Valley during the summer season. Hot dog stands are mushrooming under the redwoods along the California coast. The day is not far off when we will have a "Winter Disneyland" in the Sierra Nevada Mountains. Mass recreation has at least two major advantages over a more passive use of a unique natural area. When an area is privately owned, it is obviously to the owners' advantage to appeal to the broadest possible market. When an area is public property, public officials and Congress tend to favor the use most compatible with majority opinions for practical political reasons. In either case, the result is mass recreational development aimed at the largest homogenized market.

American society has not always proved to be worthy of the great natural endowment it was blessed with. In our lust for progress, we have destroyed much of our unique natural environment. Man's capacity to demand more is unrelenting, and the civilizing process inevitably becomes a rape. For over a century, wilderness advocates have labored to gain political support for their cause by making the public aware of the merits of the wilderness. It was reasoned that preserving wild places depended on getting Americans into the back country without saws or bulldozers so that they could see what they had been missing. But their very success in this endeavor may be their downfall, for it is entirely possible that massive recreational use of wild areas will ultimately have a more disastrous effect on the quality of the back country environment than the most grotesque strip mine ever mismanaged by man.

Congress prides itself on its right to debate major national issues, but like many of our other political institutions it is basically a slow-moving and conservative entity, except perhaps in times of obvious national crisis. The committee system, based on seniority and often dominated by a few powerful individuals, is an added impediment to needed social change. Debate over the Wilderness Act of 1964 demonstrates the undue power that can be exercised by committee chairmen who vehemently oppose bills even when there is intense public pressure for the legislation. In a very real sense the time of unlimited abundance is gone. All the demands for natural resources can no longer be simultaneously satisfied. Congress is faced with the dual challenge of formulating national priorities for the wise use of remaining wildland resources and the preservation of a diversified environment for the American people. Wildland preservation should be an inherent part of that diversified environment. Congress must find a way to fulfill its obligation to create a more adequate wilderness system before the remaining wild areas have succumbed to other demands. If it cannot succeed in this small task, there is little hope for the future of this magnificent society.

5. Controversy in the North Cascades

ALLAN SOMMARSTROM

THE most complete, diverse, and dramatic outdoor complex ever approved by Congress"—the recently created North Cascades National Park was thus described by one of its leading proponents, Senator Henry M. Jackson of Washington.[1] Congressional action followed a bitter and hard-fought controversy over this relatively untouched area in Washington State. Plans for the area varied so dramatically one might wonder whether the same area was being referred to. To some, this was a golden opportunity to develop an intensively managed mass recreation area with something for everyone; to others it appeared a storehouse of natural resources which would be wasted if not utilized commercially; and to yet others its beauty and lack of development were the prime assets that ought to be protected. Advocates of each of these approaches, and others besides, believed that their particular course of action most accurately reflected not only their own interests but the interests of society as well. Into this sea of conflicting values and interests Congress was drawn, in effect to leave its imprint on one of the last large natural landscapes in the contiguous forty-eight states.

The gap between opposing sides in the controversy is broad. As is true of many contemporary environmental problems, these disparities frequently are the result of differences in perception of the problem.

ALLAN SOMMARSTROM is assistant professor of geography at the University of Hawaii. He has worked on a study of the economic impact of Mount Rainier and Olympic National Parks and is currently completing a doctoral thesis on the creation of the North Cascades National Park.

[1] *Seattle Times*, September 18, 1968, p. 57. Walt Woodward quoting Senator Henry M. Jackson.

The roots of this lie deep in American tradition and in the striking changes taking place in American life. Rural-urban antagonisms, aesthetics versus the dollar, development versus preservation, all are important and pervasive environmental concerns evident in the North Cascades controversy. There was also a sense of urgency present prior to the passage of the legislation which suggested a recognition by the interests involved that, contrary to what is commonly heard from advertising men, technologists, and some economists, we *do* have to live with what we have; that the unlimited cornucopia of land which Americans have depended on in so many instances is found to be wanting; that somehow planning must take the place of unbridled optimism. There are also the post legislation doldrums in which concern lessens with the confidence that whatever the problems may have been; they were solved by congressional action. In the North Cascades case, as elsewhere, the forces which led to the controversy will persist and may be expected to reappear. Only the ground rules have changed.

I

The North Cascades are rugged, wild, and beautiful. Windswept ice-covered peaks alternate with deeply incised valleys in a sea of visual splendor. A glance at the landscape in midsummer will convince one that winter is the dominant season. The high country meadows awaken from winter by July or August and compress spring, summer, and fall into two months; then the snows return. Snow has less of a grip on the lower stream valleys, but the storms passing through leave flooding and a tangle of downed trees. The topography and climate of the North Cascades have made this area remote and often hazardous for man. The glaciers, which are a major element in the scenic grandeur of the area, are responsible also for the deep and rugged valleys which penetrate the mountainous core. Most human activity is concentrated in the valley streams, for it is here that access routes can benefit from the gentler terrain and milder climate.

Miners were among the first to use the valleys as natural routes to their claims in the high country. Early in this century the timber stands in the lower stream valleys began to attract the interest of lumbermen, but the building of logging roads was prohibitively expensive, and utilization had to wait until the more accessible timber stands were exhausted. Occasionally, recreationists made use of the valleys to attain their high country hiking and climbing destinations. Until recent decades, most of the region, including the critically important stream valleys, was managed by the United States Forest Service under a custodial philosophy. Demands on the area were slight, and conflicts were minimal. The wild character of the land, a focal point for the present controversy, was protected by lack of interest.

Economic prosperity following World War II brought new demands on public lands. The housing boom increased the rate of depletion of private timber and increased the interest of the industry in public timber. This interest was welcomed in the North Cascades by the United States Forest Service. Sustained yield of the area's forest resources would improve the age and growth rate of the timber, insure a relatively stable source of income for the local communities, and improve access for public recreation and fire control. According to the Forest Service, multiple-use management of the land promised many benefits to the public; recreation, wildlife, grazing, timber, and watershed values were all to be maintained and enhanced under expert management.

The economic forces which improved the market for timber were also at work on the broader fronts of personal income, leisure time, and mobility, which tended to increase the number, duration, and frequency of recreational visits. As logging sales proceeded, roads were pushed up the stream and tributary valleys. Many areas previously accessible only to the hiker were opened to automobiles, and, consequently, to vastly greater numbers of people. A midsummer place of quiet beauty for the solitary hiker became a campground full of people making a lot of noise and leaving a lot of garbage and having a lot of fun. What of the wilderness hiker? He consulted his friends and his maps and picked another lake and campsite where he could regain the values he sought; but the process could not go on forever.

Wilderness enthusiasts soon began to recognize the critical role of roads in the gradual demise of the environments they sought. While road building had other purposes, nevertheless its chief one was logging—which brought another kind of impact to the area besides increased access for recreation. Clear cutting is the cheapest form of timber harvest in the region if the most desirable tree species is to reseed naturally and make a strong return. An area is completely cleared to the ground and the brush and debris are burned. A greater visual change would be hard to imagine: trees, mosses, and ferns are replaced by stumps, scarred hillsides, and snarls of rusting cable from the logging operation. A hiker toiling up a dusty and hot trail through a clear-cut patch, if he is not from one of the surrounding lumber towns, may be hard pressed to see any advantage in this visual disaster, and may, instead, direct a pungent curse toward those responsible.

Who is responsible? Congress has charged the U.S. Forest Service with administering the lands under its control according to "multiple use" guidelines set out in the act which established the agency in 1905, and, more recently, in the Multiple Use Act of 1960. The term "multiple use" appears frequently in the land-use literature. It conveys the idea that forest lands can and should produce a number of different products simultaneously, though the 1960 act does note that sometimes only a single land use may be appropriate. But the concept is much more useful as a slogan than as a policy, for it offers no criteria to determine the proper mix of uses in a particular situation. In essence, the Forest Service can and does allocate land as it sees fit, and this places a great responsibility on local rangers and foresters who are required to make land-use decisions almost daily based on their individual technical expertise, practical experience, and value systems.

II

Why did some people rebuff Forest Service management and favor, instead, the creation of a national park in the North Cascades? A partial answer lies in the organization and staff of the Forest Service itself. By formal training in scientific forestry, and through a commitment to decentralized "grass roots" organization, officials of the Forest Service appear to some to be more sympathetic to the economic needs of the local communities than to more diffuse national needs. For example, those who were concerned about the reductions of wilderness lands in the North Cascades as a result of the growing road network, asked the Forest Service to reveal its plans for the ultimate extent of the road network. They were shocked by the response. Few, if any, of the low-lying stream valleys were to escape logging. Wilderness plans formulated by the Forest Service frequently included rock, ice, snow, and high-country meadows of limited economic value for other uses, and even those lands would be deeply penetrated by nonwilderness corridors along the stream valleys where the good timber was located. Preservationists fought for the inclusion of these corridors, pressing their arguments in Forest Service hearings and at the national level, and, occasionally, reluctant local officials were overruled from Washington, D.C., with orders to expand the initial wilderness proposals to include more territory.

In time, the Forest Service began to show increasing responsiveness to the demands of preservationists, but the pace remained agonizingly slow to those watching wilderness disappear. When the 458,505-acre Glacier Peak Wilderness Area was established in 1960, the Secretary of Agriculture made specific mention of the management of the area to the north called the Eldorado Peaks area, which is located between the 801,000-acre North Cascades Primitive Area to the north and the Glacier Peak area to the south (see fig. 3). The Eldorado Peaks area would eventually have a through highway across its northern portions, and it was the secretary's view that mass recreation was the most appropriate use of the area. Wilderness enthusiasts were frustrated in their attempts to have portions of the area reserved as wilderness.

There had been talk of a national park in the North Cascades as early as 1906, but little had come of it. Faced with a growing dissatisfaction with Forest Service performance, preservationists began in the late 1950's to give serious consideration to the alternative of national park status for portions of the North Cascades. It was recognized that a major battle would have to be fought for a national park, one involving new as well as old opponents, and one which would risk further strained relations with the Forest Service. Some were hesitant to push for a national park, because the popularity of such areas is so great that park qualities are themselves threatened through intensive use. In his recent study of the human erosion of our national parks, the ecologist F. Fraser Darling noted:

We have been under the impression throughout our survey that visitor statistics showing high rates of increase year by year are welcomed as valuable weapons in getting larger appropriations for the National Park Service. Development takes place which will encourage more visits rather than conserve the unique habitats which the parks represent.[2]

[2] F. Fraser Darling and Noel D. Eichborn, *Man and Nature in the National Parks: Reflections on Policy* (Washington, D.C.: Conservation Foundation, 1957), p. 28.

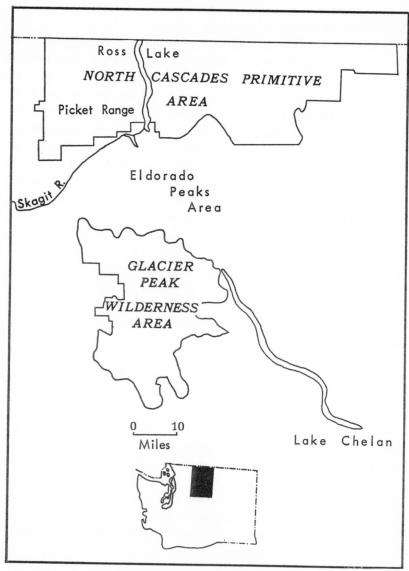

Figure 3. North Cascades prior to 1968

However, others pointed out that the designation, "national park," attracts substantial public interest which would be invaluable in generating nation-wide support for preservation. At any rate, leaders of the local preservation movement decided in 1960 to push for a national park in the North Cascades to include a sizeable amount of land not under wilderness protection.

Representative Thomas Pelly of Washington, at the request of local preservationists, requested in 1959 that the National Park Service carry out a study of the Glacier Peak area. The Forest Service was not cooperative, recommending that the study not be done. A year later, in 1960, Washington Representatives Don Magnuson and Pelly in the House, and Warren Magnuson, also of Washington, in the Senate, introduced bills "to provide that the Secretary of the Interior, in cooperation with the Secretary of Agriculture, shall investigate and report to the Congress on the advisability of establishing a National Park or other unit of the National Park System in the central and North Cascades region of the State of Washington." [3] None of these bills was acted upon. Representative Pelly introduced the same bill in 1961 with a similar result. The Secretary of Agriculture announced that no logging would take place in twenty specific areas until a management policy was formulated by that department, which showed that the park proposal was beginning to have an effect. However, the secretary relented the following year (1962) and announced that additional timber sales and new road construction would be prohibited in only ten of these areas, a statement indicating the extent of the pressure he was beginning to feel. Preservationists were enraged that the Forest Service would open areas once closed to logging when these areas were being considered for park status.

The year 1963 was eventful in the development of the North Cascades controversy. A rapidly growing preservationist group, the North Cascades Conservation Council, submitted a Prospectus for a North Cascades National Park, advocating establishment of a large 1,038,665-acre national park in the Eldorado Peaks area and a 269,521-acre Chelan National Mountain Recreation Area (see fig. 4). In the same year, a document passed over the desk of President Kennedy from the secretaries of Agriculture and Interior pledging "a new era of cooperation" in the relations between these departments. The North Cascades controversy was singled out as an example, and a joint study of the problem was proposed. The resulting study team was created with two officials from Interior, two from Agriculture, and

[3] *North Cascades Study Team Report* (Washington, D.C.: Government Printing Office, 1966), p. 185.

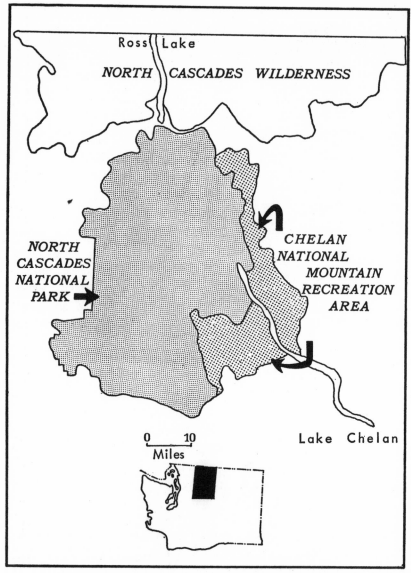

Figure 4. North Cascades Conservation Council's proposal

the chairman from the Bureau of Outdoor Recreation, which is also lodged in the Interior Department. Its goal was "to determine the management and administration of those lands that will best serve the public interest." [4]

[4] *Ibid.*, p. 154.

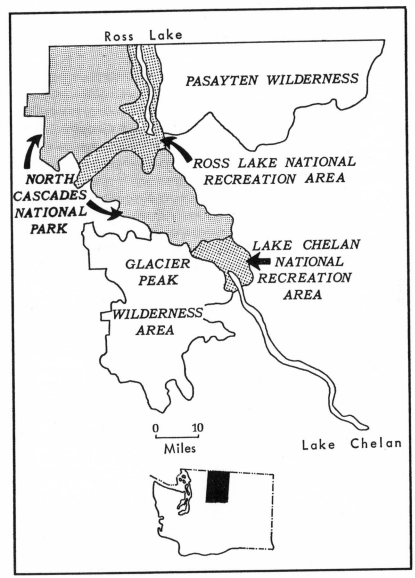

Figure 5. North Cascades Park in S. 1321 as amended

More than two and one half years later, the study team issued its recommendations. While the report dealt with Federal land management problems from the Canadian border to south of Mount Rainier National Park, the center of attention was its recommendations concerning the establishment of a North Cascades National Park. The

committee vote on the park issue neatly divided the Agriculture and
Interior representatives, with the deciding vote being cast for a national park by the chairman, who, as noted above, was also an
employee of the Interior Department. The park recommended by the
study team was largely a compromise between the two parks advocated by Interior representatives and the no-park recommendation of
the representatives from Agriculture. The park included two separate
parts—a northern section, which was already in the North Cascades
Primitive Area, and a southern section, which included the core of the
disputed area north of the Glacier Peak Wilderness Area (see fig. 5).
Many of the other recommendations were designed to make the park
proposal more acceptable to various interest groups, some allowing
timber cutting in areas where logging was not permitted previously,
and others advocating official wilderness designation for areas now in
"limited" status.[5] It is worth noting that if all recommendations of the
study team had been followed there would have been an increase in
both the annual allowable timber cut and in the acreage officially
designated as wilderness. There was literally "something for everyone"
in the study team report.

Senator Henry M. Jackson, Washington State's junior senator and
chairman of the Senate Interior and Insular Affairs Committee, held
hearings in 1966 on the study team's proposed park.[6] Following the
hearings, a North Cascades National Park bill, S. 1321, was introduced
for the administration by Senator Jackson. With minor exceptions,
principally deletions of controversial lands, the bill followed the proposals of the study team. Additional Senate hearings were held by the
Interior and Insular Affairs Subcommittee on Parks and Recreation in
Washington, D.C., Seattle, Mount Vernon, and Wenatchee.[7]

III

Although the park bill was drawn to eliminate many of the areas of
greatest conflict, much opposition to the proposed park still existed.
Those with economic interests in continuation of Forest Service management remained strongly opposed, some to this particular park

[5] *Ibid.*, pp. 85–88.
[6] U.S., Congress, Senate, Committee on Interior and Insular Affairs, *Hear-ings on the North Cascades Study Team Report,* 89th Cong., 2d sess., 1966.
[7] U.S., Congress, Senate, Committee on Interior and Insular Affairs, *Hear-ings on S. 1321,* 90th Cong., 1st sess., 1967.

proposal and others to any park whatsoever. Chambers of Commerce from the surrounding towns and cities spoke up against the proposed park because of the adverse economic impact it would have. The timber and mining industries objected strenuously to being barred from the area. The former activity is dominant in the small communities surrounding the proposed park, and access to public timber is crucial to the present economy of the area. (Although the actual amount of timber which would be removed from cutting by establishment of the park would be less than 3 per cent of the total annual allowable cut on the national forests involved, this figure is misleading because these towns rely heavily on this particular portion of the total allowable cut; the 3 per cent reduction would, in fact, react heavily on the local economies.) Although mining activity is minor in the area at the present time, opponents of the proposed park contended that new techniques for locating minerals and modern mining methods undoubtedly would change this, especially if prices for copper and other minerals continue to rise. It is imperative to the mining interests that this option not be jeopardized for anything so intangible as a national park. As one miner testified:

> When I was younger and growing up in Northwest Washington State, all the people welcomed with open arms any new industry that chose to come into our community to produce and become part of it. We knew it meant more jobs, more money, more security, and a better life. Very few people had a college education and the majority a meager schooling. We realized all wealth comes from the earth and that it must be taken from the earth by the ingenuity of man and distributed to provide for our being and welfare. Now we have college graduates by the thousands and education is running rampant through the land.
>
> It seems to me there is a deadly attack being launched against the U.S. Economy to thoroughly cripple and sabotage our economic status; whether it is by design from foreign sources or within, I know not, but the end point is the same. You cannot tax people too heavily nor can you lock up their natural resources for too long.[8]

Park proponents attempted to counter these economic fears by noting that a surge in tourism generally occurs after a national park is established. Understandably, however, many local citizens were concerned about the time lag between the reduction in logging activity and the heralded tourist boom. They also questioned whether the wage earners displaced by the park would be the same people employed to

[8] *Ibid.*, pp. 344–45.

serve the recreating public. The flexibility of jobs and location which urbanites consider normal does not exist to the same degree among residents of small mountain communities. A man with a family to feed and a twenty-thousand-dollar mortgage to pay off on his new logging truck will not have his immediate fear relieved by promises of new job possibilities in tourism.

The restrictive policies of the National Park Service preclude the kind of mass recreation developments some people want in the area. Associations of ski operators and instructors, for example, objected to a park because the National Park Service is extremely reluctant to allow permanent ski installations on park lands. Trail vehicle user groups expressed similar opposition because their activity would be prohibited throughout much of the proposed park. Hunters are highly organized, and they have strong representation in the state government. They are also the principle group whose interests would be hurt more by the establishment of a national park than by designation of the area as a wilderness under Forest Service jurisdiction, since hunting is permitted in the latter.

As a result of pressures from hunting organizations, S. 1321 was amended after the 1967 hearings to exclude 62,000 acres in the Stehekin area. (Objections of private landowners in this area was also a factor in the decision to eliminate these lands from the proposed park.) The bill which eventually passed (S. 1321) included less than 1 per cent of the State of Washington's annual deer kill and about a sixth of the annual mountain goat kill. However, hunters continued to oppose the park, arguing that the hunting which would be lost is among the highest quality in the state. This position amounted to a rephrasing of the preservationist's argument that sheer numbers of users should not be the only determinant of proper usage. Park advocates tried to convince some of these groups that they had other interests that would be best served by a park, but this was not effective. At one point in the hearings, Representative Wayne Aspinall observed in his capacity of chairman that "about the only real opposition that we have had to this legislation comes from sportsmen's groups." [9]

Proponents of the park frequently testified as individuals, rather

_____

[9] U.S., Congress, House, Committee on Interior and Insular Affairs, *Hearings on H.R. 8970 and Related Bills, Part III*, 90th Cong., 2d sess., 1968, p. 976.

than as spokesmen for a group. They argued for a different set of values, holding that the beauty of the area deserved a rich society's protection. A rapid increase in hiker use of the back country was stressed, as was the wide range of alternative sources of wood fiber and mass recreation in contrast to the steadily decreasing wilderness in the North Cascades:

> Of one thing I am sure: If the Congress were to preserve in national parks and wilderness areas the maximum amount of land that has been asked to date by any single proposal or by a combination of all proposals, the people of the year 2000 would say, "It is not enough. You should have saved us more." In 2000 they will say of the North Cascades Conservation Council, "You were too timid. You compromised away too much. You should have been more farsighted, more daring." [10]

Organizations such as the North Cascades Conservation Council, the Sierra Club, the Wilderness Society, the National Parks Association, the Mountaineers, and the National Audubon Society offered detailed testimony and encouraged their members to become involved in the battle to save the North Cascades.

The state government was hopelessly divided on the park issue. In 1967, the Washington Legislature passed a Joint Memorial supporting multiple-use management, and, if Congress should deem it advisable, a national park in the Picket Range. Various state officials spoke out in favor of a park, including the governor, who thought a wilderness park should be considered for the area between Ross Lake and Mount Baker (see fig. 3). However, the director of the State Game Commission, who is not directly responsible to the governor, preferred continued Forest Service management of the area as this would not result in loss of state control over fishing and hunting. The governor appointed a committee to study the problem. A subcommittee of three (a state government official, a timber company executive, and an individual active in preservation organizations) arrived at a compromise plan. It recommended a 335,000-acre national park in the Picket Range, an area already managed as wilderness and proposed as the northern section of the two-part park proposed in S. 1321. As a condition of their support, the state government and timber representatives required assurances from the conservation representative that his groups would not seek a larger park. In turn, they assured the

[10] Senate, Interior and Insular Affairs Committee, *Hearings on S. 1321,* p. 337.

conservation representative of the cooperation of the groups they spoke for. The pledged silences on the topic were not achieved, and the battle over the location and extent of the park continued to gain momentum.

The Senate Interior and Insular Affairs Committee passed S. 1321, as amended, and sent it to the Senate floor where it passed by an overwhelming vote. But the legislation had a much more difficult time of it in the House Committee on Interior and Insular Affairs under the chairmanship of Wayne N. Aspinall of Colorado. That committee considered H.R. 8970 introduced by Representative Lloyd Meeds of Washington, which was identical to the original administration bill; H.R. 12139 introduced by Representative Pelly, which was the 1963 plan of the preservationists for a large national park and adjacent national recreation area; and H.R. 16252 introduced by Representative Catherine May of Washington, which proposed a park slightly smaller than that of the Governor's Study Committee.

Hearings were held in Seattle on April 19 and 20, 1968, by the Subcommittee on Parks and Recreation. The subcommittee was overwhelmed by the number of people (approximately 800) requesting to testify, which moved Representative Aspinall to remark that "he had never seen anything like it." [11] Explained Aspinall:

I don't know who these people are. Are they hippies or part of a Seattle drive to get out into the country? Of course they have the right to testify, but they will repeat the same thing over and over again and will not trust their position to be stated for them by responsible officials or organizations. This whole thing has been ballooned all out of proportion here.[12]

Most of the witnesses spoke in favor of a national park. Perhaps the most crucial testimony of the hearings was given by Washington's governor, Daniel J. Evans, after he had presented the official position of the state. When asked what his choice would be between national park legislation as passed by the Senate or no national park at all, he responded in favor of the Senate bill.[13]

After the hearings Representative Aspinall promised to "do his darndest" to report a North Cascades bill in time for final congressional action during that session,[14] and to hold additional hearings in

[11] *Seattle Times*, April 21, 1968, p. 47.

[12] *Wild Cascades*, February–March, 1968, p. 3.

[13] House, Interior and Insular Affairs Committee, *Hearings on H.R. 8970 and Related Bills, Part I*, p. 80.

[14] *Seattle Times*, April 24, 1968, p. 10.

eastern Washington and Washington, D.C. The next news had a different tone. Following the hearings, Representative Roy Taylor of North Carolina, chairman of the Subcommittee on Parks and Recreation, was quoted in June as saying that he was giving "low priority to a North Cascades National Park because he had received so much mail in opposition to it." [15] Representative Aspinall concurred, indicating that action on a North Cascades National Park was "unlikely" because "there is too little time in this congressional session to resolve the continuing controversy over the project." [16] The proponents saw this as the death knell for the legislation.

A short period of inactivity was broken, however, by the news that more hearings were to be held in Wenatchee on July 13, 1968. Why this sudden reversal? During this time legislation concerning the Colorado River Basin Project, of vital concern to Representative Aspinall and other southwestern Congressmen, was being considered in the Senate Committee on Interior and Insular Affairs chaired by Henry M. Jackson of Washington. Representative Taylor was also vitally interested in the progress of legislation concerning the Blue Ridge Parkway which extended into his state. This bill was also in Jackson's committee. The Colorado River Basin Project bill was especially important to Senator Jackson because of threats that it would contain provisions for a study of the diversion of Pacific Northwest water to the Southwest. Senator Jackson would not agree to such a study and it appeared that he would block that legislation. A compromise was reached, however, enabling the Colorado River legislation to begin moving again (sans diversion study), and legislation concerning the Redwoods and North Cascades National Parks and other important conservation matters began to move again in the House.

After the Wenatchee hearings, additional hearings were held in Washington, D.C., on July 25 and 26, 1968. Representative May spoke for her bill (H.R. 16252) and Lloyd Meeds spoke for his bill. Representative Pelly submitted a statement in which he said he would vote for any of the bills, including his own (H.R. 12139). The Secretary of the Interior and the Director of the National Park Service spoke strongly in favor of the Meeds bill.

During its deliberation Chairman Aspinall made it clear to the subcommittee that no legislation would be reported out of the full

[15] *Ibid.*, June 4, 1968, p. 10.
[16] *Ibid.*, June 3, 1968, p. 6.

committee unless there was agreement among those introducing legislation. Representative May stood by her bill until she was reached by phone by Governor Evans who reiterated his earlier statement that he would prefer the Senate passed bill over no park at all (Governor Evans was alerted by Mr. Brock Evans, Pacific Northwest Conservation Representative for the Federation of Western Outdoor Clubs, who was sent to Washington, D.C., to aid in the passage of North Cascades legislation). George Hartzog, director of the National Park Service, testified that the smaller "Governor's park" was unacceptable and he would prefer no park to that alternative.[17] The deadlock was broken when Representative May then agreed to the Senate passed bill.

On September 4, 1968, the whole committee heard the testimony of Thomas L. Kimball, executive director of the National Wildlife Federation, in opposition to a national park and then unanimously passed H.R. 8970. The Senate concurred on the House amendment and passed the bill by voice vote, sending it to the White House where it was signed by President Johnson on October 2, 1968.

IV

The battle over land use in the North Cascades boiled down to whether a national park should or should not be established. The question received national attention, and the long process of moving toward legislation tended to polarize the issues. With the national park established, a majority of the interested public will probably consider one side to have "won" and the matter closed. But a great many issues cannot be resolved so easily, for there are many persistent problems.

Wilderness preservation was one of the prime motivations of those advocating a national park in the North Cascades. Parks have a dual purpose. They provide for public recreation and for the preservation of the environment. The popularity of national parks testifies to their important place in American experience, but some national parks are receiving such high levels of use that the quality of the park environment is being eroded. In a society where, all too often, bigger is better and growth is best, it is no wonder that skyrocketing visitation figures are often the Park Service's best guarantee of adequate appropria-

---

[17] House, Interior and Insular Affairs Committee, *Hearings on H.R. 8970 and Related Bills, Part III*, p. 952.

tions. Expanding developments to accommodate visitors is a short-run solution which may lead to even greater public use, and simultaneously, to a reduction of the more subtle aspects of the environment and the visitor's enjoyment of it. Wilderness is one of the first environments to go as roads and campgrounds are built to spread out the users. National parks must have areas developed for intensive recreation as well as areas of wilderness. The real question is how much of each is appropriate. The answer depends largely upon an individual's perception of the proper nature and function of national parks. Research to determine the ecological and qualitative values that may be lost when parks become overrun is just beginning. In short, if the Park Service continues to move toward intensive recreational development, the wilderness enthusiasts who fought so strenuously for the park may well have won the battle and lost the war. The need also remains for coordinated management of adjacent areas, for this can have virtually as great an impact on the park as does the internal management of the park itself. Clear cutting on lands immediately adjacent to park boundaries or the building of additional roads up the approach valleys are real threats to park wilderness. Interagency hostility is not removed by legislation. Such problems are only partially dealt with in the proposed legislation.

Conflict in the North Cascades and the institutional response to it are indicative of the strengths and weaknesses of our political system and our view of the nature of resource conflicts. In this controversy, "victory" appeared to consist of either establishing a sizeable national park or squelching such an attempt. Either outcome is a momentary equilibrium whose undoing begins the next moment. The preservationist's necessity to reach a diffuse general public forces simplification of the arguments and the scope of the goals sought. The intense controversy which often follows, once a position has been established, resembles a "last ditch stand" by either side, obscuring the many "stands" which will likely follow as values and circumstances change.

This suggests something about our changing interest in the natural environment and our ability to cope with that change. What is happening could be described as an increase in the tempo and complexity of such controversies and the legislative response. Greater pressure on timberland, mass recreation areas, and wilderness is pushing for finer incremental tuning of the decision-making process at a time when the impact of the divergent goals at the root of such problems is greater than ever. What comes from Congress addressing itself to these problems is not their solution, but the treatment of their symptoms. This becomes a continual process, lending support to a view of Congress as an environmental "fire department" constantly dousing the flames of conflict.

A recreation frontier is closing, and we no longer have apparently limitless land which can absorb conflicts before they start. This is forcing a profound change in our thinking as we begin to look inside the boundaries of the units we have established. There is ample evidence to indicate that few are willing to participate in a cooperative attack on the problem. Until such a willingness is realized, the losses society incurs will gradually build in intensity. We expect Congress to act on these controversies with omniscience, but Congress has a record of being satisfied with decisions and approaches which are stop-gap measures. Congress has not begun to articulate environmental goals. Until it begins to address itself to that topic its actions will continue to be reactions, and the price can only be measured in a growing number of apparently unrelated localized environmental conflicts. We are not yet asking the right questions.

6. Economics, Aesthetics,
and the Saving of the Redwoods

ERNEST H. WOHLENBERG

UNTIL a very short time ago the world's tallest known living organism could legally have been cut down and sawed into siding, fence posts, or picnic tables. It and many other similar trees were standing naked and without protection in California. Since several redwood national parks were first proposed by the Sierra Club in 1895, over seventy years have passed, and not until 1968 did we have a national park to preserve the redwood. Why did it take so long to get action on this matter?

The tallest, and among the oldest, living things on the face of the earth are the coastal redwoods, *Sequoia sempervirens,* which grow only in the humid, mild climate of the Pacific coastal margins of northern California. Some of these trees are well over a thousand years old. They range upward in height to a giant specimen of 367 feet, and many are taller than a twenty-story building.

Originally, California may have contained two million acres of old-growth redwoods before cutting started in the nineteenth century. The redwood tree is highly prized for its wood. Timber cutting has gone on relentlessly since the 1850's, until today the remaining virgin redwood acreage has shrunk to approximately three hundred thousand acres. In recent years, redwoods have been felled at the rate of about twenty-five acres per day, or ten thousand acres per year. Cutting has occurred on the boundaries and even within what was to

ERNEST H. WOHLENBERG is assistant professor of geography at Indiana University (Bloomington). He has worked on the economic geography of the wood pulp industry in the United States and Canada and is currently completing a doctoral thesis on the Redwoods National Park.

become the Redwood National Park.[1] At present rates of consumption, all old-growth redwoods except those protected in existing state and national parks will have been logged before the year 2000.

I

Legislation designed to preserve some exceptional stands of these fine old trees for the inspiration and enjoyment of present and future generations in a redwood national park was introduced in both the Eighty-ninth and Ninetieth Congresses. This legislation was the culmination of a series of events beginning in 1918 when the newly organized Save-the-Redwoods League proposed a national park. The idea languished, but revived again in 1946 when another proposal was presented to Congress. The National Park Service made a detailed study of areas where a prospective park might be located in 1963–64. This study was followed by an Arthur D. Little, Inc., assessment of the economic impact of the proposed national park on the local area in 1965.[2] In his 1966 message to Congress on natural beauty, President Johnson recommended immediate establishment of a redwood national park.

Various arguments favoring and opposing such a park had been articulated. The proponents of the park claimed that the coastal redwood was a threatened and vanishing species; that establishment of a national park to save them was urgent. They explained that a redwood forest presents a scene of unusual natural beauty which can be enjoyed and experienced nowhere else. As the Sierra Club noted in a pamphlet entitled, "Facts about Redwoods and the Need for A Redwood National Park," "groves of Redwoods are to the plant kingdom what the Grand Canyon . . . is to canyon scenery." Proponents also pointed out that as income, leisure time, and population increase, there is a growing need for more recreation space and the addition of more acreage to the already crowded facilities of the National Park System. The argument favoring a park is difficult to express in concrete terms. How does one place a value on the aesthetic, scenic, and recreational advantages of a redwood grove? Can one justify the largely intangible benefits of a redwood park on economic grounds?

[1] *New York Times,* October 30, 1967, p. 47.
[2] Arthur D. Little, Inc., *The Impact of the Proposed Redwoods National Park on the Economy of Del Norte County* (Washington, D.C.: Arthur D. Little, Inc., 1966).

It is much easier to describe and support the case against a park in cold, hard, economic facts. Opponents of the proposed redwoods park were alarmed that establishment would have an adverse economic impact on the local area. Nearby Del Norte County was already classified as being distressed, and had been for years. Its unemployment rate was consistently above the national average. The A. D. Little study, mentioned earlier, estimated that 33 per cent of the jobs in that county were directly related to the lumber industry. Although a specific study of Humboldt County was not made, the economic situation was similar. Establishment of a national park wherein logging was not permitted would reduce the area's timber supply and force some curtailment of logging operations, and perhaps shut down one or more of the region's lumber companies.

These were real and understandable fears of the local residents. However, increased employment by the National Park Service and construction contractors with the service could be expected to offset at least some of those losses in the short run. Other new jobs would be created in the long run as a result of an expanded tourist industry based on the park attraction. One Department of the Interior study concluded, for example, that at the end of a five-year period after establishment of a park there would be an average net annual gain of 172 jobs per year in Del Norte County.[3] Though difficult to quantify precisely, it nevertheless appeared that a park would eventually become an economic asset to the area, despite hardships during the first few years.

The park might also have an immediate adverse economic impact on the local area through the removal of private land from the local tax rolls. Opponents of the park proposal feared that unless tax rates on remaining property were increased, or other new sources of revenue found, a deterioration of local government services would be inevitable. Property-tax rates in the area were already among the highest in the state because such a high proportion of the land was already publicly owned.

Land acquisition costs presented another economic obstacle. Land was expected to cost in the neighborhood of $5,000 per acre or more for the higher quality stands, with the total reaching a figure between

[3] U.S., Congress, Senate, Committee on Interior and Insular Affairs, Subcommittee on Parks and Recreation, *Hearings on S. 2962*, 89th Cong., 2d sess., 1966, p. 21.

$50 million and $200 million. Since there were already some 50,000 acres of redwoods protected in California state parks, the question was legitimately asked whether this large sum could not be more wisely invested elsewhere—say, in big-city slums. There was also a question in the minds of some whether acquisition of land from private citizens for public recreational and aesthetic purposes was not a violation of the right to private property. Few people have difficulty accepting condemnation of private property for more utilitarian purposes such as highway or pipeline construction, for example, but not for a park.

The companies and individuals who owned the redwood lands also contended that the coastal redwoods were not a threatened species since they were carrying out extensive replanting programs. Even among the park's supporters, there was little agreement as to how large it should be and exactly where it should be located, and this tended to weaken the proponents' stand. To insure the ecological integrity of a stand of redwoods, it is essential to include as much of a complete watershed as possible within the protected boundaries, since removal or alteration of upstream forest cover may result in destructive flooding and siltation of downstream redwood groves. Also a matter of concern to the purists among conservationists was the ecological diversity of the forests to be included in the park. In their view, a park worthy of the name would include redwoods growing in many diverse settings in the flats and on the slopes, in pure stands and mixed species, and at all elevations from sea level to approximately 2,500 feet.

II

Disagreement about the specific size, location, and boundaries of the proposed park on the part of its supporters resulted in the introduction of a number of different bills in the Eighty-ninth Congress representing the desires of different groups. The Administration-sponsored bills (S. 2962 and H.R. 13009), introduced by Senator Thomas Kuchel (R., Cal.) and Representative Phillip Burton (D., Cal.), proposed the establishment of a park approximately 43,000 acres in size to be located mostly in Del Norte County, largely in the Mill Creek watershed and including within its boundaries portions of the existing Jed Smith and Del Norte Coast state parks (see fig. 6). This would have affected only one timber company. The proposal favored by the

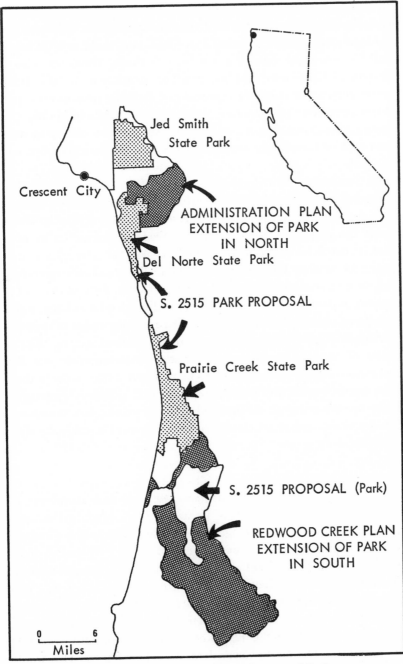

Figure 6. Proposals for a Redwoods National Park

Save-the-Redwoods League provided "economic adjustment payments" to local governing bodies. A second proposal, known as the
Redwood Creek Plan, was aimed at establishing a larger 90,000-acre
park in Humboldt County within the Redwood Creek watershed
where it was contended that the trees were of more "parklike" quality
(and, incidentally, could be expected to be more expensive). This
plan was favored by a number of conservation groups including the
Sierra Club. It was introduced in the Senate as a substitute amendment to S. 2962 by Senator Lee Metcalf of Montana; a companion
measure was introduced in the House by Representative Jeffrey Cohe-
lan of California.

A third proposal, favored by the timber industry and residents of
local communities, was the Redwoods-to-the-Sea Plan (H.R. 13042),
which was introduced by Representative Don Clausen of California in
whose district the proposed park would be located. This plan would
have linked over six million acres of Federal, state, and local lands into
a so-called "regional conservation plan." Under this proposal, the
national park would be created primarily through the amalgamation
of existing state parks with few additional acres required. Lands
available for timber cutting would remain at a maximum.

The Senate Subcommittee on Parks and Recreation held hearings
on these proposals in Crescent City, California, and in Washington,
D.C., in 1966, but no further action was taken during the Eighty-ninth
Congress. The proposals were introduced again with minor changes in
the Ninetieth Congress: the Administration Plan as S. 1370, the Redwood Creek Plan as S. 514, and the Redwoods-to-the-Sea Plan as S.
1526 and H.R. 7742. The Senate Subcommittee on Parks and Recreation as well as the House Subcommittee on National Parks and Recreation held additional hearings on these bills in Washington, D.C., in
1967.

In an attempt to resolve these conflicting proposals, the Senate
Interior and Insular Affairs Committee in October, 1967, introduced a
compromise bill (S. 2515), which, according to its proponents, included the best features of the Administration and Redwoods Creek
plans. The compromise bill included provision for a park in excess of
60,000 acres and more equally divided between Del Norte and Humboldt Counties (see fig. 6). To placate the lumber interests, minimize
the adverse economic impact on local communities, and reduce the
total expenditure for land acquisition, the compromise contained a

controversial section permitting exchange of United States Forest Service lands located in Del Norte County for private lands to be included within the boundaries of the proposed park. The compromise bill was supported by the Sierra Club, the Save-the-Redwoods League, and the local and county governments. The controversy surrounding the compromise centered on the question of whether a dangerous precedent would be established by exchanging lands administered by one governmental agency (e.g., Department of Agriculture) for private lands subsequently to be administered by another governmental agency (e.g., Department of the Interior).

Among those favoring the exchange provisions in the compromise bill were the five lumber companies in the area, various local public and private organizations, and Governor Reagan of California. Understandably, Secretary of Agriculture Orville Freeman strongly opposed the exchange provisions of the compromise bill, and he led the attack during the Senate hearings. Also opposing the exchange provisions were such prominent national conservation organizations as the American Forestry Association, the Boone and Crockett Club, the Izaak Walton League, the National Rifle Association, the National Wildlife Federation, the North American Wildlife Foundation, the Sport Fishing Institute, and the Wildlife Management Institute. With few exceptions, these organizations represent groups and individuals vitally interested in maintaining the maximum area of public lands open to hunting and fishing. Although hunting is permitted on national forest lands, it is specifically prohibited in national parks.

As a result of this opposition, an amendment was introduced by Senator Clinton Anderson of New Mexico and Senator Allen Ellender of Louisiana to eliminate the exchange provisions in S. 2515. The amendment was defeated by a vote of 30 to 52. Not unexpectedly, most of the opposition to the exchange provision came from senators from states where the forest products industry is important, or from areas where hunting on public lands is significant. The compromise bill containing the controversial exchange provisions passed the Senate and was sent to the House. But this by no means meant that opposition to the bill was dead, for the House is generally the more conservative body and more sensitive and responsive to local economic interests when these are in conflict with broader nationwide interests. The House took no action on the compromise bill during the remainder of 1967, but hearings were held again in April and May,

1968, at Crescent City and Eureka, California, and also in Washington, D.C., by the House Committee on Interior and Insular Affairs, chaired by Representative Wayne Aspinall of Colorado. Although the chairman appeared to be in no hurry to take action, time was of the essence. Logging in the vicinity of the proposed park was continuing at a rapid rate and land values and acquisition costs continued to escalate.

Finally, in early July, 1968, the House committee reported a bill, but it was vastly different from the Senate version, providing for a park of only 28,500 acres. Only the Prairie Creek and Del Norte Coast state parks and approximately 10,000 acres of connecting strips and corridors were included in the House version of the bill, although the controversial land exchange provisions of the Senate bill were retained. The House passed the bill by an overwhelming vote of 388 to 15. However, many of the yea votes were cast by representatives favoring a larger park with the understanding that the House-Senate conferees would approve a larger park. In September, the conference committee met and agreed to the establishment of a park with a maximum size of 58,000 acres, much larger than the one approved by the House and quite similar to the Senate version in size, shape, and location (see fig. 6). Both the House and the Senate agreed to the conference report, and the President subsequently signed the bill into law on October 2, 1968.

III

How effective will the act be in preserving a portion of the remaining redwoods in an unmolested state? The measure will apparently achieve its objective in the limited sense of saving some of these trees from the lumbermen's saws since timber cutting is not permitted inside the boundaries of the park. Whether this measure preserves enough of the finest trees is a matter of controversy, but most proponents seem to agree that it is an important step in the right direction. In a long-range ecological sense, however, there is some doubt as to whether the redwoods will be given sufficient protection in the national park, which includes only a narrow strip of land along Redwood Creek in the southeast. Trees inside the park may well be subjected to flooding and other destructive influences from outside its boundaries. According to a Sierra Club pamphlet, five hundred redwoods in the Bull Creek watershed of Humboldt Redwoods State Park were destroyed as a result of severe flooding in 1955 when upstream slopes outside park boundaries were denuded.

Other problems in carrying out the intent of this legislation can be expected. The bill provides for Federal purchase of lands adjoining state-owned lands contained in three California state parks—Jed Smith, Del Norte Coast, and Prairie Creek. The bill also authorizes the Secretary of the Interior to accept "only by donation" from the State of California the three state parks within the new national park. Governor Reagan is on record in opposition to this. "The State of California," he said, "must receive full, fair, and equal value from the Federal Government for any state land incorporated into the national park. . . . State land must be exchanged for equal Federal land." [4] The implication is clear, but there are no provisions for this in the act and there is little precedent for exchange of Federal and state lands.

Senator Henry Jackson (D., Wash.) is on record as stating:

. . . the Interior and Insular Affairs Committee does believe that the Redwoods National Park will reach ultimate fruition only when the Jed Smith, Del Norte Coast, and Prairie Creek State Parks are donated by the state of California and become part of the national park. . . . The committee has not made this donation a condition precedent to creation of a Redwoods National Park. Should the state not act, the national park should be created to assure preservation of additional redwood groves. In such event, cooperative management agreements should be worked out with the State of California so National and State Parks can co-exist with maximum shared contribution to the public interest. [5]

Unless the Reagan administration changes its position, it is unlikely that the state parks will be donated to the National Park Service, as envisioned by Congress. Although the Reagan administration appeared to have softened its position, it remains to be seen whether a truly satisfactory agreement can be negotiated for transfer of the state parks to Federal ownership and administration or, failing that, whether some arrangement for joint state-Federal management of the park can be established to maximize the public welfare. The latter is questionable. The elongated shape of the park is less than ideal and makes administration and protection that much more difficult. [6]

[4] U.S., Congress, Senate, Committee on Interior and Insular Affairs, Subcommittee on Parks and Recreation, *Hearings on S. 1370, S. 514, and S. 1526,* 90th Cong., 1st sess., 1967, pp. 65, 66.

[5] U.S., *Congressional Record,* 90th Cong., 1st sess., CXIII (1967), S15582.

[6] U.S., *Congressional Record,* 90th Cong., 1st sess., CXIII (1967), S15509.

The act establishing the Redwood Park authorized $92 million for land acquisition. Appropriations of $53 million were approved during 1968 in a supplemental appropriations bill. Although the act's proponents exuded confidence that the law provided financial authorizations in excess of those actually needed for land acquisition (particularly because of the land exchange provisions) some authorities feel that this amount is insufficient. According to Mortimer Doyle, executive vice president of the National Forest Products Association, the allocation for land acquisition was "totally unrealistic." He indicated that because of escalating land values the cost of private property alone may very well be more than $200 million,[7] in the absence of large land exchanges.

It was precisely because of these rapidly spiraling real estate and timber prices that one of the measure's most unprecedented provisions was included in the act. To expedite acquisition and eliminate further increases in land purchase costs, the law contained a section permitting a "legislative taking" of privately owned lands within the park boundaries. On the date of enactment "all right and title in all private property . . . is vested in the United States." Landowners must negotiate with the Secretary of the Interior to arrive at a just compensation for their property in the form of money, land, or a combination of the two. Any claims against the Federal government are to be heard in the Court of Claims rather than by a jury in a Federal district court, as is usual in condemnation proceedings. This section of the law may be interpreted as circumventing the citizens' rights to property and the due process of law, and its constitutionality has been questioned on these grounds. Whether the law will be tested in the courts remains to be seen, but if this provision stands, "legislative taking" may well become the most widely adopted method of property acquisition by governments at all levels for a wide range of purposes. In the case of the Redwoods National Park, it could go a long way to prevent, or at least alleviate, the invidious speculative spiral envisioned by Mortimer Doyle and others.

The economic health of the local area is an especially important concern because the act as passed eliminated the economic adjustment payments contained in the original administration bill. The economic difficulties are somewhat more diffuse than those of the

[7] *Ibid.*

administration bill since the economic impact will now be shared by four companies in two counties (rather than one company in one county). Some provision was made to lessen the initial adverse economic impact of the park on the local area through exchange of public and private lands, but additional Federal economic assistance for local people and communities may be necessary if minimum standards of income and services are to be maintained during the first five years of the park's existence. One of the primary concerns of the people in Del Norte and Humboldt Counties, which was brought out in the hearings, was that if a park were to be created it should be done swiftly so that development and construction of park facilities would speed the shift of the local economic base from excessive emphasis on forest products to a more even balance with tourism and recreation. It is too early to determine how well this problem will be met. There are other ways, however, that could help to ease any temporary strain on the local economy. It has been suggested, for example, that the annual allowable cut in the nearby Six Rivers National Forest could be increased to the maximum consistent with sound forest management. There are also the programs of the Office of Economic Opportunity, the Small Business Administration, and the Economic Development Administration which can be brought to bear on the problem if the need develops.

A question still unanswered in the minds of many is where, actually, are the tallest trees? It was the intention of Congress to include within the park the grove containing the tallest known trees, which have only recently been discovered. Some experts hold that a thorough survey of existing stands would disclose specimens outside the park that are taller than any now known and measured. If so, the intent of the legislation would be thwarted unless boundary adjustment can be made. Much basic ecological knowledge about the redwoods is lacking.

An overriding consideration throughout the Redwoods National Park controversy has been the matter of national versus local economic interests. According to a 1966 report of the Department of the Interior, some four thousand comments were received in response to a preliminary report of the National Park Service on the redwoods controversy. Nationwide the replies were overwhelmingly in favor of establishment of a national park to preserve this resource. Most of the opposition came from members of the forest products industry and local authorities in the northern counties of California who feared the economic consequences of a reduced timber supply.

Congress responded very slowly to the wishes of a great majority of the American public. A redwood national park did not become a reality until over seventy years after it was first proposed. Should changes be made in the American political system to make government more responsive and effective in its efforts to restore or preserve a quality environment? If an apparent majority of Americans agree that some old-growth redwoods should be preserved in a national park, what criteria can be used to determine the correct number of acres to include? At what point do all the costs of an additional acre exactly balance all the possible social benefits to be gained from preservation of that acre? For that matter, how can one measure the costs and benefits of a scenic or recreational resource?

Our present political system is inept at weighing local interest and well-being on the one hand, and the national interest on the other hand, in conservation matters. Certainly we do not want a tyranny of the majority; the economic interests of a local area or special-interest group must be considered. But this can not be to the exclusion of all other considerations. The case of the redwood national park controversy illustrates this major limitation to existing methods of decision making. Many congressmen are simply unable to weigh the long-term aesthetic and ecological implications of national park legislation because their constituencies exert heavy and constant pressures upon them to deliver more tangible benefits. Thus, short-term economic considerations often have the advantage over aesthetics and ecology.

In the context of current conservation politics, this problem is particularly pressing. If, as a nation, we fail in our efforts to save masterpieces of nature, in most cases we will not have that opportunity later. If we do not save the giant redwoods now, we will not have another chance until perhaps the year 2500. The emphasis on the possibly adverse effects on the economy in the fight to save the redwoods is disturbing. It is disturbing because it suggests the inability, or at least the unwillingness, of Congress to deal explicitly and directly with some central political issues. Localized economic distress is a problem that Congress can do something about, more or less effectively, through existing legislation and government programs. However, there is no reasonably certain method for evaluating the extent to which a redwood national park will add to the meaning and quality of life in America. The decision to create such a park required that Congress make a political value judgment to the effect that the aesthetic and recreational benefits of such a park are likely to be more meaningful to Americans than the local economic benefits from continued felling. This is to be heralded. But the fact remains that it was a compromise that gave the American people a two foot square cut out of the lower left quadrant of a famous masterpiece.[8]

[8] See p. 13.

7. Meeting the Costs of a Quality Environment:

The Land and Water Conservation Fund Act

DANIEL P. BEARD

THE outdoors lies deep in American tradition. Our literature and folklore have always shown a deep affection for the land. As one source has pointed out, since the earliest time, one of the strongest currents in that tradition has been the idea that the outdoors is a right of all Americans, "not only something to be enjoyed but vital to our spirit."[1] But as population has multiplied and become more urban, we have moved away from this traditional use of the outdoors. We have shifted from a life tied to the land, to a life where the outdoors has become a recreational experience, primarily to the city dweller. Advances in technology have also played a vital role in this transformation by increasing personal incomes, leisure time, and mobility which, in turn, have led to a rapidly increasing demand for public outdoor recreation during the last decade.

This raises several major public policy issues. How much outdoor recreation is actually needed? What kind? Where should it be located? Who should provide it? And, perhaps the most difficult and controversial question of all, who is going to pay the costs? Should the primary responsibility rest on those who recreate, or on the general public?

A good case can be made for placing the major responsibility for payment on those who use the recreation facilities. For several years

DANIEL P. BEARD is a teaching assistant in geography at the University of Washington. He is currently completing a study of the administration of the Land and Water Conservation Fund Act in the State of Washington.
[1] Outdoor Recreation Resources Review Commission, *Outdoor Recreation for America* (Washington, D.C.: Government Printing Office, 1962), p. 13.

now, user fees have been collected at a number of recreation areas. But the collection of admission fees has been limited, largely in response to the historical attitude that public lands should be freely available to all citizens. On the other hand, there are many who feel that outdoor recreation provides benefits not only for those who participate but also for the general public. According to this argument, a certain portion of the costs for meeting the increased demand for outdoor recreation areas must fall on the taxpayer. Thus, as Marion Clawson and Jack Knetsch pointed out in their recent book, *The Economics of Outdoor Recreation,* "In the final analysis, the major policy issue is the degree to which users of outdoor recreation shall pay for it individually and directly as they use it, as compared with raising the necessary revenues collectively by general or special taxes."[2]

The Land and Water Conservation Fund Act of 1965 was an attempt by Congress to deal with the rising demand for recreational lands and with the question of who should undertake the burden of payment for new recreational areas. As this paper will show, for various reasons the results fall far short of hopes and expectations.

I

During the 1950's, problems related to outdoor recreation began to become apparent to the Congress. As a result the Outdoor Recreation Resources Review Commission (ORRRC) was created to examine the nation's recreational policies and to make recommendations about the nation's future needs in outdoor recreation. The findings of the commission were reported to Congress in 1962. It was pointed out that 90 per cent of the population participated in some form of outdoor recreation. The report estimated that outdoor recreation provided a $20 billion a year market for goods and services, and, more importantly, also provided essential social benefits of inestimable importance to the individual and the nation.[3]

The commission's report also presented Congress with a perplexing dilemma. While the demand for outdoor recreation was increasing dramatically, the supply was not. The commission noted that there was very little coordination among governmental agencies in their

[2] Marion Clawson and Jack Knetsch, *The Economics of Outdoor Recreation* (Baltimore, Md.: Johns Hopkins Press, 1966), p. 313.
[3] ORRRC, *Outdoor Recreation for America,* p. 4.

efforts to meet future demands and that a number of steps would have to be taken. The commission recommended that the states should play the pivotal role in developing the nation's outdoor recreation resources, suggesting that each state develop a long-range plan "to provide adequate opportunities for the public, to acquire additional areas where necessary, and to preserve outstanding natural areas." [4] More importantly, the report urged that public agencies should create a system of user fees which could pay for a significant portion of the costs of operating and maintaining recreation areas. Finally, the commission recommended a Federal grant-in-aid program to assist the states in meeting the costs of an improved outdoor recreation policy.

Shortly after the release of the ORRRC report, President Kennedy, in his conservation message of March 1, 1962, recommended the establishment of a land and water conservation fund consistent with these recommendations. During the congressional session of 1962, two bills were introduced to meet these recommendations, but after hearings in both the House and Senate the bills were shelved. They failed to gain support primarily because no provisions were included to aid state and local governments in acquiring land for recreational purposes.

In a letter to the Speaker of the House on February 14, 1963, President Kennedy renewed his request for a land and water conservation fund:

> The land and water conservation fund I am proposing will enable the states to play a greater role in our national effort to improve outdoor recreation opportunities.
>
> . . . .
>
> Actions deferred are too often opportunities lost, particularly in safeguarding our natural resources. I urge the enactment of this proposal at the earliest possible date.[5]

Accompanying the letter was an administration bill, which was introduced in the House by Representative Wayne Aspinall of Colorado (H.R. 3846). A counterpart measure in the Senate was introduced by Senator Henry Jackson of Washington (S. 854). Significantly, they are

---

[4] *Ibid.*, p. 71.
[5] U.S., Congress, House, Committee on Interior and Insular Affairs, *Hearings, Land and Water Conservation Fund*, 88th Cong., 1st sess., 1963, p. 7.

chairmen, respectively, of the House and Senate Interior and Insular Affairs Committees.

The purpose of the bill was "to assist in preserving, developing and assuring accessibility to all citizens . . . such quality and quantity of outdoor recreation resources as may be available and are necessary and desirable for individual active participation in such recreation and to strengthen the health and vitality of the citizens of the United States."[6] To accomplish this, the bill proposed the creation of a fund from which appropriations could be made to assist in planning, acquiring, and developing areas for outdoor recreation on state, local, and Federal lands. The fund would derive revenue from four sources. The first was in the form of admission and user fees. Admission fees were to be charged for access to and use of Federal lands which had outdoor recreation as their primary use. The Golden Eagle Passport, a $7.00 a year sticker, would allow entry into any Federal area administered primarily for scenic, scientific, historical, cultural, or recreational purposes. Fees would also be collected for the use of federally administered facilities such as campsites and cooking facilities. Two other sources for the fund were revenues from the sale of surplus real and related personal property, and from the motorboat fuel taxes authorized in the Highway Revenue Act of 1956. Finally, the bill authorized appropriations from the Treasury to the fund of $60,000,000 a year, to begin in the third year following the creation of the fund, and to continue for eight years thereafter.

Money held in the fund was to be appropriated each year by Congress, with 60 per cent to be allocated to the states and 40 per cent to agencies of the Federal government. The money allocated to the states could be used for planning, acquiring, or developing outdoor recreation areas, with the states required to provide 50 per cent matching funds for each project. Before money could be appropriated for any acquisition or development projects, the individual state was required to draw up a comprehensive statewide outdoor recreation plan including an evaluation of the demand for and supply of outdoor recreation resources in the state, a program for implementation of the plan, and a consideration of relevant Federal programs. The fund also provided money for the acquisition of land and waters by the National

---

[6] PL 88–578, Section 1(b).

Park Service and the U.S. Forest Service as well as money for the acquisition of areas intended to preserve threatened wildlife species and for recreation purposes at wildlife refuges.

II

Like most legislation, the act was altered during its passage through Congress. Hearings in both the House and Senate were held early in 1963. Support for the bill was considerable. As already mentioned, Representative Aspinall of Colorado introduced the measure and was its principal proponent in the House. The bill had the full support of President Kennedy as well as President Johnson when he took office later in the year. It was backed strongly by both Secretary of the Interior Stewart Udall, and Secretary Orville Freeman of the Department of Agriculture, and also found support among state officials, conservation groups, recreation organizations, and labor unions. Support for the legislation centered around three basic ideas. The first was that the states must play the major role in developing the nation's outdoor recreation resources. Second, the proponents recognized that it was necessary to acquire large amounts of land to meet future demand, and that this acquisition should occur before lands suitable for outdoor recreation were put to other uses. Third, a reasonable portion of the acquisition costs must be met by those who are the direct beneficiaries of additional land for recreation—namely, the recreators. All three of these points were included in the bill.

There was also, of course, opposition to the bill. Of all the provisions contained in the proposed legislation, the most controversial was the imposition of admission fees to all federally administered recreation areas, a dramatic departure from the existing procedure although some precedent did exist. The proponents envisioned the admission fee portion of the bill to be a leading source of revenue for the fund, as Table 1 indicates. The bill required that the heads of Federal departments and agencies prescribe rules and regulations for the collection of such fees.

It immediately became apparent when Secretaries Udall and Freeman began their testimony before the Senate Interior and Insular Affairs Committee that most of the committee members were opposed to the admission fee proposal. The committee was composed entirely of western senators who not only feared the lax provisions for the collection of the fees but could foresee a potential threat to their political popularity if their constituents were suddenly required to pay admission into public recreation areas which had formerly been free.

TABLE 1

EXPECTED REVENUES TO THE LAND AND WATER CONSERVATION FUND
(Per Year)

Source	Revenues
Admission Fees	$ 57,000,000
User Fees	10,000,000
Sale of Surplus Property	50,000,000
Motorboat Fuel Tax	29,000,000
TOTAL	146,000,000

Source: U.S., Congress, House, Committee on Interior and Insular Affairs, *Land and Water Conservation Fund, Hearings on H.R. 3846 and Related Bills*, 88th Cong., 1st sess., 1963, p. 20.

Similar opposition developed in the hearings before the House Interior Committee. Among the most vociferous of the groups were the North Carolina and Tennessee delegations who were concerned about the imposition of an admission fee to the Great Smoky Mountains National Park. The basis for their opposition was that the deed conveying the roads entering into the park to the Federal government was given with the provision that "no toll or license fee whatsoever shall ever be imposed for the use" of the highways.[7] Yet the imposition of admission fees for entrance into the park for the purposes of recreation was not in violation of the agreement. Another group worked for the abolishment of fees at Tennessee Valley Authority and Corps of Engineers projects. Their contention was that by imposing fees for admission to and use of water bodies, the Congress would be breaking faith with the American public, by severing the historical precedent that water bodies should be open to the public without charge.

Although none of these groups were able to muster enough support to abolish the admission fee provisions entirely, the bill was compromised to meet these objections. An amendment was accepted prohibiting the charging of entrance fees to the Great Smoky Mountains National Park "unless charged at all entrances." Since this was not feasible, the amendment had the effect of upholding the objections of the congressmen from North Carolina and Tennessee. The bill was

[7] House, Interior and Insular Affairs Committee, *Hearings, Land and Water Conservation Fund*, p. 69.

also modified to provide that no fees would be charged for the use of any public waters, although access to such waters could be charged. These were only minor chinks in the legislation but they developed into a broad cleavage in later years as difficulties developed in the equitable administration of the admission fee provision with its various exceptions.

Controversy also developed over the section of the bill earmarking money for recreational purposes. The most obvious precedents were the Pittman-Robertson and Dingell-Johnson acts which established earmarked funds from Federal taxes on firearms, ammunition, and fishing tackle to assist states in financing fish and wildlife restoration projects. In the case of the land and water conservation fund, the proponents hoped that the revenues from the four sources would be similarly earmarked to provide a constant fund that would enable Federal as well as state agencies to plan ahead and give priorities to certain outdoor recreation projects. However, a crippling concession was made to those congressmen who feared that Congress would be abdicating its responsibilities by following such a course, and the final bill contained a proviso that "moneys covered into the fund shall be available for expenditure for the purposes of this Act only when appropriated thereof." [8] Thus, although revenues were earmarked to a special account in the Treasury, the appropriations from this account still depended on the Federal budget and annual appropriations made by Congress.

Finally, controversy arose over how and for what purposes the fund should be expended. The primary objective of the supporters of the bill was the acquisition of lands to meet existing and future recreational needs, and it was intended that the use of the fund for actual development of recreational facilities would be nil. Money for development, it was felt, should come from other sources. In keeping with this objective, the bill as originally introduced provided that Federal agencies could not use any of their funds for development. To placate the states, however, it was prescribed that each state could use 10 per cent of the money allocated to it from the fund. The political realities of such a provision became immediately apparent during the Senate hearings on the bill. Almost all of the senators at the hearings expressed grave misgivings about this proposal. Their concern was

[8] PL 88–578, Section 3.

understandable. In most of the western states, Federal ownership of land was extensive and many states felt that development was of more immediate concern. Opposition to this provision was also expressed by western representatives on the House Interior Committee, as well as by virtually all of the witnesses testifying from state and local agencies. Their arguments were based on the premise that local governments should have full powers in determining how the funds should be expended within their jurisdictions. As a result of these pressures, the 10 per cent limitation on state and local use of the fund for development purposes was dropped from the final bill.

The use of money from the fund by Federal agencies was another area of contention. The bill proposed to give the various agencies the power to purchase private lands including especially those within existing boundaries of the National Park System, the national forests, and other areas. The Department of Agriculture testified that the intermingling of private and public ownership within federally administered areas was a very real problem which precluded effective land management. Purchase of these inholdings would help greatly to alleviate the problem. However, a strong lobby developed in opposition to the use of *any* funds by Federal agencies for acquisition purposes. The lobby was led by the forest products industry which feared the impact of the provision in shifting timberlands to recreational uses. The major contention of this group was summarized by Ralph D. Hodges, chief forester of the National Lumber Manufacturers Association:

> We do not believe it is the intent of the ORRRC or of this bill to have the Federal Government acquire lands to provide local recreational facilities. . . . Existing procedures are fully adequate and we recommend deletion of all Federal land acquisition authority.
>
> . . . .
>
> The chief aim of the Federal recreation activities should be the development of existing Federal recreation sites to meet the demonstrated needs of the public for recreational opportunities. We strongly urge that the proposal for acquisition be completely eliminated.[9]

This view was backed by the powerful National Association of Manufacturers and the American Farm Bureau Federation, as well as by numerous western senators and congressmen. While the lobby was

[9] House, Interior and Insular Affairs Committee, *Hearings, Land and Water Conservation Fund*, p. 230.

not successful in its effort to eliminate all Federal land acquisitions from the bill, it did succeed in limiting Forest Service acquisitions to those lands within or immediately adjacent to the national forests in which outdoor recreation was of primary importance. A provision was also added requiring that at least 85 per cent of the lands acquired by the Forest Service be located east of the 100th meridian. This provision was designed primarily to appease eastern members of Congress who felt that without it most of the new Federal recreation lands would be acquired in the West; but the provision was also supported by western senators and congressmen and the timber lobby as a means of preventing any large Federal land acquisitions in the West. All of these changes had the effect of limiting the extent to which the objectives of the bill could be realized.

Just before passage of the bill, a final effort was made by these same interests to add an amendment allowing Federal agencies to use the fund for development of existing federally administered recreation areas. (There was, as already mentioned, a provision placed in the bill giving state and local governments this prerogative.) The proposed amendment was backed by members of the House Interior Committee and by numerous western senators; but the provision was clearly not in keeping with either the recommendations of the ORRRC report or the basic objectives of the legislation. The act was intended to be an interim measure to assist the state, local, and Federal governments in catching up with the great demand for recreational lands; drawing off part of the fund for the development of recreational facilities on existing Federal lands would have hindered achieving this goal. The defeat of this amendment was the greatest success sustained by the proponents as the bill proceeded through Congress. The bill, as amended, was signed into law by President Johnson on September 1, 1964.

III

The Land and Water Conservation Fund Act appears to meet several of the needs expressed in the ORRRC report. The act created a fund from which money can be appropriated to assist states in planning, acquiring, and developing outdoor recreation areas. It allocated money to Federal agencies to assist them in acquiring land. It placed the primary responsibility for supplying outdoor recreation areas on the state and local governments, and it placed a major responsibility for paying the costs of further land acquisitions on those who would benefit most by imposing user and admission fees. Nevertheless, shortly after passage, it became apparent that the act was not meeting all of the intended goals; that it was not having the impact originally envisioned.

One of the main achievements of the act has been in the area of Federal-state cooperation. It has awakened state and local governments to their responsibilities toward providing land for recreation, and it has forced state and local agencies to attempt comprehensive planning in cooperation with the Federal government. During the first three years of the program's operation the states have received $138 million for planning, acquisition, and development, while Federal agencies expended some $88 million for acquisition, and altogether around 800,000 acres were acquired by both Federal and state agencies during this period.[10] But problems have developed. Examination of the statistics discloses that a majority of the money allocated to the states has been used for development purposes. During the first three years, for example, nearly 60 per cent of the state allocations from the fund were spent on development projects, contrary to the original intent of the legislation. The ratio of acquisition to development varied, of course, from state to state. In Texas over 85 per cent of the allocated funds went to development; in New York, the figure was 95 per cent; and in Pennsylvania all of the money went for development projects.[11]

A disparity also developed between the amounts the states were qualified to receive from the fund and the actual amounts awarded. In Pennsylvania, for example, recreation agencies were qualified under the matching formula to receive $4.9 million in 1968, but were awarded only $3.8 million; in the State of Washington, after three years the disparity between qualified and awarded funds had reached $1.5 million. The reasons were twofold: in the first place, the fund was not collecting enough money; and in the second place money was not being appropriated by Congress at the authorized level.

Examination of Table 2 reveals a primary cause for the lack of

[10] U.S., Congress, Senate, Committee on Interior and Insular Affairs, *Hearings, Land and Water Conservation Fund Amendments*, 90th Cong., 2d sess., 1968, p. 51.

[11] U.S., Congress, House, Committee on Interior and Insular Affairs, *Amending Title I of the Land and Water Conservation Fund Act of 1965*, Rept. 1313, 90th Cong., 2d sess., 1968, p. 4.

money—the failure of the admission fees. As pointed out earlier (see Table 1), the fund was expected to receive approximately $146 million

TABLE 2

Revenue to the Land and Water Conservation Fund
1965–67
(In Millions)

Source	1965	1966	1967
Annual Permit	$ .7	$ 2.8	$ 3.8
Other admission and user fees	1.3	5.0	5.6
Motorboat fuel tax	4.4	27.6	31.3
Surplus real property	22.0	74.3	54.1
TOTAL	28.4	109.7	94.8

Source: U.S., Congress, Senate, Committee on Interior and Insular Affairs, *Land and Water Conservation Fund Amendments, Hearings on S. 1401 and Related Bills,* 90th Cong., 2d sess., 1968, p. 9.

yearly, but during its best year it collected only $109.7 million. The admission fee portion was expected to be one of the major producers of revenue, collecting approximately $57 million per year. During its best year, however, only $3.8 million was collected. One of the reasons for this vast discrepancy has been the nearly impossible job of collecting fees at a great number of recreation areas, largely because of the many entrances and exits. The National Park Service collected over 50 per cent of all the money derived from admission fees on Federal lands, primarily because of its ability to control ingress and egress from its parks. But other Federal agencies ran into much greater physical difficulty. The Corps of Engineers, in addition, was basically opposed to the idea of collecting fees for the use of its recreation areas and made only half-hearted efforts at collection.[12] The costs for collecting the fees also proved to be a problem. The National Park Service reported that the cost of running its fee program was about 11 per cent of the total revenues collected, while the Corps of Engineers maintained that its costs during fiscal year 1967 were $660,500 while the revenues derived were only $594,000.[13]

[12] U.S., Congress, House, Committe on Interior and Insular Affairs, *Hearings, Land and Water Conservation Fund Amendments,* 90th Cong., 2d sess., 1968, p. 12.
[13] Senate, Interior and Insular Affairs Committee, *Hearings, Land and Water Conservation Fund Amendments,* p. 97.

The Land and Water Conservation Fund has also suffered from what has become known as the growing money gap, which refers to the disparity between congressional authorization and what is actually appropriated annually. Although revenues to the fund for the first three years were $342 million, the appropriations were only $289 million. For fiscal year 1968, $142 million was requested yet only $119 million was appropriated; and, in fiscal year 1969, $130 million was sought while only $92.5 million was appropriated.[14]

Another critical problem leading to deficiencies in the fund has been land price escalation. After government agencies announce their intention to purchase land, the price of land has tended to increase sharply as a result of speculation. As historians have frequently pointed out, the history of America has been the buying of land by the acre and selling it by the front foot. In other cases, the land has been committed to other uses before the money to complete the purchase is made available. As a result, the fund has not gone as far as expected in terms of the amount of land purchased.

An indication of the extent of this problem was presented during recent Senate hearings:

> At twelve recently authorized Federal recreation areas there was an average lapse of about two years between the time a bill was first introduced in the Congress and its enactment, and an average lapse of about three years from introduction of a bill to the first appropriation of funds by the Congress for property acquisition after its enactment. The average time from enactment of a bill to the first appropriation of funds for property acquisition was about nine months.[15]

A report by the Bureau of Outdoor Recreation noted that the price of recreation land is rising at a rate of 5 to 10 per cent per year.[16] Thus by the time money is appropriated for projects which have been approved by Congress, land prices could conceivably have risen from 30 to 40 per cent. The Point Reyes National Seashore is a good example. In 1962 Congress enacted a bill creating the Seashore and appropriated $14 million to acquire the needed land. By 1968, the appropria-

[14] Conservation Foundation, *CF Letter*, March 15, 1968, p. 7; and December 16, 1968, p. 2.
[15] Senate, Interior and Insular Affairs Committee, *Hearings, Land and Water Conservation Fund Amendments*, p. 7.
[16] Bureau of Outdoor Recreation, *A Report on Recreation Land Price Escalation* (Washington, D.C.: Government Printing Office, 1967), Introduction.

tion had been increased to $19,135,000, and there were indications that the final costs could rise as high as $55 million.[17] The major factor is time. If money were made available to purchase the land shortly after the approval of a project the land price escalation problem might be averted.

IV

In an effort to overcome some of these problems, Congress passed additional legislation in July, 1968, to amend the original Land and Water Conservation Fund Act. Sponsored by Senator Henry Jackson and Representative Wayne Aspinall, the new legislation sought to bolster the lagging fund and to attack the problem of land speculation. The Bureau of Outdoor Recreation had estimated in 1967 that, considering the rate of land price escalation, the next decade would require an investment of approximately $3.6 billion to meet Federal and state outdoor recreation needs, yet expected revenues to the fund during this period were estimated at only $900 million.[18] Something had to be done if the nation's outdoor recreation program was to be salvaged.

To combat the problem of land speculation, the new legislation gave the Secretary of the Interior authority to purchase options on land authorized for inclusion in the National Park System. Under this provision the secretary could enter into an advanced contract to lease land with an option to buy. The act also allowed the secretary to enter into arrangements whereby the land could be leased back to the original owner until the need for the property arose, or could be sold back to the original owner if Congress did not appropriate funds for the purchase. A separate fund of $30 million was provided to finance the program during the first two years. This would allow the secretary to act quickly in order to forestall land price escalations during the usual two- or three-year time lag between congressional authorization and final appropriation of funds for particular land acquisitions. A provision was also included allowing the secretary to exchange Federal lands under his jurisdiction for state or private lands within the boundaries of a national park when this was deemed in the national interest.

[17] Senate, Interior and Insular Affairs Committee, *Hearings, Land and Water Conservation Fund Amendments,* p. 34.

[18] Bureau of Outdoor Recreation, *Land Price Escalation,* Introduction.

How to bolster revenues to the faltering Land and Water Conservation Fund drew the most controversy. It had become apparent that the admission and user fee system, envisioned six years earlier as the leading source of revenue for the fund, was a miserable failure. Several reasons account for this. There was the physical difficulty of collecting the fees because of the lack of control over ingress and egress at many Federal recreation areas, and the concomitant high costs of collection in relation to revenues derived. Of greater significance, however, was the nonacceptance of the admission fee concept by the general public and a corresponding reluctance of the agencies to collect the fees for public relations reasons. The admission fee concept had never been properly explained and interpreted to the public, and Congress had undermined the concept from the very beginning by allowing various exceptions. The 1968 legislation dealt it a death blow. The mandatory fee system in the original act was repealed and the imposition of fees was left to the discretion of each agency. What began as a bold new experiment in public policy ended in smoke.

Strong pressure on Congress from the U.S. Army Corps of Engineers was an important factor in the demise of the fee system. This was brought out by Representative John Saylor of Pennsylvania at the House hearings on the proposed amendments:

Now, I am delighted to hear the chairman of the full committee say that there has to be give and take on this proposition. But it disturbs me that there are certain people in the Government, and I might as well be honest with the people who are here and the members of the committee, it disturbs me no end that the Army Engineers are agitating the Members of Congress in whose areas they have projects, and saying to them that the taxpayers built and paid for these various projects and therefore we shouldn't be called upon to charge any money.[19]

As a substitute for the fee system, the new legislation, as originally introduced, proposed to divert to the Land and Water Conservation Fund *all* of the revenues derived from the Outer Continental Shelf Land Act. These receipts had totaled nearly one billion dollars during the preceding ten years, primarily from off-shore oil leasing, and they were expected to greatly exceed this amount in the ten years ahead.[20]

[19] House, Interior and Insular Affairs Committee, *Hearings, Land and Water Conservation Fund Amendments*, p. 12.

[20] Senate, Interior and Insular Affairs Committee, *Hearings, Land and Water Conservation Fund Amendments*, p. 236.

However, the proposal was met by a storm of protest principally from the congressional delegations of the coastal states who have sought for years to get these Federal receipts distributed to the states abutting the continental shelf. As a result, the proposal was blocked. The act as finally passed provided instead that Congress would appropriate sufficient money to maintain the Land and Water Conservation Fund at $200 million during the next five years, and if this amount was not met through the conventional appropriations process, the remaining balance (i.e., up to the $200 million a year level) would be credited to the fund from the Outer Continental Shelf receipts.

Despite these efforts to improve the Land and Water Conservation Fund, the major problem—the lack of money—still exists. The dilemma of the money gap will continue to plague the program and others like it until there is a genuine reorientation of national goals and priorities. To improve or even maintain the quality of the environment is a highly costly matter. The history of this legislation points up clearly that despite the reams of popular rhetoric and political oratory concerning environmental quality, there is underneath it all an unwillingness to pay for it. This was brought out clearly in a Gallup Poll conducted in 1969 which showed that 75 per cent of the nation's populace was in favor of setting aside more land for conservation purposes such as national parks, wildlife refuges, bird sanctuaries, and so forth, and a substantial percentage was willing to pay more in taxes to carry out such a program. However, only 4 per cent of those sampled were willing to pay as much as $100 a year in extra taxes.[21]

This attitude is reflected in Congress. As Representative Wayne Aspinall pointed out in the recent congressional hearings, the problem does not stem entirely from the Corps of Engineers but from the people who seem to believe that the present situation is the same as it was a hundred years ago; that land and recreation are free. "I do not think," he said, "there is a more misguided line of thinking in existence than this particular holdover from the days of the frontier." [22]

Unfortunately, the situation is not likely to get better until the shoes begin to pinch harder. Although the amendment to the Land and Water Conservation Fund allows up to $200 million to be appropri-

[21] Reported at the 1969 Annual Convention of the National Wildlife Federation in Washington, D.C., by George Gallup.
[22] House, Interior and Insular Affairs Committee, *Hearings, Land and Water Conservation Fund Amendments*, p. 184.

ated per year in an effort to accelerate the acquisition of authorized national parks, monuments, seashores, lakeshores, recreation areas and wildlife areas, the Johnson administration only proposed an appropriation of $154 million, and the Nixon administration is expected to lower this figure.[23] In an effort to counteract this trend, Representative John Dingell of Michigan and eight of his colleagues introduced a bill in the Ninety-first Congress to double the financial resources available annually for these purposes, which is more in keeping with the current needs. But the likelihood of the bill passing is remote. Until the people show a real willingness to pay for a quality environment, either through more taxes or by reordering Federal spending priorities, or both, such legislation, and that already passed, can only be viewed pessimistically.

[23] Conservation Foundation, *CF Letter,* March 12, 1969, p. 6.

8. Water Projects and Recreation Benefits

KEITH W. MUCKLESTON

In the literature of conservation politics in the United States, and particularly in connection with water resources, the Corps of Engineers of the U.S. Army and the Bureau of Reclamation of the Department of the Interior stand out as giant figures. Both agencies are primarily occupied with the design, planning, and construction of water development projects and in many instances are responsible for operating and maintaining the projects they build. Individually they are large and powerful bureaucracies. The Corps of Engineers has exercised functions relating to the improvement of navigation and flood control since the early days of the republic, and in all of its regions. Predecessors of the Bureau of Reclamation began a program of dryland irrigation and reclamation at the turn of the century in the seventeen western states. Together these agencies have brought economic growth and added wealth to numerous local communities and even entire regions. They have done so by building dams, creating reservoirs, constructing canals, and generally modifying the landscape. But the water projects constructed by these agencies have also aroused public opposition, especially in recent years. Both agencies have become conscious of their public image as destroyers of natural values and as advocates of a man-made environment, or at least one in which man and not nature is clearly dominant.

Both agencies function on the premise that water is a resource that

KEITH W. MUCKLESTON is assistant professor of geography at Oregon State University. He serves with the Water Resources Research Institute at Oregon State University, and is the author of articles on the historical geography of the Volga River in the USSR.

can and should be put to work. They have been most insistent that projects be built only if they are economically justified by a favorable ratio of project benefits to project costs. Congress has found this ratio to be a valuable guide to authorizing projects, but from time to time dissatisfaction has been expressed in Congress and among economists and conservationists with the kinds of benefits and costs that are included in determining project feasibility.

In 1965 Congress agreed to modify the benefit side of the benefit-cost equation by recognizing the legitimacy of benefits attributable to the recreation and fish and wildlife enhancement features of Federal water projects. In addition the Federal Water Project Recreation Act recognized the need for a uniform Federal-local cost-sharing formula as between the Corps of Engineers and the Bureau of Reclamation. Previously the absence of such a formula had complicated the reviewing function of the Bureau of the Budget and had made congressional appraisal and comparison of projects difficult. The act was also a response to a desire on the part of some local units of government to be given a greater role in planning, financing, and administering Federal water projects. On the face of it the act promised to reduce the autonomy of the Federal construction agencies and to bring a new set of considerations into play in determining project feasibility.

I

Water projects are designed to alter the environment. For millennia extensive irrigation projects have not only altered the regime of rivers but also changed the utilization and appearance of adjacent lands. Projects designed to enhance drainage, navigation, urban water supply, and the production of inanimate energy have left their marks on many river basins throughout the world. Until recently the drive to produce more food and material goods from water development projects far outweighted concern about the damage that these projects might cause to biotic communities or aesthetic values. Dams have altered fish habitat markedly, not infrequently blocking movements of anadromous fish; large numbers of animals have been drowned in lined but unfenced diversion canals; nesting habitats for waterfowl have sometimes been destroyed as water levels rise or fall; and scenic valleys, canyons, and waterfalls have been inundated by reservoirs.

As public attitudes toward aesthetics and recreation have changed, Congress has responded accordingly, and recent environmental legislation embraces a wide range of interests and concerns. It would seem that the role of at least small parts of the environment might be changing from "workshop to temple." But the Federal organization of and responsibility for water resource management has changed relatively little. The traditional *ad hoc* and fractionalized approach continues, often at the expense of broader environmental considerations. It is difficult for any political system to formulate the comprehensive and consistent policies required to manage the incredibly complex web of environmental interrelationships. Growth of population, urbanization, skyrocketing per capita consumption, and galloping technology all complicate the problem. The present system of water management, moreover, continues to embody three interrelated characteristics which render a balanced approach to water management exceedingly difficult if not impossible: the committee system, the constituency-orientation of Congress, and the pork barrel.

The present congressional committee system frequently produces conflicting and unsatisfactory legislation concerning the environment. For water policy alone there are no less than four committees drafting substantive legislation, and several others are indirectly involved. Interlocking committee membership offsets only part of the built-in disadvantages of this system. The complexity of the problem was summarized well in a recent article in the *Natural Resources Journal:*

Each committee can do one or two things to a river without being able to do anything else. The Public Works Committees, for example, can tell the Corps of Engineers to build a dam or navigation channel on a river or the committee can ignore the river. They cannot choose the preservation alternative. The Interior Committees can choose, in the West, between reclamation dams and scenic rivers, having only the latter option in the East, but they cannot direct the Department of Agriculture to control floods and conserve soil with a system of small headwaters impoundments—that is the province of the Agriculture Committees. The House Committee on Merchant Marine and Fisheries and the Senate Committee on Commerce legislate generally on wildlife refuge, and fishery development programs; these committees are moving toward a position of establishing specific management areas in estuaries, which will further involve them in the river basin planning picture.[1]

Moreover, the committees tend to have a disproportionate number of members representing constituencies which stand to benefit directly from the particular type of water development their committee han-

[1] Roger Tippy, "Preservation Values in River Basin Planning," *Natural Resources Journal,* VIII (April, 1968), 277.

dles. For example, in the Ninety-first Congress, seventeen of the twenty-four members of the House Subcommittee on Irrigation and Reclamation are from states where the Bureau of Reclamation is active. On the Senate Subcommittee on Water and Power Resources, which is responsible for irrigation, ten of the eleven members are from reclamation states.

The constituency orientation of Congress is a second characteristic militating against careful consideration of the interrelationships between water projects and the quality of environment. In theory a congressman may approach legislation as either a delegate who carries out instructions from his constituency or as a trustee who uses his own judgment in seeking the national interest. For much legislation he often functions as a trustee because no instructions are received, or the complexity of the legislation is beyond the comprehension of his constituents, or countervailing interest groups are about equally divided. But as Hubert Marshall has noted, "A public works bill gives the trustee no such freedom. The issue is clear."[2] The constituency will benefit substantially because of the nonreimbursable nature of Federal water projects. The congressman has no choice; he becomes a delegate. This constituency orientation of Congress, coupled with the generous subsidies enjoyed by the locality near Federal projects, has tied water development to the pork barrel. Access to the pork barrel is commonly facilitated by log-rolling, and the whole process is stimulated by the symbiotic relationship between the congressional subcommittees and the two major construction agencies, the Corps of Engineers and the Bureau of Reclamation.

Since the Corps of Engineers has had a long-standing responsibility for navigation and flood control its influence is nationwide. The Bureau of Reclamation, whose primary *raison d'etre* is irrigation, is confined by law to the seventeen western states. At the local level the corps can generate pressure and enthusiasm for Federal water projects because navigation and flood control costs are largely nonreimbursable. The Bureau of Reclamation, on the other hand, requires irrigators to repay part of the cost of Federal projects, although returns from the sales of hydroelectric power and low interest rates act as significant subsidies.

[2] Hubert Marshall, "Rational Choice in Water Resource Planning," *Readings in Resource Management and Conservation*, ed. Ian Burton and Robert W. Kates (Chicago: University of Chicago Press, 1965), p. 536.

The Corps of Engineers has a uniquely cordial association with Congress. Indeed they refer to themselves as "the engineer consultants to, and the contractors for, the Congress of the United States." [3] The Bureau of Reclamation is ultimately responsible to the President through the Secretary of the Interior. In conflicts between the two agencies, the usual alignment of forces is the corps plus Congress versus the bureau plus the President. The corps-Congress combination has proven the stronger. Not even a popular war-time President could control the engineers, as evidenced by the controversy over which agency would build the Kings Valley Project in California. President Roosevelt wrote the Secretary of War, "I want the Kings and Kern River Projects to be built by the Bureau of Reclamation and not by the Army Engineers." [4] The corps built the project. Repeated efforts to weaken this special corps-Congress relationship have been thwarted by Congress.[5] The corps is also aided by one of the most powerful lobbies in the country, the National Rivers and Harbors Congress, which includes congressmen in its membership. Hence, the lobbied are also the lobbiers. The bureau's interest-group organization, the National Reclamation Association, although influential, is no match for the Rivers and Harbors Congress. The association has not always been an automatic supporter of bureau programs.

The Corps of Engineers is especially adept at manipulating local interests to gain support for public works. As Harold Ickes, the former Secretary of the Interior during the 1930's, noted: "An Army Corps' 'Operation Santa Claus' is a two-pronged affair—the Engineers lobbying directly for an appropriation by the Congress while inciting local constituencies to bring pressure to bear upon their senators and

[3] Arthur A. Maass, "Congress and Water Resources," *American Political Science Review*, XLIV (September, 1950), 580–81.

[4] Arthur A. Maass, *Muddy Waters* (Cambridge, Mass.: Harvard University Press, 1951), p. 234.

[5] The attempts started in 1908 when President Theodore Roosevelt recommended centralization of water resource activities. In 1932 President Hoover proposed that the corps's civil functions be transferred to the Department of Interior. In 1945 President Truman asked Congress to re-enact reorganization legislation which was aimed at the corps. In 1949, the first Hoover Commission proposed that the functions of the corps and Bureau of Reclamation be consolidated. Congress has not approved any reorganization. Maass, "Congress and Water Resources," pp. 587–90, and Grant McConnell, *Private Power and American Democracy* (New York: Alfred A. Knopf, 1966), pp. 213–14.

representatives." He later summarized the corps's operations as mutiny *for* the bounty.[6] Being handicapped by repayment policies, the Bureau of Reclamation has not been able to manipulate local interests as readily.

The method by which corps projects are authorized is particularly conducive to log-rolling and pork barrel benefits. The individual projects from all congressional districts are lumped together as an omnibus rivers-and-harbors bill. It then becomes a situation of "all for one and one for all." As Grant McConnell has noted, "This process has been so notorious that some cynics have taken rivers-and-harbors as a working definition of the 'pork barrel.'"[7] Although many individual congressmen are against this process in principle, Congress as a whole has not tolerated any interference with what many members regard as a source of job security. During the first six years that President Eisenhower was in office, he vetoed 145 acts of Congress. All of these vetoes were sustained by Congress; yet with almost no debate they overrode the 146th veto, which was exerised on a public works appropriation bill.

Reclamation projects are more difficult to log-roll. Not only must each project be authorized individually, but reclamation interests are now largely limited to the West, and this reduces the opportunities for pork barrel politics. For example, as the costs of reclamation projects have become better known to taxpayers in the East, congressmen from that region have become less enthusiastic about "making the deserts bloom." The scrutiny given each project recommended by the Bureau of Reclamation, combined with these less favorable log-rolling conditions, gives proponents of nonutilitarian values a somewhat better opportunity to air their case before the nation. For example, had the Echo Park or Marble Canyon dams (which would have inundated parts of Dinosaur National Monument and Grand Canyon National Park, respectively) been included in an omnibus rivers-and-harbors bill, chances for congressional authorization would have been appreciably greater.

For over three decades, a favorable balance of benefits over costs has been prerequisite to water projects authorized by Congress. One of the overriding objectives of this country has been a continually increasing Gross National Product, and avid proponents of water

[6] Cited in Maass, *Muddy Waters*, pp. xi and xiv.
[7] McConnell, *Private Power and American Democracy*, p. 217.

projects never tire of pointing out that these investments increase the
wealth and productivity of the nation. Weighing the costs and benefits
of any capital investment is, of course, a wise approach and is frequently used by the private entrepreneurs, but there are problems
when this type of analysis is employed on public projects. In the first
place, many of the benefits and costs to the nation are either difficult
or impossible to quantify. In the second place, both the Corps of
Engineers and the Bureau of Reclamation have a stake in the outcome
of the analysis and have tended to inflate the expected benefits and
ignore certain social and intangible costs that are not easily measured
in dollars. As a result, benefit-cost analysis has become more a tool of
justification than of evaluation. The impressive calculations that go
into the analysis were summed up by one of the Second Hoover
Commission Task Force investigators as a "considerable accumula-
tion of absurdities." Since the Federal Water Projects Recreation Act
allows the construction agencies for the first time to include considerable benefits from the enhancement of outdoor recreation, fish, and
wildlife in the benefit-cost equation, an important issue is raised about
the act's potential long-term impact on the environment. Will the
inclusion of these new benefits merely result in the economic justification of water projects heretofore considered marginal and thus open
the gate further to the pork barreling of construction agencies? Before
considering this and related questions it will be helpful to take a closer
look at the act and its legislative history.

II

Early in 1963, the House Committee on Interior and Insular Affairs
held hearings to consider the lack of congressional policy on recreation cost-sharing as it related to other projects. It subsequently
adopted a resolution asking the administration not to submit any
further water projects to Congress involving nonreimbursable allocations to recreation, including fish and wildlife values, until the administration had submitted recommendations for legislation to establish
general procedures relating to cost-sharing. The Bureau of the Budget
quickly responded with recommendations which were introduced as
H.R. 9032 in the Eighty-eighth Congress. Although the bill died
without further consideration, parts of it were subsequently put into
effect as administrative policy. Early in the Eighty-ninth Congress,
however, the executive branch recommended that a different ap-

proach be undertaken to cost-sharing and reimbursement because of difficulties encountered in implementing this policy. Both the House and Senate Committees on Interior and Insular Affairs followed the new recommendations, and two separate bills, H.R. 5269 and S. 1229, were introduced in the respective chambers. Several differences between the House and Senate versions resulted in a conference committee, and S. 1229, as amended, was accepted by both houses and was signed into law as the Federal Water Project Recreation Act on July 9, 1965.

Four major differences were resolved in the House-Senate conference. First, the House version had limited the costs of recreation developments and the improvement of fish and wildlife values to 50 per cent of the total costs of a Federal water project, while the original Senate bill allowed more than 50 per cent expenditures on a project when it involved anadromous fish, shrimp, and migratory waterfowl protected by international treaty. The Senate version was adopted. Second, the Senate bill placed no ceiling on expenditures which the Corps of Engineers or the Bureau of Reclamation could make to establish waterfowl refuges near projects. The House version followed the Bureau of the Budget recommendations for a ceiling and was adopted by the conference committee. Third, a conflict existed about the disposition of land acquired by the Federal construction agencies for purposes of recreation and fish and wildlife enhancement. According to the Senate bill, if no cost-sharing agreement was reached by Federal and local governments during the ten-year period after construction of the project, the Federal agency could allow repurchase of the land by individuals and private organizations. This would have left open the possibility of cheap commercial developments around Federal reservoirs. The House version, which kept the land in Federal ownership and barred incompatible uses, was adopted in conference. Finally, the Senate bill authorized for the Department of the Interior only one half the funds provided by the House bill for the acquisition of lands and facilities to enhance recreation, fish, and wildlife at existing reclamation projects. The conference committee adopted the more liberal House version.

Favorable testimony by witnesses from several executive agencies made up the bulk of the hearings on S. 1229. Cogent arguments were made by representatives from the Bureau of the Budget, which had drafted the original bill, and by Department of the Interior spokesmen who favored the bill because it increased the authority of the Secretary of the Interior as well as that of the Bureaus of Outdoor Recreation and Sport Fisheries and Wildlife. Representative Wayne Aspinall of Colorado, the influential chairman of the House Interior and Insular Affairs Committee, was an important force in Congress behind the legislation. As a good friend of reclamation, Aspinall was able to accomplish two things by this legislation. First, the Bureau of Reclamation, with which Aspinall's committee has close ties, strengthened its position relative to that of its chief competitor for construction funds—the Corps of Engineers. Previously, the corps was able to provide recreation developments free of charge at its projects, while the Bureau of Reclamation had to receive special congressional authorization for the provision of recreation. This placed the corps in a much more favorable position vis-à-vis the support of local interest groups for its water projects. Under the new act, however, the two agencies must operate under the same cost-sharing rules. Second, irrigators benefited from the act because part of their expenses could now be assigned to recreation. Also supporting the bill were such conservation groups as the Izaak Walton League and the Sports Fishing Institute.

The most rigorous questioning of the bill came from those who feared that the provisions allowing the costs of recreation projects and fish and wildlife enhancement features to reach 50 per cent of the total project costs would allow many otherwise unfeasible water resource projects to become feasible. A representative of the Bureau of the Budget admitted that some formerly unfeasible projects would become economically feasible with the addition of these new benefits, but stressed that each individual project purpose would have to have a benefit-cost ratio greater than unity.[8] Senator Ernest Gruening of Alaska had quite a different concern about the bill. He spoke of the "negative benefits" that might occur if "extremist" fish and wildlife values were weighted more heavily at the planning stage.[9] This, he felt, might result in some highly desirable water projects being declared economically unfeasible because of greatly inflated costs of protecting fish and wildlife resources, a situation that occurred with

[8] U.S., Congress, Senate, Committee on Interior and Insular Affairs, *Hearings, Water Project Recreation Act,* 89th Cong., 1st sess., 1965, pp. 30 and 44.

[9] *Ibid.,* pp. 61–63.

respect to the Rampart Dam proposal on the Yukon River in Alaska.

Many of the committee members were also skeptical about the validity of benefits derived from recreation, fish, and wildlife. Their doubts stemmed from the "intangible character" of these benefits as opposed in their opinion to such "tangible" benefits as hydroelectricity, reclamation, flood control, and improved navigation, which can be measured in dollars and cents, and, hence, *ipso facto*, are more important and should be given greater weight in the decision-making process.

Opposition to the bill also came from various special interest groups who feared change in the *status quo*. For example, the Association of American Railroads foresaw that passage of the legislation might result in some heretofore economically unfeasible navigation projects becoming feasible, and they opposed the bill because it would result in a direct government subsidy to a competitive mode of transportation. The Mississippi Valley Association opposed the bill on the ground that, since people travel considerable distances to enjoy recreation on water bodies, it was unfair to assess the costs of developing recreational sites against the local governments near the reservoirs, implying instead that these costs should be more widely shared geographically or subsidized more heavily by the Federal government. Finally, some objections came from state fish and game departments, which generally oppose any measures they judge will erode state jurisdiction over these resources. For example, state agencies responsible for anadromous fish have been particularly vehement in their opposition to water resource development projects involving dams that would harm the spawning migrations of these species of fish, and, in this particular case, the California Fish and Game Commission flatly opposed the entire bill as "bad" with no other explanation.[10] However, opposition to the bill was generally fractured and unorganized, and had only minor impact on the substance of the bill.

III

Although the Federal Water Project Recreation Act exhibits many of the weaknesses inherent in the existing system of policy formation, it is not entirely without merit. It gives legislative recognition to the idea that recreation and fish and wildlife values must share equal consideration with the traditional and more utilitarian benefits from

[10] *Ibid.*, p. 36.

water development. It recognizes that man, the ecological dominant, has the technological and political means not only to alleviate environmental damage caused by water projects, but also to improve selected desirable aspects of his biophysical surroundings. And, by further encouraging establishment of user fees, it forces upon the average recreationist a greater respect for the quality of at least those parts of the environment that he must pay to use. But the act also contains provisions which may tend to lower the quality of the environment. The whole system of assessing benefits favors quantitative over qualitative criteria, which could have the effect of encouraging overcrowding and the further degradation of the already deteriorating quality of recreation. Mass recreation might not only conflict with high-quality outdoor experiences, but may also prove to be incompatible with certain types of fish and wildlife which are also supposed to be available at many Federal water projects.

The impact of the act on the environment depends in no small part on the way it is implemented. The act requires nonfederal governments to pay for half the separable costs and all of the operation and maintenance costs of improving recreation and/or fish and wildlife at major Federal water projects.[11] Many state and local spokesmen have been less than enthusiastic about this requirement. Outdoor recreation at Federal water projects is no longer a windfall for nonfederal governments. While local and state governments have generally applauded "creative federalism" aimed at giving them a greater voice in the planning and management of government programs, they are markedly less enthusiastic about the increased financial responsibilities this entails.

Although not enough time has elapsed since passage of the act to make positive statements about its implementation, trends are apparent. According to the Bureau of Reclamation, as of June, 1968, a letter of intent or an agreement with a nonfederal public body had been obtained for thirty-one planned and authorized projects, while on only two occasions was it unable to secure the required letter. The Corps of Engineers has received letters of intent for twenty-five major projects, which is about one half of the total projects authorized for the corps since the Federal Water Project Recreation Act was pas. ... represen-

---

[11] Separable costs are defined in the act as the difference between the capital costs of the entire multiple-purpose project and the capital cost of the project with the purpose omitted.

tative Wayne Aspinall pointed out that there was no evidence of resistance to the implementation of the act, and that none should be expected because state or local public agencies receive more value and benefits from dollars spent under the provisions of this act than from any other program providing for assistance to recreation development.[12] Former Secretary of the Interior Udall stated in a letter to Senator Henry Jackson that the act was working quite well as of June, 1968. He attributed a less positive response in the Pacific Northwest to the bountiful outdoor recreational opportunities already existing in the region.

On the other hand, there is evidence that many state and local agencies may be much less enthusiastic about the Federal Water Project Recreation Act than is indicated by these remarks. In response to an inquiry, the National Council on State Parks reported that many state parks and recreation agencies indicated it was too early to assess the full impact of this law on state park programs, but that at least two states, Kentucky and California, reported the act was working a hardship. Moreover, state agencies in the Pacific Northwest, have revealed that for Idaho, Montana, Oregon, and Washington, costs well might be too great to allow full participation in many Federal water projects. A number of state fish and game departments have also reported to the Bureau of Sports Fisheries and Wildlife that cost-sharing under the terms of the act is too expensive.

At the annual meeting of the National Council on State Parks in September, 1967, two resolutions were passed opposing major parts of the act. In the first resolution the council favored rescinding the section of the act requiring nonfederal governments to pay 50 per cent of the costs attributable to recreation and fish and wildlife values; and in the second, the group favored acquisition by the Federal construction agencies of all lands to be set aside for recreational purposes and the installation of all facilities at Federal expense before they are turned over to the political subdivisions for administration.

In addition, the act raises a number of legal and constitutional questions. The Texas Parks and Wildlife Department, for example, has not agreed to participate in any of the numerous Federal water projects authorized in Texas because the act involves the obligation of state revenues not yet appropriated, which is against state law. This

[12] Data concerning progress were obtained through correspondence with the respective agencies, and with Representative Aspinall.

does not apply to county or city governments in Texas, and a number
of local governments have signed letters of intent. A similar situation
exists in Oregon, Virginia, and Missouri. Local governments and
agencies which decide to participate in cost-sharing must, however,
have the authority to do those things required under the act, including
the power to contract with the Federal government, to engage in the
development of recreation and/or fish and wildlife, and to tax. These
requirements may preclude many local governments from participation. But the mere fact that many state and local governments have
submitted letters of intent even though they will incur considerable
expense indicates that they find the act advantageous, and it appears
that implementation of the act may well be quite extensive.

IV

   The specific nature of the impact of the act on the environment is a
moot question. In some cases, implementation of the act will have a
marked favorable influence on traditionally nonutilitarian values. For
example, although the principal purpose of the Garrison Diversion
Unit of the Missouri River Basin Project is the irrigation of 250,000
acres of land in North and South Dakota, another 147,000 acres were
acquired for waterfowl habitat. Prior to the construction of the unit,
waterfowl production in the area fluctuated widely in accordance
with the precipitation in this droughty region. But with water from
the unit supplying seventy waterfowl units there will be adequate
water for much more sustained production. In this particular case
both irrigation and migratory waterfowl production are complemen-
tary. The Federal Water Project Recreation Act was designed to foster
this kind of complementarity.
   On the other hand, there is evidence that the construction agencies
may be using provisions of the act to manipulate benefit-cost analysis
at the expense of some valuable wilderness recreation areas and other
aesthetic values. The Bureau of Reclamation's proposed Bumping
Lake Enlargement in Washington is a case in point. Bumping Lake
was originally created as a single-purpose storage reservoir for the
Yakima irrigation project, which is one of the most successful of all
bureau projects. The lake lies in the rugged Cougar Lakes Area to the
east of Mount Rainier. The reservoir is only two to three hours by car
from 1.5 million people, most of whom are clustered along Puget

Sound. Bumping Lake is a popular jumping off point for back country users. Over 55,000 hikers are estimated to have used the area in 1967. Intensive water-oriented recreation is all but eliminated midway through the summer season as irrigation demands draft the reservoir. Because of these extensive early drawdowns, the U.S. Forest Service has invested only limited funds in facilities to accommodate intensive recreational use of the reservoir, which is located on National Forest lands.

The proposed project would enlarge the storage capacity of Bumping Lake almost fourteenfold. According to the bureau's preliminary report the major benefits from the project would be first, an adequate supply of irrigation water; second, better anadromous fish runs in the Yakima River and its tributaries; and third, creation of "one of the most attractive recreation areas in the state." [13]

Using calculations made legitimate by the Federal Water Project Recreation Act the proposal to enlarge Bumping Lake Reservoir has a very favorable benefit-cost ratio of 2.56 to 1. It is noteworthy that approximately 60 per cent of the costs of this reclamation project are charged to fish, wildlife, and recreation benefits, and well over 90 per cent of these costs will be borne by the Federal treasury.

Implementation of the act has not produced as a rule such a heavy reliance on fish and wildlife benefits to justify a project. In most cases the act specifies that the costs attributed to recreation, fish, and wildlife may not exceed one half of the total project costs. The Bumping Lake project, however, will enhance an *anadromous* fishery, which nullifies the 50 per cent limit. Because anadromous fish are migratory, which diffuses benefits over a large area, improvements are largely financed by the Federal treasury. In addition, the costs of enhancing outdoor recreation are nonreimbursable in this case because the reservoir is on National Forest land. Accordingly, almost all local and many regional interests are solidly behind the project.

Opposition to the project stems largely from proponents of wilderness. Since 1962, the Federation of Western Outdoor Clubs and the Sierra Club have been on record as favoring the establishment of a Cougar Lakes Wilderness Area. Bumping Lake lies in the heart of this

[13] United States Department of Interior Joint Report, Bureau of Reclamation and Fish and Wildlife Service, *Bumping Lake Enlargement, Yakima Project Washington,* Boise, Idaho, January, 1966, Statistical Summary, page a.

area. According to their position, if hundreds of thousands of visitors are drawn to the reservoir for intensive recreational activities as projected in the preliminary reports, the wilderness will be destroyed. The project opponents cogently argue that the sizeable project funds for the creation of intensive recreation development at Bumping Lake could be used more efficiently either at four other mountain reservoirs in 'the Yakima River Basin that do not have precious wilderness qualities, or at the huge Priest Rapids reservoir on the nearby Columbia River. But alternatives to providing water for fish enhancement and irrigation are not presented in the preliminary bureau report. Enlargement of Bumping Lake is presented as the plan in a take it or leave it fashion. The costs of losing a potential wilderness area are not entered on the cost side of the bureau's ledger. It is unlikely that a revised bureau report would differ in this respect. As long as Congress allows construction agencies to place economic values on mass recreation while ignoring other less intensive forms of recreation because they are both intangible and difficult to measure, advocates of these latter forms of outdoor recreation will suffer.

Another example is the corps's proposed multiple-purpose Snoqualmie River storage project on the rugged, heavily timbered western flanks of the Washington Cascade Mountains. The dam sites on the fast-flowing Middle and North Forks of the Snoqualmie River are less than an hour by car from the Seattle Metropolitan area; accordingly the area is heavily used by outdoorsmen, hikers, fishermen, and white water buffs. Once the Snoqualmie breaks into the lowlands it meanders through picturesque farmland. Its periodic floods have created a greenbelt by impeding the sprawling developments that are common around the peripheries of American cities. The Snoqualmie joins the Skykomish River to become the Snohomish, continuing until it empties into Puget Sound at Everett. Highwater periodically causes extensive damage to some residential and commercial property in the flood plain of the lower Snohomish. Earlier studies by the corps were unable to justify flood control projects. However, the Federal Water Project Recreation Act now makes the project feasible. By projecting mass recreational use of the proposed reservoirs while ignoring the cost of destroying the established recreation uses at the sites, recreation becomes the single most important benefit of the flood control project. According to the corps's calculations, recreation is credited with 33 per cent of the total annual benefits, flood control with 32 per cent, and power with about 26 per cent. Since the benefit-cost ratio is not quite 1.2:1, recreational benefits obviously swing the entire project into the economically feasible category.

Critics of the project charge that the projected recreational use of the proposed reservoirs is grossly exaggerated because the area has hundreds of similar bodies of water. They point out that a scarce recreational and asethetic resource will be sacrificed in the name of enhancing mass recreation. The chief beneficiaries, they contend, will be downstream land speculators who will reap the benefits of increased land values resulting from flood protection. The Corps of Engineers recommended full authorization of this project but as a result of these criticisms rescinded this in March, 1969, and recommended instead that further consideration be given to alternatives which considered the preservation of the natural environment. The outcome of the project is uncertain, but it illustrates clearly the potential for misapplication of the Federal Water Project Recreation Act.

The Bumping Lake enlargement has been endorsed by the Washington Department of Game, which is acting as the nonfederal entity required by the Federal Water Project Recreation Act as a participant in cost-sharing. The Snoqualmie River flood-control project has the formal approval of King County, as the participating local authority. The existence of considerable opposition to both of these projects brings into question the extent to which approval by a unit of state or local government represents the real involvement of nonfederal interests in water project planning. The financial contribution of the Department of Game to the Bumping Lake project constitutes a major expenditure for a single state agency, probably slightly less than a million dollars. However, the benefits of the project as proposed by the Bureau of Reclamation make the investment one that Game Department officials can hardly afford to refuse. Like most state agencies, the Department of Game is mission-oriented and the values it seeks to attain are limited. It is at best questionable that the Federal Water Project Act, in providing for participation by a state or local entity, adequately takes account of all the nonfederal interests affected by and with a legitimate concern about water projects. In the case of the Snoqualmie River project, King County as a governmental unit with broader jurisdiction than a single mission-oriented agency also inadequately represents the full range of local opinion. The formal approval of the county commissioners clearly conflicts with other local interests.

No system of decision making could take full and formal recognition of all of the interests relevant to these two projects and produce a decision to satisfy everyone. In the past Federal water projects have been largely, if not entirely, the product of Federal agency initiative. They have been built with Federal funds, they have seldom taken account of ecological considerations and the quality of the environment, and they have co-opted a narrow set of local interests instead of giving full and careful consideration to a broad range of local opinion. By seeking to involve state and local governments in the process of decision making, by giving nonfederal entities an economic stake in projects, and by modifying the range of values considered in the calculation of costs and benefits, the Federal Water Project Recreation Act attempts to break away from the traditional method of water project decision making. While the attempt is to be commended, it is unfortunate that Congress did not go further in seeking to modify the behavior of the Federal construction agencies.

The Corps of Engineers and the Bureau of Reclamation are still in the business of evaluating sites for the construction of water projects. The Federal Water Project Recreation Act did not give these agencies the authority to evaluate sites with a view to recommending no construction or the establishment of a wilderness recreation area, for example. The major weakness of the act is that the construction agencies may interpret it as a mandate to continue recommending projects as long as they can sell them to a nonfederal unit of government as a sound investment, and provided they take explicit account of recreation and fish and wildlife values in calculating benefits and costs.

What mechanisms are available to modify or at least place some constraints upon the enthusiasm of the corps and the bureau? Clearly, direct political action to oppose projects such as that in the Snoqualmie River Valley can have a delaying effect and may even halt a project. Taking a more long-term perspective, and assuming that there is some merit in a planned and coordinated approach to water resources development, the Water Resources Council and regional river basin commissions, or their counterparts, could serve to introduce into individual agency planning some of the national and subnational interests that would make Federal water projects more than just attractive morsels from the pork barrel. Ecological considerations and the quality of the environment must eventually receive formal endorsement by Congress as considerations to which construction agencies should give priority. Experience with the Federal Water Project Recreation Act indicates that for the moment Congress is content with arrangements for administering water resources programs that perpetuate *ad hoc* programs and piecemeal projects at the expense of broader environmental policy goals.

9. Water Quality: A Question of Standards

PHILIP P. MICKLIN

WATER pollution is a problem of national scope. Congress, traditionally, has been loath to involve itself in this area on the constitutional grounds that such matters are primarily a state and local responsibility. The sad experience of the last half century has been that state and local governments, for a variety of reasons, are unequal to this challenge. Thus, hesitantly and only as a last resort, Congress over the past two decades has become deeply embroiled in the matter.

No doubt the most important and, at the same time, most controversial action taken by the national legislature regarding water pollution control was passage of the Water Quality Act of 1965 (PL 89–234). This measure involved Federal authorities in the field of water-quality management, traditionally a state and local preserve, far deeper than ever before. Consequently, it was the subject of lengthy, acrimonious congressional debate, raising anew the old issue of the balance of power between the Federal government and the states. Nevertheless, despite the boldness of the measure, one may question not only the legislation's adequacy to resolve the water pollution problem in the United States but, in a larger sense, the whole approach to waste management it symbolizes.

I

Although the Federal government has been involved in the water pollution control field nearly seventy years, it has played a quite minor

PHILIP P. MICKLIN is a research fellow in geography at the University of Washington. He has taught at Western Michigan University and is the author of a paper on resource use conflicts in the USSR. He is currently completing a doctoral thesis on Soviet efforts at conservation of the Caspian Sea.

role over most of this period. Indeed, until relatively recently the national government's responsibility was defined by three acts: the Rivers and Harbors Act of 1899, forbidding the discharge or deposit of materials into waterways that would be hazardous to navigation; the Public Health Service Act of 1912, which contained provisions authorizing investigations of water pollution related to the diseases and impairments of man; and the Oil Pollution Act of 1924, forbidding oil discharges in coastal waters. Since the 1930's efforts have been made to enact comprehensive Federal water pollution control legislation. These culminated in success with the passage of the Federal Water Pollution Control Act of 1948.[1]

This pioneer piece of legislation was experimental, and initially limited to a five-year period. At the end of the trial period, the law was extended for an additional three years until June 30, 1956. The act was implemented under the direction of the Surgeon General of the U.S. Public Health Service. However, the legislation clearly stated that the prime responsibility for water pollution control still rested with the states, and it provided mainly a supporting and advisory role for Federal authorities. Evidently, the feeling was that the development of comprehensive programs in cooperation with the states toward eliminating or reducing the pollution of interstate waters, making loans available for construction of treatment works, and providing money to state and interstate water pollution control agencies, would solve the major part of the water pollution problem. The law did provide for Federal enforcement action against polluters, although an abatement suit could be brought only when pollution originating in one state endangered the health or welfare of persons in another, and only then at the request of the governor in the affected and/or originating state. Moreover, the adjudication procedure was both time-consuming and highly complicated.

In 1956 Congress passed the Federal Water Pollution Control Act Amendments. This law both strengthened and made permanent the 1948 legislation. The emphasis remained on a cooperative approach, with the states retaining the primary responsibility for pollution control. For the most part, the amendments provided more monetary and technical assistance to the states, although abatement procedures against interstate polluters were also simplified and made more worka-

[1] Frank Graham, Jr., *Disaster by Default: Politics and Water Pollution* (New York: Evans, 1965), pp. 236–37.

ble. The most significant of the 1956 modifications was the substitution of a grant program for the earlier loan program to provide money for construction of municipal sewage treatment works.

This experiment in federalism during the late 1940's and 1950's had only partial success. Thus, although the construction assistance and technical research programs were significant Federal contributions toward the fight against water pollution, the overwhelming majority of states failed to live up to their responsibilities. Only a few states developed comprehensive pollution control programs, and those that had water-quality standards failed to enforce them. The states seldom asked the Federal government's help in establishing such standards, and, in light of the extent of the pollution problem, they requested surprisingly little Federal aid in enforcing pollution abatement (ten suits between 1948 and 1963). A parade of witnesses at the field hearings of the Senate Select Committee on National Water Resources held from October, 1959, through May, 1960, in twenty-two states convincingly pointed out the numerous failures of the water pollution control program. Information presented here and elsewhere increased congressional sentiment for a more direct Federal role in controlling water pollution. To use the lexicon of Daniel R. Grant, a need was felt to place more reliance on the stick and less on the carrot in future legislation.[2]

This mood was clearly apparent at the National Conference on Water Pollution held in Washington, D.C., in December, 1960. At that meeting, two national legislators, Representatives John Blatnik and William C. Cramer, chairman and member, respectively, of the Rivers and Harbors Subcommittee of the House Public Works Committee, which handles water pollution legislation, bluntly called for an extension of Federal powers regarding water pollution control.[3] This call was reflected in the Federal Water Pollution Control Act Amendments of 1961. Although this law in many of its provisions continued the past cooperative approach to water pollution control (i.e., increasing grants for construction and research purposes), it broke significant

[2] Daniel R. Grant, "Carrots, Sticks and Political Consensus," in *Environmental Studies,* ed. Lynton K. Caldwell (2 vols.; Bloomington: Institute of Public Administration, Indiana University, 1967), I, 19–41.

[3] "The Legislator Looks at Water Pollution," in U.S. Department of Health, Education, and Welfare, Public Health Service, *Proceedings, The National Conference on Water Pollution, December 12–14, 1960* (Washington, D.C.: Government Printing Office, 1961), pp. 41–46.

new ground regarding Federal abatement authority. In the first place, Federal jurisdiction was expanded to include both interstate and navigable waters.[4] This made pollution of nearly all waters in the United States a Federal concern, although the national government's abatement power differed, as we shall see, depending on whether pollution caused intra- or interstate damage. Secondly, pollution of interstate or navigable waters having consequences solely within the state of origin now came under the purview of the law, with the proviso that Federal abatement action was to be initiated only upon request of the state's governor. Finally, and most importantly, the Secretary of Health, Education, and Welfare, who had been directly invested with enforcement responsibility, was now empowered to request that the U.S. Attorney General bring an abatement suit without the express consent of state officials if pollution endangered persons' health or welfare in a state other than where the discharge originated.

This last modification to the Water Pollution Control Act had great potential for alleviating the water pollution impasse. The Federal government could not now be prevented from bringing an abatement suit against interstate polluters by recalcitrant governors. Nevertheless, the new enforcement provision did not live up to expectations. There were two major problems. First, the Federal government had to prove interstate damage to people's health and welfare to obtain an abatement order. This was extremely difficult to do, since the matter of what constituted pollution of such seriousness was a subject of great debate. Secondly, the Public Health Service, responsible for investigating pollution and recommending remedial action, was laggard in its duties; considering the extent of the problem, it did relatively little investigating and recommended few abatement proceedings.

By the early 1960's, however, a substantial section of the populace had become aware of the gravity of the water pollution problem. This led to the exertion of sustained pressure on Congress for an effective control program. The public was in no mood for a continuation of the palliative programs of the past; they demanded bold new approaches. The popular media played a key role in the development of this

---

[4] Interstate waters are those flowing across or forming a part of state boundaries; navigable waters are those used or suitable for use for the transportation of persons or property in interstate or foreign commerce.

militant attitude by forcefully calling the public's attention to the
water pollution mess. For example, articles on the subject appearing
in large circulation journals during the early 1960's left the over-all
impression that water pollution in the United States threatened not
only wildlife but human health; that water quality was deteriorating
rapidly all across the nation; and that, in the majority of cases, state
and local officials as well as industry were unwilling or unable to take
appropriate action to alleviate the crisis.[5]

The stage was set for more legislative action at the national level. At
the opening of the Eighty-eighth Congress in January, 1963, Senator
Edmund Muskie of Maine, chairman of the Special Subcommittee on
Air and Water Pollution of the Public Works Committee, along with
eighteen other senators, introduced S. 649, a bill to amend the Federal
Water Pollution Control Act. Similar bills were introduced in the
House. Although these bills contained the traditional provisions increasing grants for construction and research purposes, their most
important, and, one might add, most controversial, sections were
aimed at more clearly defining as well as strengthening the Federal
role in water pollution control.

II

Any significant piece of Federal legislation is influenced by many
pressure groups, each seeking to promote certain defined interests.
The Water Quality Act of 1965 is no exception to this rule. At the
public hearings held in the Senate (June, 1963, and January, 1965),
and in the House (December, 1963, February, 1964, and February,
1965), representatives of numerous organizations testified. Many
points of view were expressed, and few of these organizations, as
indicated by their representatives' testimony, held exactly the same
position on the proposed legislation. Nevertheless, there is enough
similarity in much of the testimony to permit a broad distinction
between those generally opposed to the legislation and those for the
most part favoring it.

In the former category, one can place first and foremost the water-

---

[5] See, for example, Rachel Carson, "How Safe is Your Drinking Water,"
Redbook, August, 1961, pp. 48–49; Rusty Cowan, "Mystery of the Walleyes
and the Water," *Sports Illustrated*, November 6, 1961, pp. 26–27; William
L. Rivers, "Politics of Pollution," *Reporter*, March 30, 1961, pp. 34–36; and
"Wastes Spoil Once Pure Sources," *Life*, December 22, 1961, pp. 72–73.

using and polluting industries and their lobbying appendages. Included here were the pulp and paper, chemical, and oil companies, the National Association of Manufacturers, the Pulp and Paper Association, and the Manufacturing Chemists Association. These organizations were against all provisions of the Muskie bill, although certain of its sections bothered them much more than others. They, of course, saw the bill as a tool that could and no doubt would be used to force them to abate their pollution of interstate waters at great cost. Also in substantial opposition to the bill were state and interstate agencies charged with water pollution control functions. These included, for example, the Texas Water Pollution Control Board, the Pennsylvania, Kansas, and Kentucky departments of health, and the Interstate Sanitation Commission of New York, New Jersey, and Connecticut. These groups were not entirely opposed to the measure, favoring certain aspects of it such as the provisions increasing grants for construction of sewage-treatment facilities and expanding research activities. They did, however, object strenuously to the key sections of the legislation, and for this reason lobbied against passage of the bill. To them the bill appeared to be a further erosion of their prerogative in (and one more step toward Federal domination of) the water pollution control field. Finally, a diversity of other groups, such as professional engineering societies and farm lobbies, for a variety of reasons, also opposed the measure.

Among the organizations supporting the proposed legislation, and instrumental in having such a bill introduced, were conservation organizations such as the National Audubon Society, the National Wildlife Federation, and the Izaak Walton League. Certain of these groups, notably the Izaak Walton League and the National Audubon Society, had some reservations about the bill. However, their doubts were not about the intent and purpose of the measure, but stemmed from a desire for a stronger act, along with some doubts about the effects of certain provisions. Because of their concern with protecting and preserving the natural environment, these organizations felt the need for more positive action regarding water pollution control. They saw S. 649 as a vehicle to this end. Joining them in general support of the Muskie bill were such diverse groups as the League of Women Voters and the National Council of Mayors, who also realized the necessity of more adequate pollution control to improve the quality of American life.

There was disagreement to one degree or another on almost all sections of the bill. However, only three parts were the subject of major disputes: (1) the statement of purpose, (2) the provision setting up the Federal Water Pollution Control Administration, and (3) the provision empowering the Secretary of Health, Education, and Welfare to promulgate water-quality standards for interstate waters. The heated controversy over these sections of the bill led to significant modifications in two of the three sections and no change in the other.

The statement of purpose in the original bill postulated the concept of "keeping waters as clean as possible" rather than "attempting to use the full capacity of such waters for waste assimilation." Industry strenuously objected to this language, interpreting it to mean as clean as "technically" rather than "economically" feasible. This, they said, was completely unrealistic, and could be obtained only at immense cost and economic hardship to them. On the other hand, conservation groups such as the Izaak Walton League and the National Audubon Society supported the statement because it seemed to offer a "positive" approach to water quality improvement, and urged that it be retained. The industry viewpoint prevailed, and, when S. 649 was reported out of the Senate in October, 1963, the original language had been changed to the more ambiguous declaration of purpose: "to enhance the quality and value of our water resource and to establish a national policy for the prevention, control, and abatement of water pollution."

The section of the Muskie bill establishing the Federal Water Pollution Control Administration within the Department of Health, Education, and Welfare, and charging it with handling and coordinating all governmental activities concerned with water pollution, was the center of a sharp controversy.[6] Representatives of industry and industrial lobbies opposed the creation of the FWPCA to a man. Many individuals representing state health departments, and state and interstate water pollution control organizations, also testified against the creation of the FWPCA to a man. They contended no distinct

[6] On May 10, 1966, a presidential reorganization order transferred the FWPCA to the Department of the Interior. However, HEW retained responsibility for public health related aspects of water pollution. See U.S., Department of the Interior, Federal Water Pollution Control Administration, *Federal Water Pollution Control Act (Public Law 84–660); Oil Pollution Act, 1924* (Washington, D.C.: Government Printing Office, 1967), Appendix A.

Federal organization with water pollution control authority was needed, since the Public Health Service, through its division of water supply and pollution control, was already doing an adequate job. It was also maintained that the Public Health Service over the years created a rapport with the state and interstate agencies concerned with water pollution control. A new agency would not have this support, and would make Federal-State cooperation on pollution problems much more difficult. As Mr. George Olmsted of the American Paper and Pulp Association succinctly put it:

The establishment of a Federal Water Pollution Control Administration appears to us unnecessary, and, in fact, undesirable at this time. The existing agencies have built up a backlog of experience and knowledge concerning the problem involved, and have developed to a high degree the necessary cooperation with state and interstate agencies.[7]

The conservation organizations provided the main support for this section of the bill. Their case was based on three considerations. First, they argued the Public Health Service was mainly concerned with health aspects of water pollution, which were a diminishing menace, and tended to ignore the contemporary problems caused by the aesthetic, recreational, and ecological consequences of water-quality deterioration. A new agency was needed, in their view, to approach the problem from the over-all viewpoint of environmental quality rather than from the narrower viewpoint of health protection. Second, they argued the Public Health Service had not been sufficiently aggressive in applying Federal authority to abate interstate water pollution. This, it was contended, reflected the agency's research orientation which influenced its personnel to shy away from enforcement actions involving political controversy. Also, because of the close "rapport" that had developed between the Public Health Service and state and interstate water pollution control agencies, the former was wary of entering into the latter's traditional domain. Finally, creation of a Federal Water Pollution Control Administration, it was claimed, would make the program more readily identifiable by the public and Congress, and, therefore, more responsive to both public support and criticism. These arguments were effective. The provision setting up the FWPCA and transferring Federal water pollution control functions to it remained

[7] U.S., Congress, Senate, Special Subcommittee on Air and Water Pollution of the Committee on Public Works, *Hearings, Water Pollution Control*, 88th Cong., 1st sess., 1963, p. 533.

intact in the bill as finally passed, despite the strenuous opposition.

The most controversial part of S. 649, however, was the section directing the Secretary of Health, Education, and Welfare, after reasonable consultation with affected parties, to issue water-quality standards applicable to interstate waters of the United States. Opposition came from many corners; industry, state and interstate water pollution control agencies, as well as certain mayors and governors, were the most outspoken. This group contended that existing state and interstate authorities vested with water pollution control functions were in a better position to set water-quality standards than the Federal government because they were "closer to the problem" and, thus, could develop more viable programs. Certain witnesses, particularly those from industry, also maintained that the existing control agencies were doing an excellent job regulating water pollution and needed no guidance from Washington. The need to preserve a "cooperative Federal-State relationship" and to protect states' rights were other common arguments employed against the provision. Finally, a fear was voiced by a number of industrial representatives that uniform water-quality standards would be set for all interstate waters, and that these would be so high as to lock up many water bodies from industrial use.

Public support for this highly controversial section came primarily from conservation-oriented groups, although some confessed to certain reservations about it.[8] Senator Muskie was adamant about the necessity of the provision, and he fought hard to preserve it intact. Indeed, proponents viewed Federal standards as absolutely necessary to prevent the worsening of the national pollution situation and to bring about water-quality improvement. Their chief argument was that the establishment of fifty sets of state standards, based on local assessments of the pollution problem and greatly influenced by the polluters themselves, would result in chaos, since regulations would no doubt vary widely from state to state. Furthermore, in light of past experience, there was skepticism that the states would establish adequate standards if left alone. On the other hand, the opposition's

---

[8] Two such organizations were the National Audubon Society and the Izaak Walton League. The former thought that the measure would provide a "potentially useful tool," but felt the authority should be optional rather than mandatory. The latter feared standards might be set at a level allowing further deterioration of the quality of certain very pure waters.

contention that absolutely uniform standards would be set for the whole country was dismissed as fallacious; federally set standards, it was asserted, would take into account local conditions.

A number of attempts were made to amend the standards section as S. 649 moved through the Eighty-eighth Congress. The Senate withstood these efforts and passed the bill with this section essentially intact on October 16, 1963, by a roll-call vote of 69 to 11. However, the language had changed slightly; the secretary could now promulgate standards only if, after his request, the states failed to develop acceptable regulations themselves. This provision did not fare as well in the House. When the bill was reported out of the House Committee on Public Works (September 4, 1964), they had cut the heart out of the standards section through an amendment empowering the secretary only to "recommend" water-quality standards to the states. Congress adjourned before the House voted on the modified bill. A number of factors contributed to this action by the House. First, the pressure to tone down this section had been intense, no doubt because the opposition forces saw this as their best and perhaps last opportunity to moderate the intent of the bill. No less than forty-four individuals or organizations testified against the standards section at the House hearings, as compared to only eleven at the Senate hearings.[9] Secondly, John Blatnik, chairman of the Rivers and Harbors Subcommittee of the House Public Works Committee handling the bill, was personally opposed to Federal standards; as a result, the type of strong leadership provided in the Senate by Muskie did not exist in the House. Third, it seems certain that the publicly expressed opposition of Secretary of Health, Education, and Welfare Anthony J. Cellebreeze to "mandatory" standards did not enhance the chances of passing the provision in the House without amendment.

Senator Muskie introduced a new bill (S. 4) into the Eighty-ninth Congress containing the same provisions concerning water-quality standards as S. 649 passed by the Senate in 1963. Drastic attempts were made to amend this section on the Senate floor by John Cooper of Kentucky and John Tower of Texas; again they were unsuccessful. Nevertheless, the bill as passed by the Senate on January 28, 1965, by a roll-call vote of 68 to 8, did provide more judicial and administrative

[9] U.S., Congress, Senate, Committee on Public Works, *Report, Federal Water Pollution Control Act Amendments of 1965,* Rept. 10, 89th Cong., 1st sess., 1965, pp. 14–15.

recourse for states if they felt the federally set regulations were unreasonable, a concession to the opposition forces. At this juncture, both the Secretary of Health, Education, and Welfare, and Representative Blatnik gave unqualified support to the whole bill. Strong opposition to the standards provision continued, however, from state and interstate water pollution control agencies and from various industrial interests; hence, intense pressure was applied at the House hearings on the bill in February, 1965, to remove or weaken the measure. The House responded by again cutting the heart out of the standards section, although somewhat more subtly than was the case in 1964. The amended bill provided that states must submit within ninety days after enactment a letter stating their intent to establish water-quality criteria on interstate waters by June 30, 1967. The penalty for failure to comply would be loss of Federal construction and research grants related to water pollution control. This bill passed the House unanimously on April 28, 1965.

Over the next four and one half months, a joint House-Senate conference committee attempted to reconcile the disparate views on the matter. Proponents of the House version held out for a mild standards section that would give the states a chance to act,[10] while Senator Muskie insisted that, to make water-quality standards effective, the Federal government had to have a say in setting and enforcing them. Compromise was finally achieved in September, 1965. It was a victory for the Senate, and advocates of a strong bill, in that it preserved the power of the Secretary of Health, Education, and Welfare to promulgate and enforce water-quality standards. Nevertheless, significant concessions had been made to the opponents of Federal water-quality standards. First, the states were given one year from the date of the law's enactment to file a letter of intent that they would adopt suitable water-quality regulations for interstate waters, including a plan of implementation and enforcement. Only in the event that a state did not file such a letter and did not develop acceptable standards by June 30, 1967, could the secretary step in and promulgate Federal criteria. Before this could be done, however, the Federal government was required to go through a number of proce-

[10] However, the bill, as introduced by Muskie, did state that the Federal government would act only if the states, upon request, failed to come up with adequate standards. Thus, it is not clear what the House wanted in this regard.

dural steps, including reasonable notice to the concerned parties of the contemplated action, the calling of a conference of affected groups to establish acceptable standards, and a waiting period of six months from the date of publication of the standards to allow the state one last chance to enact adequate regulations on its own. Second, the secretary's authority was further limited by giving the states recourse to an impartial hearing board if they felt the Federal standards were unreasonable. Finally, the section provided for an informal conference between the Federal government and the violator before action could be filed and a full judicial review of the standards by the courts when charges were brought against a violator.

Although this section was still a bitter pill for many to swallow, it had been sufficiently moderated to pass both the Senate and the House. Congressman Blatnik and Senator Muskie said they were entirely satisfied with the final version of the bill. President Johnson signed the bill into law on October 2, 1965, with a strong statement of support and a promise of bolder legislation in the future.

III

The Water Quality Act of 1965 is a milestone in Federal conservation legislation. It not only continued and expanded the policy established by earlier congressional action to make monies available to the states for pollution control programs, but also broke important new ground. For the first time, an organization charged solely with water pollution control was established at the Federal level, and for the first time the Federal government was empowered to take an active role in formulating and enforcing standards of water quality. But how effective will the legislation be in meeting the water pollution problem? Will it accomplish its purpose "to enhance the quality and value of our water resources and to establish a national policy for the prevention, control, and abatement of water pollution?"

Certainly the provision requiring the states to develop water-quality standards for interstate waters acceptable to the FWPCA, or have the Secretary of the Interior establish them, is a most effective new tool. The value of this measure depends on the stringency of standards required, and even more importantly, on how forcefully the standards are enforced. The original guidelines published by the FWPCA (May, 1966, revised January, 1967) to aid the states in formulating acceptable standards were tough. For example, guideline one, in line with the

1965 act's declaration of policy, stipulated water-quality standards be designed to "enhance the quality of water," and declared, without exception, that in no case would standards providing for less than existing water quality be acceptable.[11]

This provision has been the center of a bitter controversy. Conservationist groups in the summer of 1967, arguing that standards for some of the first ten states approved violated guideline one, succeeded in delaying action on other states' standards.[12] This matter was supposedly resolved in February, 1968, when Secretary Udall decided that all states' standards to receive approval must contain a nondegradation provision promising to maintain the quality of interstate waters where it is above state standards at the time standards become effective. However, he went on to say that these and other waters of a state can be lowered in quality if "it has been affirmatively demonstrated to the state water pollution control agency and the Department of the Interior that such change is justifiable as a result of necessary economic or social development and will not interfere with or become injurious to any assigned uses made of, or presently possible in, such waters."[13] This compromise seems to have borne out, to a degree, the fears expressed by the Izaak Walton League at the Senate hearings on the Water Quality Act in 1963, that the setting of water-quality standards might be used to justify the lowering of water quality in some cases. Certainly, the addition of this variance loophole appears to violate the intent of the water-quality enhancement policy established by the 1965 law.

In spite of being a retreat from the original guidelines, Udall's statement was adversely received by the states, polluting industries, and some in Congress. They saw it as preventing industrial or other economic activities that would in any way cause the lowering of water quality without unusual justification and specific Federal approval. This, it was claimed, would involve the national government in every

[11] U.S., Department of the Interior, Federal Water Pollution Control Administration, *Guidelines for Establishing Water Quality Standards for Interstate Waters* (Washington, D.C.: Government Printing Office, 1967).

[12] "Standards for Water Quality," *Resources,* No. 27 (January 27, 1968), p. 5.

[13] U.S., Department of the Interior, Federal Water Pollution Control Administration, *Compendium of Department of the Interior Statements on Non-degradation of Interstate Waters* (Washington, D.C.: Government Printing Office, 1968), pp. 1–2.

controversy where a plant was being proposed that would degrade existing water quality, make it very difficult to locate new industries on pristine waters, and thus impede economic growth. Although Udall, in congressional testimony during April and May, 1968, stated that fears of such things as pervasive Federal interference in industrial site selection were greatly exaggerated, he confirmed that the new policy statement was literal and aimed at preventing any lowering of water quality, particularly of presently pure waters, except under very extenuating circumstances. Quite rightly, he pointed out that if this were not the intent of the act, then it was a water degradation and not an improvement measure.[14] Opposition to the "nondegradation" provision notwithstanding, nearly all states have incorporated such a statement into their standards as attested by the acceptance of forty-eight of the fifty states' standards as of January, 1969.[15]

Enforcement of water-quality standards may prove the more difficult task for several reasons. In the first place, even though the established standards are, in effect, Federal regulations, initial enforcement responsibility remains with the states.[16] Past experience has shown the states to be notoriously lax in pressing polluters for abatement. However, since the Federal water pollution control functions have been moved from the relatively ineffectual Public Health Service to a new Federal Water Pollution Control Administration in the Department of the Interior, and since the states also are required to submit plans of enforcement and implementation for their water-quality criteria, a climate may have been created in which the states will realize that they not only can, but must, deal harshly with polluters. Certainly the influence of the polluters' old threat to the states that they would rather move than clean up their waste has been greatly weakened, for now all parts of the United States are subject to federally approved water-quality standards.

A second set of problems arises over the enforcement procedures.

[14] Thorough coverage of the controversy over this provision is provided in *ibid.*

[15] "Water Quality Standards almost Wrapped Up," *Department of the Interior News Release*, January 19, 1969. The remaining two states, Kentucky and Kansas, were expected to receive approval after some improvements in certain of their standards.

[16] U.S., Department of the Interior, Federal Water Pollution Control Administration, *Water Quality Standards: Questions and Answers* (Washington, D.C.: Government Printing Office, 1967), p. 6.

According to the letter of the law direct or indirect discharge of matter into interstate waters, which reduces the quality below the established standards, is subject to abatement. A network of monitoring stations is to check for violations. However, there are ambiguities in the enforcement procedures. On the one hand, the Secretary of Health, Education, and Welfare may at his discretion request the U.S. Attorney General to bring an abatement suit. It is assumed he would act if state and local officials did not, but he is not obligated to do so. On the other hand, by the terms of the 1961 amendments to the Water Pollution Control Act the secretary may request Federal suits on his own initiative when there is evidence of interstate pollution harmful to public health and welfare; otherwise he must get the permission of the governor to act. Violation of water-quality standards in one state because of discharges originating in another would appear to be sufficient grounds for the secretary to act under this provision, although this is not explicitly stated. But when the quality of an interstate stream falls below the standards of a state at one point and meets the standards again before leaving the same state it appears that the secretary may not act without gubernational permission. Just how this difficulty in abating intrastate pollution of interstate streams affects the viability of the whole water-quality standards program is not at all clear.

It is apparent that state cooperation is needed to institute a workable program.[17] A policy of noncooperation with the FWPCA by the states because of jurisdictional jealousy would seriously hinder, if not make impossible, accomplishment of the law's intent. That such dilatory tactics would be adopted on a wide scale seems unlikely, but only time will tell.

IV

The 1965 legislation represents a major step forward. However, the law is not a final solution to the water pollution problem in the United States. On the contrary, further action will be needed to handle old problems more effectively and to meet new challenges. This process is already under way, as indicated by the passage of another piece of water pollution control legislation, the Clean Waters Restoration Act,

[17] Allen V. Kneese, *Approaches to Regional Water Quality Management*, Resources for the Future Reprint No. 64 (June, 1967), p. 31.

in November, 1966.[18] This new measure provided increased grants for construction and research purposes, and encouraged the development of comprehensive water-quality programs for entire river basins. The latter provision is of particular note since it indicates an increased awareness on the part of Congress of the importance of an ecological approach to the nation's water pollution problems. One would hope that future legislation will incorporate this concept to a much greater degree so that more attention will be given to other means of maintaining water quality than merely construction of treatment works. Such alternate methods include river-flow regulation; direct treatment of streams through oxygenation; subsurface and off-site disposal; use of certain rivers as "sewers" to preserve the quality of others along the lines of the German model; and even such radical proposals as modification of industrial processes and land-use controls to prevent or lessen production of wastes in the first place.

Even if this level of sophistication were reached in congressional thinking on water-quality management, an essential point is still being missed. The key issue is not just water pollution, which is merely one aspect of the much broader problem of waste disposal. Congress should be considering the interrelations and ramifications of water, air, and land pollution to avoid the not infrequent occurrence where piecemeal legislation, aimed at reducing one of these, results in a worsening in the others. What is involved is simply a transfer of wastes from one disposal medium to another. As the recent National Academy of Sciences–National Research Council report on waste management and control states:

The systems approach must consider the interrelationship of land, air, and water. Too often, municipalities get rid of solid wastes by incomplete burn-

[18] The Ninetieth Congress did not pass any water pollution control legislation even though a number of such bills were considered. S. 2760 aimed at combating lake, mine, and oil pollution was passed by the Senate in December, 1967, but was not acted upon by the House prior to adjournment. During the second session, the chief provisions of this bill along with some features culled from measures introduced in the House were put together in S. 3206. This bill passed both houses in late 1968 but in substantially different form. A conference committee was not able to work out a satisfactory compromise and the bill died with adjournment. A similar measure (S. 7) was introduced at the beginning of the Ninety-first Congress. Known as the Water Quality Improvement Act of 1969, it proposes tough regulations on oil spills and discharges of sewage from vessels, encourages research on acid mine drainage, and requires certification that federally licensed activities will not unduly contribute to pollution.

ing, which may solve the land disposal problem but fouls the air. We must consider the assimilative capacity of water, air, and land taken together as a single entity and in relation to the plants and animals that live there.[19]

To be realistic, however, it is doubtful that Congress, given its present set-up, can act on the basis of a systems approach to water pollution control, let alone the much broader subject of waste disposal. Legislative responsibility regarding water, water pollution, and waste disposal problems is fragmented among numerous committees, and this militates against rational systematic action in these matters. Moreover, the local constituency orientation of Congress and its *ad hoc* approach to environmental problems makes the development of well-planned programs on a national basis extremely difficult.[20]

The whole concept of federalism may prove to be an even greater barrier than the archaic organization of Congress to the institution of a viable water pollution control program. Past experience indicates that to be effective a water-quality management program must be run on a national basis.[21] Nonetheless, congressional attempts to establish

[19] Committee on Pollution, National Academy of Sciences–National Research Council, *Waste Management and Control, A Report to the Federal Council for Science and Technology* (Washington, D.C.: Government Printing Office, 1966), p. 5. At least one European country (Bulgaria) has adopted such a comprehensive approach to the pollution problem. See E. R. Malakoff, *Water Pollution Control: National Legislation and Policy, A Comparative Study* (Rome: FAO, 1968), p. 3.

[20] On the other hand, congressional funding practices are a stumbling block to the implementation of national programs. When a law is passed funds necessary to carry it out are authorized for appropriation for some years in the future. Each year, however, specific appropriations must be approved by Congress. They cannot appropriate more than was originally authorized, but can appropriate less. This is exactly the case with the construction grants program (to aid states and municipalities build treatment works) under the Water Pollution Control Act. For example, $7,000,000,000 was authorized for this program for fiscal 1969 by the Clean Waters Restoration Act of 1966; nevertheless, only $214,000,000 was appropriated (National Wildlife Federation, *Conservation Report*, No. 3 [1969], p. 20). This "money gap" approach of Congress has made it impossible for the states and municipalities to carry through their construction programs, which were planned around the original funding authorizations.

[21] Indeed, if one accepts Boulding's concept of the earth as one huge closed system whose proper functioning is essential to human survival, even an internationally run, world-wide water-quality program is not an unreasonable or irrational objective. Certainly, this would simplify the solution of pollution problems involving international waters, particularly the oceans. See Kenneth E. Boulding, "The Economics of the Coming Spaceship Earth,"

a comprehensive national program are stymied by the Constitution and its reservation of undelegated powers to the states. Thus, Congress has been forced to write legislation to satisfy constitutional strictures, rather than to create the most effective program. This is clearly seen in the provisions of the Water Quality Act which permit the establishment of federally approved water-quality standards *only* for interstate waters. Constitutionally, Congress could have included navigable waters as well, encompassing nearly every significant water body in the nation. However, this was not done, one surmises, because of the difficulty of enforcing quality standards for other than interstate water bodies. It will be recalled that federally initiated abatement actions can be taken only when pollution from one state endangers the health or welfare of persons in another. This, of course, is possible only on interstate water bodies. Federal pollution abatement proceedings for intrastate water courses require state approval. The upshot is that the Federal government has direct power to enforce water-quality standards solely on interstate waters. Federal enforcement action on other waters would be at the discretion of state governors, who, as a group, have shown little enthusiasm in the past for intrastate water pollution control.

It appears that some innovative legislative approaches to the water pollution problem are in order. Certainly, great progress has been made in this sphere over the last twenty years by the passage of such measures as the Water Quality Act. Nevertheless, the approach to the matter is still piecemeal and "hung up" on the Federal-state relationship. To eliminate these shortcomings and institute the most efficacious national water-quality program would seem to entail nothing less than a thoroughgoing revamping of Congress and perhaps even of our Federal system. The political costs of such changes would be high. But the environmental costs incurred by muddling through with our present outdated institutional arrangements will be far higher.

---

in Henry Jarett, ed., *Environmental Quality in a Growing Economy* (Baltimore, Md.: Johns Hopkins Press, 1966), pp. 3–15.

10. Junked Autos: An Embodiment of the Litter Philosophy

ROBERT J. BARNES

THE litter that disfigures and distorts the American landscape is a direct result of individuals' refusal to cooperate as a societal body. It further represents an apathy toward aesthetic values as well as a rejection of the right of others to enjoy a pure aesthetic experience. The health hazards created by quantities of roadside and urban litter are even more ignored, and any awareness of ecological interruption is limited to that educated minority who possess the knowledge of ecological systems and who are often emotionally touched by the very thought of litter. Such people are inclined to view littering as analogous to defecating in one's living room. In every sense of the word littering constitutes a very serious form of environmental pollution because it is a conscious action. Though it may not be performed in a spirit of malice, the attitude held by anyone who practices littering can hardly be regarded as being thoughtful, communal, friendly, socially concerned, or good-natured.

Of course, society has recognized for some time that not all men's actions are of a rational nature, and therefore along with a system of government, laws were and are created to cope with divergent attitudes about how man, and in this case, Americans, should treat their earth-home. There are probably few individuals who, if offered the choice, would prefer a landscape composed of superhighways, telephone poles and wires, exhaust fumes, auto debris, guard rails, billboards, highway exit signs, and assorted highway litter to a pure wilderness landscape apparently untouched by man. For sure, this is a

ROBERT J. BARNES is a teaching assistant in geography at the University of Washington.

mere speculation, and therefore we might look to some indicator of public sentiment and action to see more precisely how people regard physical landscapes, as well as what types of factors have developed their attitudes. At that point it may be possible to see how popular attitudes might be influenced or otherwise changed and to determine whether such influence is a desirable thing.

A great deal of insight is not necessary to perceive that very often in the past hopeful attempts to clean up the landscape and otherwise enhance the appearance of the countryside have met overwhelming opposition on the legislative battleground from those political and economic forces dedicated to an expanding economy, with only minor secondary concern for the effects that such economic growth will precipitate in the environment. Certainly, the proponents of expanding the economy at all costs cannot be accused of being insincere. On the other hand, sincerity is also an attribute of those groups variously known as humanists, aesthetes, conservationists, occasionally socialists, and more often well-meaning people whose ideas are rejected out of hand as being too radical or even un-American. The ideological cleavages fostered by these opposing forces are not easily reconciled within the democratic legislative process, for it is often difficult or impossible to assess adequately what values constitute the desires of the popular majority, whether the values of the popular majority are legitimate, or what is meant by the phrase, "maximization of human welfare." The concerned citizen is an enthusiastic citizen, and depending on any number of conditions ranging from what he has had to eat for breakfast to what his teachers taught him at elementary school, his view of the earth-home is just as valid as yours or mine. This milieu of the average individual is recognized by legislators, and in fact it might be anticipated that, in the form of a margin of error, the legislator or elected official seeks to educate or re-educate his constituency more or less according to the frame of reference through which he himself experiences the world. (Mendel Rivers is probably the classic prototype of such a legislator.) This is not to say that a legislator's in-office history represents his life style, but certainly one's voting record must be some indication of feelings toward specific value controversies.

Perhaps Senator Paul Douglas of Illinois had this same educational intent in mind when he enthusiastically proposed the Junked Auto Disposal Act of 1966 aimed at developing a physical environment cleansed of some thirty million junked auto bodies which currently adorn the landscape. He was probably also thinking about the additional six to eight million junked autos that are discarded annually and how to keep them from becoming an environmental nuisance. But, if Senator Douglas was worried about the probable success of his bill, he had good cause.

I

The initial roots for the creation of the Junked Auto Disposal Act are specifically lodged in two prior legislative proposals of environmental enhancement which were subsequently enacted by Congress. These prior laws, enacted with a fundamentally prophylactic intent, were more often realized during implementation as half-baked approaches to environmental pollution which contained a variety of loopholes and calculated risks. This legislation, in fact, proved to have as much coverage as a piece of Swiss cheese in terms of healing the landscape, and the optimistic enthusiasm which had been exerted in hopes of combating a growing blight in the rural-urban scene quickly dissolved into a recognizable condition of congressional antipathy. In this respect, prior legislation served to mold the attitude of Congress in regard to the probable success or failure of further junked auto legislation. A brief review of this history will help to place the issue in a clearer perspective.

President Johnson's initiative in the 1965 legislative program included an omnibus proposal to improve the quality of the highway system. The eventual outcome was the passage in October, 1965, of the Highway Beautification Act, though the strong opposition forces in Congress produced a bill that was considerably weaker than the initial draft bill which had been proposed. (The passage of this act is analyzed in detail in Chapter Three.) Among the primary provisions of the act were controls on outdoor advertising, controls on the placement and shielding of junk yards, and increased Federal efforts aimed at landscaping and other means of scenic improvement. More specifically with respect to junked autos, the act provided for the screening of junk yards within 660 feet of the nearest edge of the right-of-way of interstate and primary systems. It also provided exemptions from junk-yard stipulations if the areas were zoned industrial, or if unzoned areas were used for such purposes, and it allowed a period of five years for compliance with the junk-yard controls and a 75 per cent compensation to the owners to cover the cost of compliance. The enforcement provisions of the legislation were vague and left much to local interpretation and local zoning regulations. As a consequence, compliance with the junk-yard provision of the act was characteristically slow or absent in many instances.

When Senator Douglas proposed the Junked Auto Disposal Act, he specifically noted that the Highway Beautification Act did not get rid of junked autos, rather it merely hid them or provided for their removal to other areas. Since the Highway Beautification Act provided no controls on non–federal-aid highways, Senator Douglas maintained that the provisions of the act merely allowed the transfer of junked autos from main highways to secondary roads at the taxpayers' expense.[1] While the interstate and primary systems represent some 280,000 miles of highway, secondary highways account for 600,000 miles. The effect was apparent, and it was Senator Douglas' hope that the situation could be remedied by means of the Junked Auto Disposal Act.

Also enacted in October, 1965, was Public Law 89–272, which amended the Clean Air Act to require standards for controlling the emission of pollutants from certain motor vehicles (Title I), and to authorize a research and development program with respect to solid-waste disposal (Title II), in which junked auto bodies were included. As passed into law, Section 201 provides that Title II may be cited as the Solid Waste Disposal Act. Section 202 states that the purposes of this act are

. . . to initiate and accelerate a national research and development program for new and improved methods of proper and economic solid-waste disposal, including studies directed toward conservation of natural resources by reducing the amount of waste and unsalvageable materials and by recovery and utilization of potential resources in solid wastes; and to provide technical and financial assistance to State and local governments and interstate agencies in the planning, development, and conduct of solid-waste disposal programs.

Section 210 of the Solid Waste Disposal Act authorized appropriations for program implementation to the extent of over $90 million, to be divided between the Department of the Interior between 1966 and 1969. In addition, the general fiscal supplement signed into law October 31, 1965 (PL 89–309), approved a figure of $4 million for Public

[1] U.S., Congress, Senate, Committee on Public Works, *Hearings, Air Pollution*, 89th Cong., 2d sess., June, 1966, p. 6.

Health Service grants to encourage the development of new and improved methods of solid-waste disposal, and also provided $1.4 million for research by the Interior Department's Bureau of Mines to develop economically feasible methods for utilizing junked automobiles.

Provisions for the disposal of junked autos were only implicit in the Solid Waste Disposal Act, since the basic intent of the legislation was aimed at stimulating research and development into possible alternative solid-waste disposal means and facilities. In an apparent attempt to focus more legislative powers on a still nebulous issue, Senator Douglas proposed the Junked Auto Disposal Act on May 25, 1966. Introduced as Senate bill S. 3400, it proposed to amend the Solid Waste Disposal Act in order to provide explicitly for the disposal of junked automobiles.

S. 3400 was based on the principle that every car should carry with it funds for its own disposal, whether by burial, cremation, or total immersion. In a very real sense, the legislation attempts to develop a body of theory advanced by Hans Landsberg, an economist with Resources For the Future, who maintains that at least one course of action in preserving environmental quality would be to tax the basic pollutants before they reach the consumer or point of consumption.[2] More specifically, the President would have the authority to develop a program for the purchase, storage, and resale of scrap from old and wrecked automobiles. The bill would also encourage development of improved scrap processing techniques and assist states and localities in creating practical programs for the disposal of junked autos. In short, the bill was designed to provide for the disposal of junked autos wherever they might be found, and it was based on the contention that such a program could be accomplished via a minimum 1 per cent Federal excise tax on the sale of new automobiles. As provided by the bill, the tax revenue would create a fund that could be funneled, in part, to subsidize scrap dealers so as to provide the necessary economic incentive for the collection of junked autos and to assimilate them into the scrap-steel cycle. The bill did not describe the specific details, techniques, or methods the President could employ to solve the junked auto problem. It merely provided him with the authority to

[2] Hans H. Landsberg, "The U.S. Resource Outlook: Quantity and Quality," *Daedalus, Journal of the American Academy of Arts and Sciences* (Fall, 1967), pp. 1034–57.

carry out the disposal through the aforementioned tax mechanism, which would yield between $190 and $200 million annually.

II

After the Junked Auto Disposal Bill was introduced, it was referred to the special Subcommittee on Air and Water Pollution of the Senate Public Works Committee, and, on June 7, 1966, hearings began. In his presentation before the committee, Senator Douglas noted that junked and abandoned autos are a highly valuable resource now largely neglected in this country for both economic and technological reasons, and are also a serious and growing environmental health hazard that must be brought under control if this country is to achieve the goals set by the Solid Waste Disposal Act. Senator Douglas believed that the presence of tens of millions of discarded autos along the nation's highways contributes directly to health and welfare hazards by providing breeding places for insects and rodents and by polluting land, air, and water resources.[3]

Senator Douglas' reference to air pollution was based on the methods used to dispose of motor vehicles, which very often involves open burning to get rid of rubber, upholstery, insulation, and other combustible automotive parts which would otherwise serve to decrease the blast furnace efficiency. This portion of his argument was seriously deflated when evidence was given by industry representatives concerning the new (1965) Prolerizing process now used in steel industries in Houston, Kansas City, Los Angeles, and Chicago (consuming approximately one million gross tons of scrap per year).[4] This new process makes it possible on a commercially feasible basis to take the impurities out of scrap without resorting to burning the auto bodies in the open air. It appeared from the testimony that in the not too distant future there no longer may be any economic reason for open-air burning of scrap autos, or even for accumulating unsightly stockpiles of the scrap autos.

During the course of the hearings, Wesley Gilbertson, Chief of the Solid Waste Disposal Office, Department of Health, Education, and Welfare, testified that the Title II provisions of Public Law 89–272 were being rapidly implemented, that considerable progress had been made in research for junked auto disposal since passage of the 1965

[3] Senate, Committee on Public Works, *Hearings, Air Pollution*, p. 7.
[4] *Ibid.*, p. 367.

Solid Waste Disposal Act, and that he regarded the problem as primarily one of metallurgical technology rather than environmental contamination.[5] Gilbertson was hesitant to make a specifically hostile appraisal of S. 3400, but he was also equally careful not to lend it his endorsement.

The dissent to the bill which Gilbertson had failed to voice was made clear by representatives of the large-scale scrap iron dealers who rely on junked autos for raw material. Even at the onset of the hearings, the realization that S. 3400 would prove to be a serious economic thorn in the side of large-scale scrap dealers precipitated the expectation that their contingent at the hearings would be large. The initial testimony of William Story of the Institute of Scrap Iron and Steel developed the general consensus among scrap iron dealers that there was no need for the expenditure of the public's money to construct scrap processing plants or subsidize processors in the belief that the private sector did not presently possess the capability to fulfill that function.[6] Furthermore, Mr. Story maintained that the Solid Waste Disposal Act was adequate and that no additional legislation was needed. The scrap iron industry believed the problem in the United States could be solved if Congress addressed itself to the primary bottlenecks at the consumption end of the scrap cycle where processed scrap is converted into raw steel, and at the roadblocks that exist in collecting the car hulks and getting them to the processor.[7]

The inherent problem in scrap auto processing seems to be achieving satisfactory economies of scale in the actual collection of the scrap autos. While the scrap industry and the steel industry both possess capacity sufficient to assimilate most junked autos, only marginal revenue would be derived by the scrap industry in the collection of smaller stockpiles of junked autos in lots of one to twenty-five. The cost of transportation borne by the scrap industry in relocating the junked vehicles to their processing plants would result in increased prices of scrap to the steel industry. The bottleneck obviously develops at the transfer point between the scrap industry and the steel industry, and the associated risk the scrap industry might have to underwrite in order to accumulate those small-scale stockpiles of scrap autos.

[5] *Ibid.*, p. 350.
[6] *Ibid.*, p. 358.
[7] *Ibid.*, p. 355.

Senator Edmund Muskie (D., Maine), as chairman of the Subcommittee on Air and Water Pollution and an advocate of S. 3400, raised three critical questions with regard to the implications of Mr. Story's testimony. What is the capacity of the scrap industry for converting automobiles to scrap? What is the capacity of the steel industry to absorb the material as scrap? If there is a discrepancy between these two, what can be done about eliminating it so that the steel industry absorbs all that is being discarded?[8] Mr. Story proceeded to cite evidence to the effect that both the scrap and steel industry were indeed achieving an equilibrium, as shown by the fact that seven million cars were assimilated by the scrap industry in 1965, while only five and one half million were discarded. Mr. Story claimed that the existing privately owned processing facilities now have the capacity to convert every auto hulk into scrap, and, in preference to the proposed Junked Auto Disposal Act, he suggested the Federal government would be more prudent to pursue a more positive program of action which might include tax incentives at the point of consumption: additional research into uses for auto hulks (as in Title II of PL 89–272); breaking the bottleneck created by present auto-titling laws, which often make it difficult and time-consuming for the scrap industry to obtain auto disposal rights; expanding the export market; and improving transportation facilities and rates to the processor.[9]

In commenting upon Senator Muskie's questions, Benjamin Schwartz of the National Federation of Independent Scrap Yard Dealers voiced opposition to S. 3400 in both principle and practice. In principle, he believed the powers granted to the President in the bill to be unnecessary and unwarranted, in view of the fact that the organization of the scrap steel industry was sufficient to accept all available junked autos and process them (a point which Senator Douglas had denied) without the creation of new facilities, without any special privileges, and without any subsidies, direct or indirect. In practice, Schwartz opposed S. 3400 because it would create the opportunity of tampering with the "law of supply and demand" and the movement of strategic raw materials.[10] Furthermore, it would create the potential of a new bureaucracy having something to say about how a free enterprise industry is run. Statements unfavorable to the

[8] *Ibid.*, p. 363.
[9] *Ibid.*, p. 356.
[10] *Ibid.*, p. 369.

bill were also submitted by the National Auto and Truck Wreckers, the Institute of Scrap Iron and Steel, Kilmer Auto Parts, and A&C Auto Wrecking. This terminated the testimony, and, on June 15, 1966, the hearings stood adjourned.

S. 3400 was never brought up for vote, nor was the House companion bill (H.R. 15436) brought up on the agenda for hearings or vote. The Junked Auto Disposal Act of 1966 had itself been junked.

III

The reasons why S. 3400 failed enactment are not readily apparent; however, several major problems with the legislation are easy to assess. The explicit 1 per cent tax proposal, which was the crucial mechanism of the bill, was not under the jurisdiction of the Subcommittee on Air and Water Pollution, and, consequently, the merits and defects of the proposal were not debated. Since the legitimacy of the tax could not be considered, a formative block was created as to the actual feasibility of this legislation. In addition, while the end goal of the bill was unquestionably desirable, the means proposed to that end involved one of the more unpopular political mechanisms—namely, a general tax. Such a proposal did not engender optimism as to the probable success of the bill.

Senator Douglas' testimony disparaging the efficiency and intentions of the scrap steel industry apparently contained many statistical discrepancies and biases, and Douglas suffered several embarassing moments in the course of the hearings when the facts and figures were revealed. For example, Douglas commented that "the industry most familiar with the problem, the Institute of Scrap Iron and Steel, basically supports the bill," but upon cross-examination it was found that, of the four basic premises of the bill, the institute supported only a portion of one of those four, the provision for research and development.[11] Basically, the institute was quite opposed to the bill. At another point in the hearings, Douglas mentioned that "other public spirited groups such as the U.S. Conference of Mayors, the United Auto Workers, the National Consumers League, the National Farmers Union, and the American Institute of Architects support the proposal." Discounting their credibility as "public spirited groups," the fact remains that there is no written or oral testimony from any of these groups contained in the hearings record, only hearsay. In addition,

[11] *Ibid.*, p. 359.

major discrepancies appeared in the data submitted by the Department of Health, Education, and Welfare and the Institute of Scrap Iron and Steel concerning the annual assimilation of junked autos into the scrap cycle, more precisely a matter of some three million units. The error was eventually recognized in favor of the scrap industry's estimate. Again Senator Douglas suffered a setback in that his inaccurate data resulted in his making several unwarranted assumptions.

The primary intent of the proposed Junked Auto Disposal Act was to cleanse the landscape. Douglas' claims that air pollution would also be alleviated by the act were squelched early in the testimony, and, if he meant to imply that the mere presence of junked autos constituted an air pollution menace, he advanced no evidence to support such a stance. The Subcommittee on Air and Water Pollution was a poor proving ground for this legislation, since the subcommittee was not created to consider legislation of this nature.

The scrap steel industry viewed S. 3400 as a serious threat to its solidarity and continued survival. The idea of the excise tax was not as unacceptable as was the provision to create a government agency with presidential authority to regulate scrap steel processing and probably prices. By the same token, the bill was considered a serious affront to the integrity and efficiency of the Department of Health, Education, and Welfare. Douglas' bill implied that the Solid Waste Disposal Office was slack in carrying out its functions, among which were research projects on possible junked auto disposal. Provisions of the bill also overlapped those of the Solid Waste Disposal Act in that both provided for establishment of research and development agencies to carry out the same basic function. In the course of the hearings, Mr. Gilbertson of HEW expressed the view that the Solid Waste Disposal Act was being implemented as rapidly as possible, and that the provisions of S. 3400, while supplementary to PL 89–272 to some extent, did not originate with the same goal in mind, and, as such, were not properly termed pollution control measures. The net result was that the Department of Health, Education, and Welfare did not endorse Senator Douglas' bill.

A most obvious flaw was Douglas' timing of the hearings on S. 3400. The Interior Department's Bureau of Mines had not as yet published its report on feasible uses of junked autos, and no apparent attempt had been made to determine the progress achieved on that study or to assess other progress in research and development financed under the

Solid Waste Disposal Act. The effect produced by Douglas' premature introduction of S. 3400 was one of congressional unrest, since it implied that the findings of the Solid Waste Disposal Office and the Bureau of Mines would have little relevancy to the solution of the junked auto problem. The popular criticism that would follow a successful passage of S. 3400 was more than apparent.

IV

While the Junked Auto Disposal Bill never made its way through Congress, the bill points up certain inherent conflicts and problems in attempts to enact legislation of this type. It illustrates a case wherein the ability of Congress to evaluate proposed legislation can be seriously questioned. Owing to a lack of accurate information, Senator Douglas' presentation at the committee hearings seemed poorly organized and produced confusion rather than clarity. As was brought out at the hearings, the central issues were not primarily of an economic nature, but rather of a conceptual nature relating to the broader question of environmental quality. Yet there was no representation from the groups generally associated with the promotion and retention of these values. This lack of support at a crucial point in the legislative process was a major contributing factor to the bill's defeat. Why Senator Douglas did not build these bridges prior to the introduction of the bill is not known, but, given the situation, Congress had little choice but to turn thumbs down on the bill.

While the legislation failed to pass, the bill was a novel approach to the problems of environmental pollution. It attempted to delegate responsibility for the success of junked auto disposal to a recognizable and accountable entity in the person of the President. The bill was based on the archaic notion that by focusing responsibility on a single person the efficiency of the administration of the program proposed in the bill would be at a maximum. But the danger of allowing the President to overextend his field of power is also clear. In a subtle sense, the constant reinforcement of presidential power can lead to a breakdown of the whole philosophy upon which the democratic process is based, and, as noted by the majority of witnesses who testified against S. 3400, such legislation puts a great deal of authority in the hands of one person. The checks and balances procedure, while fostering a system which is susceptible to only slow change, supposedly results in a system which is more just and equitable than one with an authoritarian base. By and large, a process of give and take has characterized the American legislative process. Congressional inaction on S. 3400 would seem to indicate that Congress was reluctant to disturb this balance of power between the legislative and executive branches.

Referring to the organization of Congress itself, the Department of Health, Education, and Welfare charged categorically that the Junked Auto Disposal Bill should not have been referred to the Subcommittee on Air and Water Pollution. Assuming this charge valid, where did the bill belong? What sort of legislative outlet does the congressional system possess to allow a fair and adequate evaluation of such a bill? The essentially economic basis of the American political system has left little room for the consideration of aesthetic or scenic values *per se*. The passage of measures involving these values too often develops into a struggle between those who believe that this nation has reached a stage in economic growth where we can and must seriously consider aesthetic values, and those who do not. A blatant conceptual divergence appears to exist. How do we integrate aesthetic and economic values? Where is the priority? The congressional committee system is just not organized to deal effectively with such a basic issue as this.

Strange as it may seem, the conceptual economic framework underlying S. 3400 is subject to different interpretations by people with diametrically opposed views. From one point of view, the actual mechanics of the bill were highly efficient, albeit of a bureaucratic nature. In the cold reality of pragmatism, the bill waved a high benefit-cost flag. It attempted explicitly to compound the responsibility of the private sector to look after itself. In its simplest terms, the buyer of a car would assume responsibility for the ultimate disposal of that vehicle once it ceased to be functional for him. The costs involved would be collected as a tax on the price of the car. This is little more than an extension of one's garbage tax, and makes responsibility for the disposal of the car an integral part of vehicle ownership.

In a sense, the bill also attempted to establish the scrap iron industry as a pollution control agency in the private sector. The bill did not imply that scrap resources would be nationalized by action of the President; rather it provided a tax, the revenue from which would be used to speed up the assimilation of junked autos into the scrap-steel cycle. The tax revenue, as stated in the bill, would be employed to subsidize the cost of transporting scrap autos to the furnaces, and thus to remove the major economic bottleneck to scrap removal. However, the implications of the effect of this subsidy on the price per ton of scrap autos and the subsequent decrease in total revenue to the scrap industry should not be overlooked. The effect of the bill would be to hasten the furnace consumption of the scrap autos stockpiled around the country, presently estimated at about twenty million units. In terms of ecological contamination, the obvious course of action is the one that moves these auto hulks off the land and into the furnace. This was the intent of the Junked Auto Disposal Bill. The shortcoming in this type of supply and demand analysis is that it is based upon the gross output of steel and not on the rate of using up the junked autos as steel production inputs. Nor does it take account of the substitutability of steel production inputs, such as in the substitution of scrap autos for iron ore. It can be assumed that not only does the steel industry attempt to put exactly the right amount of current factors in the form of scrap iron to work in each time period, but also that the industry exhausts the units of the resource, namely the scrap auto stockpile, only to the extent that it does not deprive itself of better returns from the scrap in later time periods. The result of implementing the Junked Auto Disposal Bill could be an excess of scrap iron in the form of junked autos ready for furnace consumption. The scrap iron market could be flooded with junked autos, the disposal of which would be subsidized by enactment of the bill. The ecological problem would have been solved but a new economic crisis created. Even if the auto hulks were merely removed from the landscape and held for the furnace, owing to the sudden excess of supply over demand, it could be expected that scrap iron prices would decline to such an extent that executive intervention would be needed to restore a price equilibrium between scrap dealers and steel producers. The problems raised by the bill are much more complex than Senator Douglas indicated before the subcommittee. The market mechanism cannot be assumed to be adequate to cope with the consequences of political action that is guided by noneconomic values.

Viewed from a different perspective, S. 3400 provides an example of the thinking characteristic of a newly evolving economic frame of reference. Assuming that the bill was passed as proposed and that the onus of responsibility for implementation was left in the private sector, the annual scrapping of between six and seven million autos would represent a sizeable material input to the steel industry. If it is assumed that this raw material source could be assimilated by the steel industry on a continuing basis over a period of years, the adverse economic effects of facing the steel industry with a huge stockpile of scrap autos could be avoided. The principle involved here is that of constantly recycling scrap and waste materials into the economy by allowing the market mechanism to determine the amount of scrap of various kinds that is consumed each year. The new Prolerizing technique for disposing of scrap autos might well be economical enough from the steel industry's point of view to ensure that annual consumption of scrap autos would be sufficient to reduce the number of scrap autos which now litter the landscape. Over time, the recycling of waste can be expected to have two results. In the first place, there would be a reduction in the amount of waste left untreated and in the amount of waste discarded. There would be less waste to contaminate the environment and despoil the countryside. Second, the quality of the natural environment would be preserved because there would be less need to extract new sources of raw material for the steel industry, for example. Looked at in this way, the Junked Auto Disposal Bill and the Solid Waste Disposal Act represent calculated attempts to maintain environmental quality by investing in the recycling of what is now largely unprocessed waste material. The Solid Waste Disposal Act was implemented with precisely this intention. S. 3400 was an attempt to force a more far-reaching approach to solving the waste disposal problem.

There is no doubt that the annual United States production of steel is large enough to absorb the inputs available each year in the form of scrap autos. The question is whether or not the steel industry can assimilate the scrap at a rate that is acceptable to the industry, from an economic viewpoint, and to the advocates of a quality environment, from the viewpoint of what is aesthetically desirable. Even if the principle of continuous recycling of wastes were adopted, it can be anticipated that at some point the efficiency of the recycling process may break down and that costs will exceed benefits. At this point, society again faces a decision in which economic and aesthetic values are in conflict. In the past, decisions have tended to follow the logic of economics. In many cases there has hardly been what could be termed a contest. To a large extent this is because the proponents of a quality environment have failed to communicate their point of view or to gain the serious attention of those committed to monetary values. Sooner or later, Congress and the nation will have to face the possibility that problems such as the disposal of junked autos may not have solutions which are economic in the long run.

11. Wild and Scenic Rivers:
Private Rights and Public Goods

DENNIS G. ASMUSSEN and THOMAS P. BOUCHARD

It is doubtful if the sponsors of the Wild and Scenic Rivers Act to establish a national wild rivers system thought of the legislation as a bold new advance in social legislation. At face value, neither the provisions of the act nor the tools for implementation seem a departure from the usual. There is nothing new in the establishment of public recreation lands, nor is there anything unique about using Federal condemnation authority to acquire lands for public purposes. But in the 1968 wild rivers law, because of the location and nature of the waterways in question, there is a dramatic legislative confrontation between the needs of the public for recreation and the sanctity of private real estate. In providing condemnation authority, the sponsors of the legislation were suggesting in concrete terms what has been only superficially confronted in the dialogue of the "new conservation" of the 1960's: that the public good, by virtue of an expanding population and a scarcity of recreation opportunities, must someday transcend the private property rights of the few.

A more familiar and related issue in the controversy over wild rivers legislation is that of development versus nondevelopment; whether the economic benefits from developing a river and the adjacent land

DENNIS G. ASMUSSEN is a teaching assistant in geography at the University of Washington. He has worked on a study of the Massachusetts Conservation Commission movement.

THOMAS P. BOUCHARD is a National Science Foundation trainee in geography at the University of Washington. He has worked on the economic impact of national parks in Washington and is currently completing work for his doctorate.

resources should be foregone in the interest of keeping a stream unspoiled, and, if so, who should bear the costs of nondevelopment. The issue has a decided regional character. As long as the wild rivers legislation focuses attention on western rivers largely running through public lands, the disruption of existing economic activities and land ownership patterns is minimized. Opposition here is primarily from those economic interests who see the potential future uses of these rivers for hydropower development, irrigation, stock watering, and the like. But when wild rivers are included which flow outside the boundaries of Federal lands and through developed and populated areas, as is the case with most of the proposed eastern seaboard rivers, the debate runs headlong into the private property issue. Thus, the difficulties of the wild rivers legislation mount as the more settled regions in the East are considered; yet it is just these regions that have the greatest need for public access to outdoor recreation.

In hindsight, now that the nation has a wild rivers law, it was the combination of these forces in opposition that succeeded in the Eighty-ninth and Ninetieth Congresses to forestall passage of the legislation to establish a national rivers system. And more conflict may be expected, especially with reference to the issue of recreation use versus wilderness preservation within wild river areas. Neither past nor future issues of this order come to easy solution, as an examination of the history of wild rivers legislation demonstrates.

I

In the past, a few rivers possessing aesthetic and recreational values have been protected under the management of the National Park Service, but the concept of protecting several rivers in a national system did not receive Federal recognition until 1961, when the Senate Select Committee on Water Resources acknowledged the desirability of protecting several rivers that had significant scenic and recreational value. In 1962, the Outdoor Recreation Resources Review Commission, a bipartisan commission established by Congress to evaluate the outdoor recreation needs of the nation, recommended that certain rivers of unusual scientific, aesthetic, and recreational value be allowed to remain in their free-flowing and natural setting. Based on these recommendations, the Departments of Agriculture and the Interior, in cooperation with the various states, initiated a wild rivers study in 1963. After screening 650 rivers, 22 were selected for detailed study and consideration as national wild rivers.

In 1965, President Johnson, in his message to the Congress on natural beauty, suggested that it was time "to identify and preserve free flowing stretches of our great scenic rivers before growth and development make the beauty of the unspoiled waterway only a memory."[1] Shortly thereafter, an initial wild rivers bill containing many of the rivers studied by the Departments of Agriculture and the Interior was submitted to the Congress by the administration. Early in 1966, the Senate passed an amended version by a vote of 71 to 1, but the House did not act during the Eighty-ninth Congress, and the bill died in committee.

In January, 1967, the President, in his message to the Ninetieth Congress on protecting our natural heritage, reiterated his hope that a portion of the nation's scenic rivers might be preserved. Following the President's plea, several new proposals were introduced. These included two for the administration, H.R. 6166 and S. 1092; one by Congressman John Saylor (R., Penn.), H.R. 90; another by Congressman Wayne Aspinall (D., Colo.), H.R. 8416; and also the re-introduction of the earlier Senate-passed bill, S. 119. In October of 1968, following a joint conference held to resolve the differences between Congressman Saylor's bill and the Senate's revised S. 119, a compromise S. 119 passed both houses and was signed into law. Altogether, some seventeen bills were introduced in the Eighty-ninth and Ninetieth Congresses, aimed at the establishment of a national system of scenic and recreational rivers, or the identification of individual rivers.

The National Wild and Scenic Rivers Act provides for the establishment of a rivers system which includes segments of eight rivers, makes provision for future additions to the system, and encourages state participation in the preservation of scenic rivers. The stated policy of the act is the preservation, in free-flowing condition, of rivers and their immediate environments which possess scenic, recreational, geologic, fish and wildlife, historic, cultural, and other related values. A river having one or more of these values is eligible for inclusion in the system, and, if not in a free-flowing condition, will be restored to that condition.

The act includes a classification system, which defines the relative

[1] Quoted in North Cascades Conservation Council, *The Wild Cascades* (Seattle, Wash.: North Cascades Conservation Council, 1965).

wildness of each river in the system. Three classes are designated:

1. Wild River Areas: rivers or sections of rivers that are free of impoundments and inaccessible except by trail, and with shorelines and environment in an essentially primitive state, and with waters unpolluted.

2. Scenic River Areas: rivers or sections of rivers free of impoundments, and essentially primitive, as above, but accessible in places by roads.

3. Recreational River Areas: developed rivers or sections of rivers, readily accessible by road or railroad, and which may have undergone impoundment.

The wild rivers law identifies eight rivers or their segments as national wild or scenic rivers, including the Salmon, Idaho (105 miles); the Rio Grande, New Mexico (50 miles); the Rogue, Oregon (85 miles); the Saint Croix in Minnesota and Wisconsin (185 miles); segments of the Clearwater, Idaho (190 miles); a segment of the Wolf, Wisconsin (24 miles); the middle fork of the Feather, California (miles not available); and a part of the Eleven Point, Missouri (35 miles). For these designated rivers, the administering secretary (either the Secretary of the Interior or the Secretary of Agriculture, or in some cases both) must establish detailed boundaries, determine the classifications, and prepare development plans by October 2, 1969 (one year after enactment).

Additions to the system are to be an ongoing concern of both secretaries. The law charges them with the study and submission to the President and the Congress of proposed additions which fit the guidelines of scenic rivers. Twenty-seven potential additions to the system are listed in the act. These "study rivers" were selected from seventy-nine of the basic rivers reviewed in the wild rivers study of 1963. Thirteen of these are in the East, nine are in the heavily populated and settled region of the Northeast industrial region, four are in the Midwest, and the remainder are in the Mountain and Pacific states. Three of the study rivers are segments of rivers initially included in the bill. In most cases, the study rivers must be surveyed and reported on within ten years of the enactment of the bill.

The act authorizes the Secretary of the Interior to acquire land or an interest in land along designated rivers through purchase of fee title, or through the use of conservation easements which allow the title to remain in private ownership but reserve access and other rights for the public. The law allows for boundaries of up to 320 acres per mile along the banks of a river, but fee title acquisition is limited to only 100 acres per mile. Condemnation of desired land along a wild river is restricted to privately owned lands in river areas where less than 50 per cent of the entire river area acreage is owned by the Federal government, a state, or other political subdivisions. No public lands may be condemned as long as the governing body is maintaining the land under a management plan in accordance with the purposes of the Wild and Scenic Rivers Act. Aside from a provision specifying exchange of Federal land for desired private land on the basis of equal value, initial acquisitions are to be funded with a maximum of $17 million from the Land and Water Conservation Fund.

The drafters of the act attempted to safeguard the rivers in the system through various control mechanisms. Under provisions of the act, for example, the Federal Power Commission cannot license construction of dams, water conduits, reservoirs, powerhouses, transmission lines, or other water projects which would directly affect any of the listed rivers, including those in the study category, for a period of eight years. Nor can any department or agency of the Federal government authorize any water projects that would directly and adversely affect any of the values for which a river was established as a scenic river. This provision also applies to the rivers under study for inclusion in the wild rivers system.

Mineral rights established before the enactment of the bill are unaffected, but rights perfected after enactment are subject to the regulations of the administering agency. This means that no mining rights will be issued in the Class I category of wild rivers, and those mineral rights issued in other classes of rivers are restricted to the bare minimum disturbance of the environment necessary to exploit the mineral resource. These provisions are modeled after those in Wilderness Act of 1964, the source of many of the restrictive principles of the Wild Rivers Act.

With the above safeguards, the river system appears to be secure from flagrant violation of the values for which the rivers were chosen. One noticeable weakness, however, is the ambiguity with which allowable development, upstream and downstream from a designated area, is defined. In the act's terms, water projects, pollution, and the like must not invade the river area or diminish its scenic or recreational value. Although there are other Federal laws on the books to limit pollution, the act is obscure on this point. It is conceivable, for example, that industrial development situated upstream from a scenic river area could initially appear to be a very small threat to the area but later through cumulative effects damage it greatly. Decisions in this vein are left to the secretary administrating the river area.

II

Analysis of the House and Senate hearings on the bill prior to its passage reveal the kinds of controversial issues which have characterized the discussions of wild rivers legislation.

First, as noted above, the wild rivers legislation provides for the condemnation of private property, and this was the issue to which most private citizens and landowning organizations spoke. On this issue, the landowning opposition to the bill had a regional identity. In the West, where public domain land is the rule, little if any opposition to condemnation authority was raised; the concern here was largely concentrated on the development potential that would be foregone through the establishment of wild and scenic rivers. But to the land-owners in the valleys of eastern rivers, where the creation of a Federal river reserve required taking of private land, the legislation loomed as a great threat.

Some of the most vocal opposition to the taking of private land for public recreation purposes came, for example, from West Virginia landowners in connection with the proposed inclusion of the Cacapon and Lost rivers, and from Florida interests in regard to the Suwannee River. Inclusion of these three rivers was considered of critical importance by the sponsors of the wild rivers legislation. Nine separate groups of landowners from the two states presented testimony at the congressional hearings, and they claimed the tacit support of national affiliates with total membership in the hundreds of thousands. Their protestations resulted in the exclusion of the three rivers from the original wild rivers system, which testifies to the strength of land-owners in the halls of Congress.

In stating their opposition to the condemnation authorization in the bill, the landowners based their chief concern on the values implicit in the ownership of private property, and in doing so identified one of the two polar positions on the private property issue. For the land-owner, the position was uniformly one of opposition to the concept

that the needs of the public in recreation and leisure are more important, given present population pressures and the scarcity of open
space, than the rights of American citizens to own and maintain real
estate. As one West Virginia farmer stated: "Clean air, water, food,
and shelter are necessary to life. Recreation and public enjoyment,
although desirable, are not; yet the ever recurring concept of condemnation seems to be negotiated in the currency of public recreation." [2]
Others of the same persuasion called the wild rivers legislation a
luxury the United States could ill afford, as one bit of dialogue
between Congressman Roy Taylor of North Carolina and a witness
illustrates:

TAYLOR. Do you object to using eminent domain in acquiring recreational
lands?
WITNESS. Yes, sir.
TAYLOR. Do you regard recreation not as a public necessity but only as a
sort of accoutrement to our society?
WITNESS. I feel that outdoor recreation is an accoutrement, to use your
term.
TAYLOR. And as more of our people move into cities, and open spaces are
becoming scarcer and scarcer, you still regard it as unnecessary?
WITNESS. I regard the basic essentials of life as food, shelter, and clothing.
TAYLOR. That wouldn't include roads and schools, then?
WITNESS. That is true, sir. [3]

Some landowners went to great lengths to corroborate the correct-
ness of their opposition to the bill. A Garden Club representative from
Charles Town, West Virginia, charged that the opening of former
private lands to the public would greatly increase the incidence of
litter on river lands, and since the National Association of Garden
Clubs was anti-litter, the bill must be opposed.[4] Their concern is
justifiable in part. The very concept of a scenic rivers bill hinges on
the kinds and intensity of use of river areas by the public, and
presents a conflict between preservation and accessibility.

With the evolution of the act, the sponsors attempted to resolve the
conflict between recreation and preservation through the development
of the river classification system. But there were two widely different

[2] U.S., Congress, House, Committee on Interior and Insular Affairs, Subcommittee on National Parks and Recreation, *Hearings, A National Scenic
Rivers System*, 90th Cong., 2d sess., p. 447.
[3] *Ibid.*, p. 448.
[4] U.S., Congress, Senate, Committee on Interior and Insular Affairs, *Hearings, Wild and Scenic Rivers*, 90th Cong., 1st sess., 1967, p. 241.

positions on this question. The active recreationists, such as represented by the canoeing associations, fishermen, boaters, and the like, perceived river areas to be largely recreational in purpose and scope. They envisioned campgrounds, launching facilities, and private concessions of every kind for the public. From this position, the point was also made that the private area surrounding the river could expect much economic benefit from scenic river establishment.

The Sierra Club, the Audubon Society, the Wilderness Society, and other more preservation-oriented groups had a much different notion of the bill's purposes. As one witness said: "Must we destroy our quality environment so that the richness of human life is denied our own generation and generations to come?" [5] For the members of these clubs, the stakes were large; if the Federal government would not preserve wild rivers in their primitive condition, such rivers had little chance of surviving development and despoliation for all time to come. Almost all of the wilderness-oriented club members and representatives believed that the scenic rivers legislation should, above all else, emphasize the maintenance of established rivers in their natural condition. The administration, as represented by Edward C. Crafts of the Bureau of Outdoor Recreation, echoed this view during the hearings by asserting that scenic river areas were not to have the extent of recreation development normally expected in recreation areas. [6]

III

The classification included in the final act was an effort to compromise these two divergent concepts of scenic river protection. The system generally assigns a value of "wildness" to each river and stipulates the extent of development, if any, to be permitted, as well as the kinds of public recreational use acceptable to the purpose of a given river segment. Besides the organizational and identificatory value of the classification system, it allows the accommodation of differing concepts of outdoor recreation and wilderness. For the purist and wilderness lover, the inaccessible upper stretches of river can be established as a Class I wild river. This will secure it from development and provide a quality of recreation that would be lost if all rivers in the system were made equally accessible and developable. The

[5] *Ibid.*, p. 235.

[6] House, Committee on Interior and Insular Affairs, *National Scenic Rivers System*, pp. 152–53, 361.

less-demanding recreationist may well find satisfaction in the much more easily accessible lower stretches of a Class III river. Crowding in existing national parks and recreation areas, and the resulting destruction of the natural environment, has prompted research by recreational psychologists and others on the notion of graded recreation systems.[7] The conclusions have been that both crowding and its adverse ecological impact can be avoided if recreation areas are rationed and delimited for different kinds of uses. Probably the wisdom of the framers of the wild rivers legislation in adding the classification system was due as much to the diverse pressures of the bill's proponents in matters of river purposes as by knowledge of this research.

Although the classification system helps to resolve conflicting problems of river usage among the proponents of outdoor recreation, it does little for those primarily interested in the development of a river. Even the least restrictive classification (i.e., Class III, Recreation River Areas) presents hindrances to the developer. In league with the developer are those who express the philosophy that local and private management are preferable to Federal control. At the congressional hearings, for example, representatives from the Suwannee River area repeatedly extolled the virtues of the private recreation development along the Suwannee's banks. They maintained that more facilities for campers, boaters, and other recreationists already existed along the river than were needed. Their own communities, they asserted, had taken care of the needs of tourists and sporting enthusiasts in the past and could do so in the future while maintaining the high quality of the river.[8] Probably closer to the truth, however, was the statement by a Minnesota proponent of the wild rivers legislation who noted the tendency of riverside communities in recreation areas to engage in competition for tourism with the ultimate effect of downgrading the quality of recreation. The local community, he pointed out, is usually much more interested in its tax base than in the preservation of river quality or public access to it.[9]

[7] See, for example, Robert C. Lucas, "Wilderness Perception and Use: The Example of the Boundary Waters Canoe Area," *Readings in Resource Management and Conservation,* ed. Ian Burton and Robert W. Kates (Chicago: University of Chicago Press, 1965), p. 363.
[8] House, Committee on Interior and Insular Affairs, *National Scenic Rivers System,* pp. 289–98.
[9] *Ibid.,* p. 345.

Representatives from western states expressed a more concrete objection to the locking-up of rivers in federal preserves, and they were joined in their objection by the Corps of Engineers, the Bureau of Reclamation, and the Federal Power Commission. What western enterprisers want is control of water resources for agriculture, hydroelectric power, and other practical uses which these Federal agencies can make possible through dam-building and river-dredging. Critical sums of money are involved in the annual appropriations to the corps, the Bureau of Reclamation, and other Federal construction agencies, and in this sense these agencies along with their clientele form a powerful lobby for water developments. There was a passive acceptance of the wild rivers legislation by this lobby, but this is likely to change in the future when river segments of real concern to these interests are considered for inclusion in the system.

One of the benefits of the wild rivers legislation is that it established and codified the interests of nonlocal citizens, interests which, though different from those of the indigenous population, may well be of equal or greater importance. At the hearings, for example, one committee member asked a pro–local-control witness about his interest in a certain "hole" in Arizona, a mile deep and lined with rocks of brilliant and variegated hue. Would the witness feel that he had a right, as an American citizen, to determine to what use that "hole" was put? Congressman Rogers Morton of Maryland asked the question another way: "Do you think we have arrived at a point . . . when we need a national rivers system to preserve the natural beauty and the scenic characteristics . . . and purity and so forth of . . . rivers in America?" The witness felt the time had come, but not in his area.[10]

The acknowledged sympathy of the House of Representatives for local as well as development interests was evident in the tone of the subcommittee's conduct with the witnesses throughout the hearings. Committee chairman Wayne Aspinall was the most outspoken in this regard. With many local interests, especially those who did not represent some clearly economic force, the chairman was in full agreement with the contention that the Federal government should not be called in to administer areas unless all else failed. Beyond that, Aspinall felt that the determination of local interest was a matter for local control, and that for Congress to step in and take over was tantamount to local people giving up their birthright. Along with this concern was a

[10] *Ibid.*, p. 297.

jealous guardianship by representatives in the House of regional pre-
rogatives and power; and members of the committee spoke freely of
their ability and right to trade rivers or delete them from the bill when
they concerned a representative's own region.[11]

Despite these attempts to mollify local interests, some of which
were successful, the sponsors of the bill and the administration implic-
itly agreed that private enterprise, local pride in a river area, and local
management were not sufficient to safeguard the treasury of remaining scenic rivers.[12] Had it not been for their tenacity, there would be
no national program today for the preservation of the nation's few
remaining wild and scenic rivers. The legislation was a matter of
compromise, but at least it represented a start.

IV

Now that the legislation has been enacted, it faces the challenges of
implementation. One problem is the procedure for the addition of
rivers to the system. It takes a report to Congress and the President
from the Secretary of the Interior or Agriculture, and the action of
Congress to add a river to the system. Whether this process will prove
an insuperable barrier to the inclusion of controversial rivers remains
to be seen. Congressional action in opposition to the inclusion of such
rivers as the Susquehanna may well foreshadow the difficulty of
adding rivers in the industrial and heavily developed East. The West
presents another kind of problem. The partnership of private development interests and the Federal water agencies interested in serving
them, such as the Corps of Engineers, the Bureau of Reclamation, and
the Federal Power Commission, could well eliminate the possibility of
including rivers in regions having potential for irrigation, dam construction, or electric power generation. An additional problem in
implementation of the act may result from the weak safeguards
against pollution, for it will be difficult for the administering secretaries of a river segment to enforce pollution and water-quality regulations either up or downstream from a scenic river area.

Funding for land acquisition presents another problem. While it is
not likely that the program will tax the financial ability of the Federal
government during the first few years, this situation will change as

[11] *Ibid.*, pp. 243, 365.
[12] *Ibid.*, pp. 286–87.

new rivers are added to the system. Many of the rivers in the study category, and others which have been recommended for inclusion in the system, are located in the more densely populated regions of the United States. These will demand much heavier expenditures for the acquisition of private lands and scenic easements. The initial $17 million authorized in the act for land acquisition may be sufficient in the short run, but it will be necessary to go beyond this if the intent of the act is to be fulfilled. The Land and Water Conservation Fund is the logical source for this financing, but given the problems confronting the fund, as brought out in Chapter 7, the future is not rosy.

Whatever the problems of implementation, the wild rivers legislation has some new and encouraging implications for public recreation. The recreational use of this nation's water resources has traditionally been a secondary consideration. Federal agency water resource development, dam building, and reservoir construction have always had subsequent meaning for mass recreation, but never has the planning of such projects hinged on recreational possibilities; and certainly until very recently water development interests have not considered the disbenefits of development to some types of recreation. The new act changes this, especially with its stipulation prohibiting the further development of selected rivers.

Equally important may be the side effects for all public recreation of the qualitative grading of rivers. The tailoring of recreation areas for a variety of users seems now to be a more pressing need than ever before. The crowding and despoliation of public recreation areas renders them less satisfying for all, and, for some, unusable. Planning for outdoor recreation embraces more than a crude approximation of a diverse public's needs. Perceptions of wildernesss are as varied as the people who hold them. For some, the totally unspoiled and uninhabited region or waterway has no substitute. For others, a happy throng of water skiers and swimmers on a heavily used river or lake is wilderness enough.

Finally, private property rights have been legislatively challenged. Until passsage of the wild rivers act, private property stood in the face of all but the most utilitarian social welfare needs. In the past, schools, public roads, and at most, multiple-purpose Federal projects could challenge the individual's right to a given piece of real estate. But now, for the first time, man's need in leisure has the possibility of equal status.

12. Aircraft Noise Abatement:

A Case of Congressional Deafness

VICTOR L. MOTE

A RECENT symposium on noise pollution rated noise—commonly described as unwanted sound, or sound without value—as America's toughest pollution problem. The presence of unwanted sound in the environment has troubled mankind since Hellenic times. In the hectic, crowded urban environment of modern America noise is an unpleasant fact of life and perhaps one that people take too much for granted. Aircraft noise has become a characteristic of many suburban areas located near airports. The prospect of travel at speeds greater than the speed of sound threatens to lay a crisscrossed pattern of sonic booms all across the United States regardless of urban, suburban, or rural distinctions. According to a report published by the Citizens League Against the Sonic Boom, a single SST supersonic flight across the United States would boom an area of 100,000 square miles containing approximately 10,000,000 people. And if overland supersonic flight is permitted, 500,000,000 persons in America, Europe, and Asia may be jolted every hour, day and night, by sonic booms from SST aircraft flying international commercial routes.[1]

The case of the SST and sonic boom poses the problem of noise pollution, and the related problem of noise abatement, in its most dramatic and frightening form. The abatement of noise from commercial jet aircraft already in service has been receiving attention from

VICTOR L. MOTE is a graduate student in geography at the University of Washington. He is currently working on noise pollution and completing work for his doctorate.

[1] William A. Shurcliff, *SST and Sonic Boom Handbook* (Cambridge, Mass.: Citizens League Against the Sonic Boom, 1968), p. 19.3.

the Federal government for some time. A few state and local governments have enacted noise abatement statutes and ordinances, though generally these efforts have had very limited effectiveness. Individual citizens have sought legal remedies against the intrusion of noise but there is no consistency among state courts in judgments concerning noise. Until passage of the 1968 Aircraft Noise Abatement Act, there was no Federal noise abatement legislation. Excessive noise is unpleasant, may damage property, and is injurious to human health. Evidence to this effect is massive but not widely known. The sonic boom of the SST simply highlights a much more general and serious noise pollution problem. It could prompt Congress into responding to a major environmental hazard before the situation reaches crisis proportions. The indications are, however, that Congress is either not listening or cannot hear.

What is noise? The lowest sound that can be detected by a keen human ear in utmost quiet is called a decibel (db). Decibels are measured on a logarithmic scale. Thus, a level of 100 db is really 10 to the 10th power times as intensive for the eardrum as 1 db. So-called "ordinary" community noise frequently measures 85 db, an injurious level if experienced eight hours per day for protracted periods. Kitchen noises range from 56 db to 93 db on the average. Aircraft noise is measured in perceived noise decibels (PNdB) which are like normal decibel measurements, except that they are adjusted to give more weight to the increased annoyance factor found in frequency components of an aircraft's complex noise. (PNdB figures are thirteen units higher than the regular decibel scale.) The worst every-day offenders for America's city dwellers are traffic noise and construction noise, especially from trucks, motorcycles, sports cars, air traffic, and jackhammers. Congressional attention to noise pollution has focused on aircraft noise partly because a Federal agency, the Federal Aviation Administration (FAA), has major responsibilities for aircraft and airport safety and operating regulations, and partly because of the huge Federal investment in the development of the SST.

I

In its August, 1968, newsletter the Conservation Foundation observed that when the history of the struggle for environmental quality is written, 1968 may be noted as the year that Congress and the administration at least began facing up to the noise pollution problem.[2] Congress had been considering and shelving aircraft noise abatement bills for almost ten years. Between 1960 and 1968 more than ninety such bills were introduced and all except one died in committee. This record was deplorable. Pressure on Congress to act increased appreciably as demands for additional funding of the SST program brought strong counterdemands for attention to sonic boom as a crucial public issue. President Johnson warned in his 1968 message to Congress on natural resources that complacency was an inadequate response to the ever-mounting volume of noise. Also in 1968, the Department of Health, Education, and Welfare for the first time organized a national conference on noise as a hazard. And in 1968, Stewart Udall, author of *The Quiet Crisis*, and at that time Secretary of the Interior, appointed a blue-ribbon panel to investigate the effects of the not-so-quiet crisis of noise and sonic boom.[3] Public disfavor continued to be expressed by groups such as the Citizens League Against the Sonic Boom and the Sierra Club. This mounting pressure was reflected in the introduction of thirty-three noise abatement bills in the Ninetieth Congress.

The ultimately successful bill, H.R. 3400, was sponsored by the chairman of the House Subcommittee on Transportation and Aeronautics, Representative Harley Staggers of West Virginia. The bill authorized the Secretary of Transportation to do three things: first, to prescribe standards for the measurement of aircraft noise and sonic boom; second, to prescribe regulations for abatement of this noise; and third, to apply noise control standards in the certification of aircraft as an extension of his authority to apply safety standards. The bill was later amended to require the administrator of the Federal Aviation Administration to discharge these functions because it is he and not the Secretary of Transportation who has jurisdiction over air safety standards. The bill did, however, recognize the ultimate authority of the secretary over research and development relating to aircraft noise and required that he be consulted before abatement standards were enforced. The bill contained no guidelines by which the administrator of the FAA could implement his new authority, although these

[2] Conservation Foundation, *CF Letter*, August 30, 1968, p. 1.
[3] The report of this panel is now published as U.S., Department of Interior, "Report to the Secretary of the Interior of the Special Study Group on Noise and Sonic Boom in Relation to Man," Washington, D.C., 1968 (multilithed). See also, Federal Council for Science and Technology, "Noise —Sound Without Value," Washington, D.C., 1968 (multilithed).

were furnished by a subsequent subcommittee amendment to the bill.
The subcommittee also acted to provide stronger protection for those
owning aircraft already certified by the FAA, and it included in the
bill a specific statement that the purpose of the legislation was to
afford the public relief from unnecessary noise and sonic boom.

In all, the subcommittee met seven times to review the legislation.
Approval of H.R. 3400 was received from each pertinent Federal
agency and was considered by each to be the best of eleven bills
before the subcommittee. After perfunctory debate, during which
Representative Lester L. Wolff of New York made an abortive attempt
to amend the bill with a clause aimed at prohibiting sonic booms, the
legislation passed the House by a vote of 312–0. It was referred
immediately to the Senate Committee on Commerce, which was already considering a similar bill introduced by the chairman, Senator
Warren Magnuson of Washington. Less than two weeks after holding
a hearing on the House measure, the Senate Commerce Committee
unanimously reported the bill without amendment to the floor of the
Senate. During Senate debate on the bill Senator Clifford Case of New
Jersey offered an amendment that would have banned all overland
flights at supersonic speed in the United States by nonmilitary aircraft.
The amendment was defeated by a margin of more than four to one.
Shortly afterwards on the same day the bill passed the Senate by voice
vote. It became a law a few days later as the Aircraft Noise Abatement
Act of 1968.

The aircraft noise problem basically involves a conflict between two
groups of interests. On the one hand there are those whose livelihood
is tied to the air transportation business and who are interested in
promoting it; on the other hand are the people who live and work in
communities near airports or in other urban areas lying along flight
approaches to the airports. Some of these people cannot enjoy nor
reasonably use their land because of noise resulting from aircraft. It is
this group that has largely been responsible for the aircraft noise
abatement bills brought before Congress since 1960, and for the
lawsuits estimated to total $200 million now pending before the
courts.[4] In general, the busier the airport, the greater the volume of
complaints. It is not surprising, then, that congressional representatives of New York (especially from New York City) sponsored fifty-

[4] Donald F. Anthrop, "Environmental Noise Pollution: A New Threat to
Society," *Bulletin of the Atomic Scientists*, XXV (May, 1969), 13.

two aircraft noise abatement bills between 1960 and 1968. Residents of the County of Queens situated between Idlewild (now John F. Kennedy) and La Guardia airports provided the impetus. Their grievances provided the basis for a 1959 House resolution establishing a congressional investigation of aircraft noise problems.[5]

The study involved nine public hearings held in New York, Washington, D.C., San Francisco, and Inglewood, California, between 1960 and 1962. Early in 1963, a full report of the hearings was issued. The conclusion was clear. Something had to be done about aircraft noise.

Since the 1963 House report, the air carrier fleet of the several commercial airlines has been converted from a piston fleet to one predominantly powered by jet turbines. During the same period (i.e., from 1963 to 1968) the number of jet aircraft, including the smaller jet planes used by business executives, has been growing at the rapid rate of over 175 per year and are expected to reach a total of around 3,300 by 1973.[6] This represents a solid contribution to the national economy. Nevertheless, as is the case with many other instruments of economic benefit, the positive economic effects are offset by a number of undesirable social and environmental consequences for which protection has been sorely lacking. For five years the 1963 House report languished while Congress was either unable or unwilling to act on aircraft noise abatement.

II

The history of the 1968 Aircraft Noise Abatement Act was marked by three important controversies. First, can aircraft noise be abated without impeding the safety and maneuverability of the aircraft? Second, who should take the responsibility for aircraft noise abatement? Third, what, if anything, can be done about sonic boom?

During the hearings opponents argued that the bill concentrated mainly on reducing noise at the source and gave little or no attention to alternative solutions. Their arguments were not altogether unjustified, for, while expounding the need for "at source" modifications to

[5] U.S., Congress, House, Committee on Interstate and Foreign Commerce, *Hearings, Aircraft Noise Problems,* 86th and 87th Congs., 1963.
[6] U.S., Congress, Senate, Committee on Commerce, *Aircraft Noise Abatement,* S. Rept. 1333, 90th Cong., 2d sess., 1968, p. 2.

mitigate noise the bill made no mention of other possibilities.[7] Among these were the possibilities for developing new flight patterns for take-off and landing that would aurally affect as few people as possible on the ground, and the adjustment of land-use patterns near airports in order to minimize noise pollution. This controversy resulted in a heated debate between aircraft operators and airport managers. The Air Transport Association (ATA), strongly opposed to the bill, instead supported another which would have given less weight to the reduction of noise at the source and more emphasis to one of these alternative approaches.[8] The ATA, along with the Air Line Pilots Association (ALPA), concluded that the state of the art precluded any further technical alterations in aircraft to abate noise. Moreover, neither group could see any possibilities for further adjustments in flight procedures without impeding the safety of the aircraft, passengers, and crew. They contended that the only realistic solution was to adjust people and airports to the airplane through zoning and compatible easements. The Airport Operators Council, on the other hand, predictably retorted that the ATA proposal was completely unacceptable, and it fully supported the "at source" noise control provisions contained in the bill.

Secretary of Transportation Alan Boyd, attempting to mediate, averred that his department would formulate regulations governing the flight of aircraft based on the principle that noise abatement is second only to safety. The ATA and the ALPA were further pleased to hear that the secretary was convinced that there never would be a quiet airplane and that people must learn to live with airplane noise and sonic boom in the way they have learned to live with other unpleasant manifestations of progress.[9]

These statements by the official charged with ultimate authority for noise abatement as provided in the bill caused certain congressmen to take a second look at who should be charged with the responsibility for implementing aircraft noise legislation. Congressmen Donald M. Fraser and Clark MacGregor of Minnesota, Theodore R. Kupferman

[7] U.S., Congress, House, *An Act to Amend the Federal Aircraft Noise Abatement Regulation and for Other Purposes*, H.R. 3400, 90th Cong., 2d sess., 1968, pp. 1–2.

[8] U.S., Congress, House, Committee on Interstate and Foreign Commerce, *Hearings, Aircraft Noise Abatement*, 90th Cong., 1st and 2d sess., 1968, p. 84.

[9] *Ibid.*, pp. 30 and 72.

of New York, Charles H. Wilson of California, Senator William Proxmire of Wisconsin, and Senator Clifford Case of New Jersey all
wanted to have jurisdiction over noise control put under a different
governmental agency. Since the FAA is by law the chief advocate and
director of development for the SST, placing the responsibility for
sonic boom regulation (especially for overland flights) under the FAA
was, as Senator Case so tersely pointed out, "putting the fox in the
chicken coop." [10] Curiously, the subcommittee gave very little consideration to any authority other than the FAA.

Throughout the hearings the controversy over the sonic boom problem was kept under the table. It was mentioned by Representatives
Fraser, MacGregor, Kupferman, Wolff, and Roman C. Pucinski of
Illinois, but was quickly subordinated to the safety issue. More explicit
disclosure of the sonic boom problem came only when the bill reached
the Senate floor. At that time Senator Case, backed by the Sierra Club
and the Citizens League Against the Sonic Boom,[11] made his move to
place the issue in its broader perspective, but, as mentioned earlier,
with no success. The arguments against the sonic boom were expressed both before and after passage of the Aircraft Noise Abatement
Act by a relatively few organized interest groups. The Citizens
League Against the Sonic Boom stated flatly that passage of the act
did nothing to alleviate their concern. The Sierra Club continued its
campaign against sonic boom as if the act did not exist. On the other
hand, most people are probably unaware of the act and its limitations.
Congressional debate on the bill occupies only thirty-two pages of the
Congressional Record, and publicity about the act has been extremely
limited. The President, for all his concern about aircraft noise abatement, made no public comment when he signed the act.

The act placed the Johnson administration in an embarrassing
position. On the one hand the administration had actively supported
development of the SST, while on the other hand it was on record as
deploring excessive aircraft noise and favoring its abatement. As of
March 1968, the FAA had provided the Boeing Aircraft Company
with $653 million for SST development. Altogether, the FAA has
committed about $1.3 billion, or around 83 per cent of the estimated

[10] U.S., *Congressional Record*, 90th Cong., 2d sess., CXIV (1968), S8523.
[11] Personal correspondence with Dr. William A. Shurcliff, Director of Citizens League Against the Sonic Boom, Cambridge, Massachusetts, November,
1968, and with the Sierra Club, San Francisco, California, October, 1968.

development costs, for production of an American prototype; the eventual total cost of the program is likely to be at least $3.5 billion. Congress has been asked to appropriate the balance of these costs (on top of the more than $650 million already allocated) in the expectation that sales will amount to somewhere between $20 and $48 billion.[12]

Undoubtedly, the huge government investment required for the SST program has had no small impact on the views of Secretary of Transportation Boyd and FAA Administrator General William McKee in their efforts to minimize the sonic boom problem, and their views in turn have had an impact on Congress. In the House, for example, several congressmen voted to approve the aircraft noise abatement bill even after stating their objections to placing the abatement responsibility in the hands of the FAA. In the Senate, resistance to the bill was more adamant. Senator Proxmire, who was frequently a critic of the Johnson administration despite his Democratic label, pointed out that according to studies by the FAA itself, the economic feasibility of the SST program was doubtful if the planes were banned from overland flights. Another estimate by the Institute of Defense Analysis indicated that if supersonic travel is restricted to overwater flights, anticipated sales of the aircraft would fall to less than half of those expected under conditions where no restrictions existed.[13] If this is the case, the SST program is likely to be an economic boondoggle. Thus, Senator Proxmire foresaw increasing economic pressure upon the FAA to lift or moderate whatever ban it might impose on noise. In such a situation the public would be the losers and Congress would be guilty of allowing technology to gain the upper hand. Senator Case came directly to the point when he described the FAA as a "narrow, single-minded instrument for the development of aviation."[14] In defense of its awkward position, the administration argued that no one fully understands sonic boom, and that the FAA was better qualified than any other agency to study the situation and set regulations.

The need for a full-scale investigation to determine if sonic boom effects are physiologically or psychologically harmful to people was rejected as redundant in light of the continual investigation of sonic

[12] Anthrop, "Environmental Noise Pollution," pp. 15–16.
[13] U.S., Department of the Interior, "Report to the Secretary . . . on Noise and Sonic Boom in Relation to Man," p. 35.
[14] U.S., Congressional Record, 90th Cong., 2d sess., CXIV (1968), S8423.

boom problems undertaken by the Federal government since 1958. Senator Case could not accept this and pressed for an investigation involving the Departments of Health, Education, and Welfare; Housing and Urban Development; Commerce and Interior; as well as the National Aeronautics and Space Administrator and the National Academy of Sciences. He did not believe that the FAA had any special competence to determine the general effects of sonic boom on the American environment, and indeed, as mentioned earlier, he saw reason to suspect the motives of the Department of Transportation and the FAA. However, his insistence that Congress had a responsibility to look beyond the economics and air safety of an SST program found only twelve supporters when his amendment was defeated by the Senate.

At least five groups favored the idea that people can and must learn to live with sonic boom: the Department of Transportation, the FAA, ALPA, the ATA, and the Association of Machinists and Aerospace Workers. Generally adverse reactions to this approach came from the National Aircraft Noise Abatement Council, the National Academy of Surgeons, and the National Academy of Sciences. The last of these had persistently advocated that more research was needed to reach a decision but in a recent report was convinced that the sonic boom might be less than desirable.[15] Other anti-boom groups included the American Speech and Hearing Association, the Sierra Club, the Wilderness Society, New York City Council, and the City Council of Santa Barbara, California.

The Department of Transportation has summarized the argument in favor of the SST as follows:

Government and Industry have conducted a great number of studies. These studies show that the SST sonic boom will do no physical harm to man or animal; also that no significant property damage would be caused to sound structures by the SST sonic boom. The SST is designed to minimize its sonic boom, but it is unlikely that sonic boom can be eliminated.[16]

This statement implies that this sonic boom has been grossly exaggerated. According to some researchers, mild booms may even be good for houses![17] The opposition, varying in emotional intensity, retorts

[15] Shurcliff, *SST and Sonic Boom Handbook*, p. 25.2.
[16] U.S., Department of Transportation, *The United States Supersonic Transport* (Washington, D.C.: not dated), p. 4.
[17] *Seattle Times*, April 23, 1969.

that the boom will have serious and adverse effects on people, structures, animals, and the natural environment.

In response to reports that certain national monuments had been
damaged following the booms of military jets, Secretary Udall appointed a team of scientists to evaluate the problem of noise and sonic
boom in relation to man. The study is, perhaps, the most objective to
date. It concluded that many of the contentions about the sonic boom
were based upon hearsay, emotion, or prejudice rather than upon fact,
logic, or analysis, but it also warned that the psychological, sociologi-
cal, and political reactions of millions of people from the sonic boom
will be extremely adverse and may be of sufficient magnitude and
prevalence to cause partial, if not complete, curtailment of the overland operation of the SST. It stresses that some sort of middle ground
must be found between the two intransigent views on the sonic boom,
but the report made no specific recommendations as to how this might
be achieved.

Under the present legislation the FAA has the full responsibility of
deciding whether or not the supersonic transport will be allowed to fly
overland. Presently, spokesmen for the FAA aver that the SST may be
restricted to flight over the oceans and other unpopulated areas. But
even this is the subject of argument. Bo Lundberg, former Director
General of the Aeronautical Research Institute of Sweden and a
member of the Citizens League Against the Sonic Boom, has posed
the question, "Why assume that people on ships can accept booms
many times stronger than the level acceptable to people on land?" [18]
Given that the SST will probably follow great circle routes, roughly
the same as those followed by ocean-going vessels *en route* to foreign
destinations, the population under the bang zone could still be quite
large. By the same token, outdoor recreation and wilderness enthusiasts are deeply concerned about the potential impact of the boom on
these values if the SST traffic is routed over land areas with low
permanent populations. Secretary Udall stated, for example, that the
decision on overland supersonic flights was simply too important to
leave to the FAA. In favoring the Department of Health, Education,
and Welfare or the Department of Housing and Urban Development
for that responsibility, Udall concluded: "The FAA should no more

[18] *New York Times,* June 17, 1967.

make a decision on this than the Bureau of Reclamation should make the decision on dams in the Grand Canyon."[19]

III

The Aircraft Noise Abatement Act is hardly a panacea for the nation's noise ills. Some call it tokenism. At best it is a step in the right direction, a recognition by Congress of the rising concern about noise pollution. The act is obviously insufficient as a means of curbing sonic boom but it possesses the potential for adequately coping with aircraft noise. In light of events which have transpired since its enactment, however, even the law's most auspicious supporters have been shaken.

The FAA for several years has had a relatively small team of sixteen specialists, including two regional noise abatement officers (East and West) and fourteen other employees of the Office of Noise Abatement. These men are responsible for research and development to minimize aircraft noise and sonic boom, to develop minimum noise operational procedures, to analyze economic implications of noise reduction actions, and to promote compatible land usage near airports. The Aircraft Noise Abatement Act has required the additional staffing of three acoustical engineers (two in the field and one in Washington) to administer noise certification rules promulgated by the FAA, observe noise certification flight tests, and evaluate aircraft noise reports submitted by applicants for aircraft certificates.

The problems confronting the Office of Noise Abatement are, indeed, enormous. Initially, their problem is how to stand firm in the face of strong opposition from powerful aerospace and airline industries who claim to have been spending large sums of money on quieter engines for a number of years. While this claim can be verified, the results of the industries' labor have been far from satisfactory. One of the reasons for their lack of success is that substantial noise reduction is a very difficult and expensive undertaking. NASA tests indicate that take-off noise can be reduced by 15 PNdB. Static tests, using acoustical linings in the engine, have obtained noise reductions of up to 40 PNdB. However, the airlines argue that equipage of existing turbo-jets with such engines would cost $6 million per plane, an exorbitant figure. In spite of their contentions, Dr. Donald Anthrop, in a recent

---

[19] *Seattle Times,* November 22, 1968.

article in the *Bulletin of the Atomic Scientists,* contends that the government should require these industries to equip their planes with engines manifesting a 40 PNdB decrease in noise level on take-off. Since the decibel scale is logarithmic, any reduction of the noise level would be a relatively large reduction in terms of net impact upon the human ear. People can perceive 20 PNdB alleviations, but the relative merits of such an abatement is debatable unless the total noise level is near 100 PNdB or lower. Anything above this level is both annoying and harmful to man.

In January, 1969, the *New York Times* reported that the Office of Noise Abatement had formulated its first regulation authorized by the new act. The rule, subject to appeal by airlines and plane manufacturers, specifies that new aircraft in approaches for landing will not be allowed to exceed 102 to 108 PNdB, depending upon their weight. Take-off noise will be limited to 93–108 PNdB. A spokesman for the office declared that such reductions would about halve the noise presently heard near airports, but he concluded that although such reductions may be noticeable, "there won't be a real lot of difference." [20] In their appeal against the new regulation, the ATA and the Aerospace Industries Association called the rule "unacceptable" and proposed an alternate which would increase the allowable noise level by 2 PNdB. Supporting their alternative, these groups stated the increase could not be perceived by humans.[21] The Office of Noise Abatement's ultimate objective is an 80 PNdB engine, but given this kind of opposition and logic, their objective may be difficult to achieve. In fact, Charles R. Foster, head of the office, concedes that it will take a long time to get any really noticeable noise reduction.

In regard to the FAA's role in regulating noise from supersonic transports, the Office of Noise Abatement stated that because of the extreme complexity of the rule-making procedures, these rules will be forthcoming "at a considerably later date." [22] Simply because the American SST is yet to be manufactured, its priority may be last on the list of proposed rule making. Sonic boom promises to be the worst noise offender, but the American public is inadequately protected from this menace by the Aircraft Noise Abatement Act. If the FAA

[20] *New York Times,* January 7, 1969.
[21] *Seattle Times,* May 21, 1969.
[22] Personal correspondence with the Office of Noise Abatement (FAA), Washington, D.C., October, 1968.

waits until the SST rolls out of its hangar or until a foreign-made craft takes to American air space to formulate sonic boom regulations, then as Senator Case has warned, it may be too late to gain passage of effective legislation.

IV

Unwanted sound permeates every corner of every street in urban America. The advent of supersonic travel threatens to extend truly devastating noise to the relatively quiet countryside; and noise in general promises only to become more abundant and louder. The answer to the problem lies not with complete elimination but with effective controls. Dr. Leo L. Beranek, a noted acoustics expert, has pointed out that except for sonic boom, there is no noise generated by science that science cannot suppress.[23] Given enough money, scientists can break the "unwanted sound" barrier. People's desire for silence, thus, wears a price tag, but many persons, including the majority of congressmen, are not ready to pay it.

After a decade of investigations, public hearings, reports, and debates, Congress has a reasonable awareness of the not-so-quiet crisis. It has been informed of the dangers of the sonic boom. Yet, a number of congressmen would have the nation believe that the economy will collapse and national prestige will be delivered a dreadful blow unless an American SST is put into the air. Unrestricted SST flights will more probably collapse much of the world around us. The passage of a weak act to quiet opponents of noise has only intensified opposition to overland supersonic travel and to the over-all SST program. Even though SST proponents claim the plane will never be allowed to fly overland, feasibility studies indicate that such a ban may spell doom for the program economically. In the absence of clear legislative and administrative safeguards, the SST will prove to be another "exigency" of today which provokes an emergency tomorrow. Sonic boom tests have already been conducted over Oklahoma City, St. Louis, and Chicago to gauge the impact on the citizenry. Since some legislators have gone so far as to call all talk about the adverse effects of the sonic boom "phoney," why not stage the next test at night over Washington, D.C.? It could be the last hope for opening congressional ears.

[23] Conservation Foundation, *CF Letter*, December 29, 1967, p. 7.

13. International Control of the Ocean Floor

PHILIP S. KELLEY

Under no circumstances, we believe, must we ever allow the prospects of rich harvest and mineral wealth to create a new form of colonial competition among the maritime nations. We must ensure that the deep seas and the ocean bottoms are, and remain, the legacy of all human beings.

THIS expression of sentiment by President Johnson at the commissioning of the research vessel *Oceanographer* in July, 1967, might have been interpreted as a suggestion that the United States was prepared to consider steps necessary to prevent the colonial competition referred to by the President. Subsequent events suggest otherwise; the United States is extremely cautious about committing itself to any specific program for controlling access to the ocean floor. This is well illustrated by the reaction of the United States Congress to a recent and highly controversial proposal to place the ocean floor and its resources under international control.[1]

PHILIP S. KELLEY is a research fellow in geography at the University of Washington. He was for some time an official of the United States Public Health Service and is currently working on the international aspects of resource conservation with special emphasis on the resources of the ocean floor.

[1] This discussion considers only the physical sea floor and legal regimes pertaining to it; the vast and complicated problems of fisheries are not within the scope of the present paper. Several specific proposals for sea floor internationalization have been made; these are concisely summarized by Eugene Brooks, "International Organization for Hydrospace" (mimeographed paper submitted to the Third Annual Conference of the Law of the Sea Institute, Kingston, R.I., June 24–27, 1968) and by Elisabeth Mann Borgese, "The Ocean Regime," *Center Occasional Papers*, Vol. I, No. 5 (Santa Barbara: Center for the Study of Democratic Institutions, 1968).

I

The ambassador to the United Nations from Malta, Mr. Arvid Pardo, proposed, on August 17, 1967, that the General Assembly of the United Nations should include on its agenda consideration of a proposal entitled, "Declaration and treaty concerning the reservation exclusively for peaceful purposes of the sea bed and of the ocean floor underlying the seas beyond the limits of present national jurisdiction, and the use of their resources in the interests of mankind." In the explanatory memorandum accompanying his proposal, Ambassador Pardo suggested that immediate steps should be taken to draft a treaty embodying at least four principles: that those areas of the sea floor not presently under national jurisdiction not be subject to further national appropriation; that sea floor exploration be undertaken in a manner consistent with the philosophy of the United Nations Charter; that use of the sea floor beyond the present limits of national jurisdiction be undertaken with the safeguarding of mankind's interests as a primary aim (specifically, that any net financial benefits resulting from such use be used to assist developing countries); and that the sea floor beyond present national limits be reserved for peaceful purposes exclusively.[2] Pardo also suggested that an international agency (he did not specify the United Nations, *per se*) should be created to assume appropriate authority over the sea floor and to oversee the use of the sea floor in a manner consistent with the treaty specifications. The Malta proposal was referred by the General Assembly to the First (Political) Committee, which, after considerable debate, created an *ad hoc* committee to survey the issue in detail. This *ad hoc* committee made a report to the General Assembly in the fall of 1968.[3] On December 18, 1968, the General Assembly passed a resolution creating a permanent forty-two-member Committee on Peaceful Use of the Ocean Floor.[4]

[2] Pardo subsequently modified the title of his proposal so that no mention was made of the words "declaration" or "treaty."

[3] United Nations, General Assembly, 23rd Session, 1968, *Report of the Ad Hoc Committee to Study the Peaceful Uses of the Sea-Bed and the Ocean Floor Beyond the Limits of National Jurisdiction*, A/7230.

[4] Resolution 2467A, XXIII, as reported in *U.N. Monthly Chronicle*, VI, No. 1 (January, 1969), 56–62. Resolutions 2467B, C, and D, passed at the same time, dealt respectively with marine pollution, a report to be prepared concerning the machinery required for international control for resource exploitation from the deep ocean floor, and a statement of support for the U.S.-proposed International Decade of Ocean Exploration.

The preparation and execution of a treaty such as that proposed by Malta would be a lengthy process; one need only recall the nearly ten years required to execute the Outer Space Treaty or the six years needed to put in force the Geneva Convention of the Continental Shelf. Also, such a treaty would be binding only on those countries ratifying it; and in the case of the United States the Senate must approve ratification. Nevertheless, the Malta proposal provoked a strong and immediate response in the United States Congress. Specifically, twenty-three almost identical House joint resolutions, all expressing opposition to the Malta proposal, were introduced in the House of Representatives during the first session of the Ninetieth Congress between September 13 and October 31, 1967. These resolutions, their sponsors, and dates of introduction are listed in Table 3. In the Senate, opposition appeared in the form of Senate Joint Resolution 111, introduced by Senator Norris Cotton of New Hampshire. This resolution was identical to most of the House resolutions listed in Table 3.

With minor exceptions, the resolutions in Table 3 all used identical wording. Each resolves that "it is the sense of the Congress that any action at this time to vest control of deep ocean resources in an international body would be premature and ill-advised," and that Congress should urge the President to instruct the American representatives to the United Nations to oppose any such action at this time.[5] Each resolution gives five reasons for its opposition to internationalization: (1) pressure has been placed on the United Nations to take action on the matter of control of the sea floor beyond the continental shelf; (2) the United States presently has no clearly defined position on the matter of ocean floor development; (3) there is a serious lack of understanding of how to exploit the ocean floor; (4) the Marine Resources and Engineering Development Act of 1966, already in force, has as an objective the clarification of points (2) and (3) above;[6] and (5) certain highly responsible national organizations

[5] U.S., Congress, House, Committee on Foreign Affairs, Subcommittee on International Organizations and Movements, *Interim Report on the United Nations and the Issue of Deep Ocean Resources, together with Hearings*, H. Rept. 999, 90th Cong., 1st sess., 1967, p. 1.

[6] The act provided for two cabinet-level bodies. The National Council on Marine Resources and Engineering Development has issued three annual reports; the most recent is *Marine Science Affairs: A Year of Broadened Participation* (Washington, D.C.: Government Printing Office, 1969). The

TABLE 3

HOUSE JOINT RESOLUTIONS IN OPPOSITION TO
THE MALTA PROPOSAL, NINETIETH CONGRESS,
FIRST SESSION

H.J.R. No.	Sponsor	Date of Introduction (1967)
816	Byrne (D., Pa.)	September 13
817	Clark (D., Pa.)	September 13
818	Downing (D., Va.)	September 13
819	Garmatz (D., Md.)	September 13
820	Hanna (D., Cal.)	September 13
821	Helstoski (D., N.J.)	September 13
822	Lennon (D., N.C.)	September 13
823	Rogers (D., Fla.)	September 13
824	Reinecke (R., Cal.)	September 13
828	Pelly (R., Wash.)	September 14
829	Utt (R., Cal.)	September 14
830	Lennon (D., N.C.)	September 14
834	Fountain (D., N.C.)	September 18
835	Gross (R., Iowa)	September 18
837	Fuqua (D., Fla.)	September 20
840	Clausen (R., Cal.)	September 21
843	Rogers (D., Colo.)	September 25
844	Willis (D., La.)	September 25
850	Leggett (D., Cal.)	September 27
856	Hall (R., Mo.)	September 28
865	Gurney (R. Fla.)	October 3
876	St. Germain (D., R.I.)	October 5
916	Bush (R., Tex.)	October 31

have expressed strong opposition to allowing the United Nations, in
particular, to control the ocean floor.[7] The opposition in the House did

---

Commission on Marine Science, Engineering, and Resources has issued its
final report and recommendations, entitled *Our Nation and the Sea* (Washington, D.C.: Government Printing Office, 1969).

[7] H.J.R. 835 and H.J.R. 856 differ from the others in that they omit reference to the present time conditions; the implication is that the United States
should at no time, either presently or in the future, consider supporting
internationalization proposals. H.J.R. 876 and S.J.R. 111 omit the prefatory
reference to the highly responsible national organizations. H.J.R. 830 expressed the same opposition as the majority of the resolutions, but offered
as well an amendment to the Marine Resources and Engineering Development Act of 1966, which specified that a detailed study of sea floor resources
be undertaken with particular reference to definition of policy. Because of
this amendment, H.J.R. 830 was referred to the Committee on Merchant
Marine and Fisheries instead of the Foreign Affairs Committee.

not appear to be especially marked by partisan politics. As can be seen from Table 3, fifteen of the twenty-three resolutions were introduced by Democrats, eight by Republicans. Perhaps of more significance is that all but one of these resolutions were introduced by representatives from coastal states, and also that ten of the twenty-three resolutions were sponsored by members of the House Merchant Marine and Fisheries Committee.

In marked contrast to the sheer number of resolutions opposing internationalization, there were but four resolutions introduced in the House supporting action of this kind. These four House Concurrent Resolutions are listed in Table 4.

TABLE 4

HOUSE CONCURRENT RESOLUTIONS IN SUPPORT OF THE MALTA
PROPOSAL, NINETIETH CONGRESS, FIRST SESSION

H.C.R. No.	Sponsor	Date of Introduction (1967)
558	Bingham (D., N.Y.)	October 25
576	Brown (D., Cal.)	November 7
577	Scheuer (D., N.Y.)	November 7
580	Matsunaga (D., Hawaii)	November 9

The four resolutions are all identical in wording and call for ocean floor resource development through international cooperation, initiation of action to this end in the United Nations and in the United States Government by the President, and studies to find the most desirable means of achieving these goals. In the Senate, two resolutions also supporting international control and development of the sea floor were introduced by Senator Claiborne Pell of Rhode Island. The first of these, Senate Resolution 172, resolves that because marine technological capabilities and the possibilities of legal confrontations over questions of sea floor jurisdiction are increasing, the United States ought to encourage the United Nations to license, regulate, use, and conserve the resources of the sea floor. The resolution suggests that the proper way to accomplish this is an international agreement governing the sea floor, including clauses covering licensing and use, arms control, definition of the continental shelf, and enforcement machinery. Senator Pell's second resolution, S.R. 186, called for the President to instruct the American delegation to the United Nations to press for consideration and passage of a resolution embodying the general principles set forth in S.R. 172, and it contained the draft of a proposed international agreement.

II

Five hearings on the resolutions introduced in the House were held during September and October by the Subcommittee on International Organizations and Movements of the House Committee on Foreign Affairs, chaired by Representative Dante Fascell of Florida. In the Senate, one hearing on the three resolutions introduced was held by the Foreign Relations Committee with Senators John Sparkman of Alabama and Claiborne Pell of Rhode Island presiding. The House hearings were more extensive and detailed than the Senate hearing, but the real difference between them was one of attitude: the Senate Foreign Relations Committee devoted most of its time to Senator Pell's proposals favoring internationalization, while the House dwelt mainly on the House Joint Resolutions opposing such action. The hearings in both houses accepted written or verbal testimony from the Departments of State, Defense, and the Interior; from representatives of some nonprofit research organizations (Resources for the Future, the World Peace through Law Center, and the Commission to Study the Organization of Peace); from individuals prominent in the field of international law; from representatives of private industry and national organizations; and, of course, from the sponsors of some of the resolutions. Among the basic questions raised at the hearings were the following: What is the nature of the resource base of the ocean floor? What is the present meaning of the limit of the continental shelf adopted by the Geneva Conventions of 1958? What would be the economic effects, both internationally and within the United States, if the ocean floor were to be placed under the control of an international body? What is, or should be, United States policy on issues relating to ocean floor use?

Faced with both House and Senate resolutions opposing internationalization, as well as favoring such action, the State Department chose the middle of the road and recommended that no action be taken on any of the resolutions. Representatives from the State Department explained that present United States policy was, in fact, similar to the very cautious approach proposed in the resolutions opposing an international approach. Consequently, there was no real need for passage of such resolutions. The Department of State opposed the passage of the Pell resolutions favoring internationalization but did not specify exactly why. David H. Popper, Deputy Assistant Secretary of State, commented on the various favorable proposals for internationalization. "Interesting and suggestive as these ideas are," he said, "we would consider it quite premature at this stage to espouse any particular type of arrangement for the deep sea bed or to make any commitments with respect to a definitive legal regime for the ocean floor." [8]

On the question of policy, representatives from the Departments of the Interior and Defense deferred to the State Department's judgment in the matter and indicated they found its position generally satisfactory. However, the Defense Department took a somewhat stronger position in opposition to Senator Pell's resolutions for internationalization. As Assistant Secretary of Defense, Paul C. Warnke, put it:

. . . the Department of Defense supports the need for care which is reflected in Senate Joint Resolution 111, rather than the proposals in Senate Resolution 172 and Senate Resolution 186 . . . it would be less than candid for me not to advise this committee that it seems obvious, even based on this preliminary study, that the Department of Defense could not support all aspects of Senate Resolution 186.[9]

The remainder of the testimony from government agencies came primarily from the Department of the Interior, and consisted largely of factual information about sea floor resources and legal aspects of Interior's leasing arrangements for sea floor exploration.

The testimony from nongovernmental sources was more varied. The nonprofit research group representatives were solidly in favor of efforts toward reaching an international agreement of some kind. They stressed that the issue is one of urgency, requiring early action to establish some sort of international agency to guide sea floor use. Clark M. Eichelberger, representing the Commission to Study the Organization of Peace, succinctly stated why. "I would not attempt," he said, "to outline the kind of agency that should be created. But I want to say that unless one is created, the world will be faced with anarchy, with untold competition, which could deprive the United

[8] House, Committee on Foreign Affairs, *Interim Report*, p. 52.
[9] U.S., Congress, Senate, Committee on Foreign Relations, *Governing the Use of Ocean Space, Hearing on S.J.R. 111, S.R. 172, and S.R. 186*, 90th Cong., 1st sess., 1967, pp. 36–37.

States of the very security which it needs to develop the sea's resources."[10]

In marked contrast to this internationalist position was that of the American marine-oriented industry, represented as a group by the National Oceanography Association. Early in his statement, Senator Norris Cotton of New Hampshire, sponsor of S.J.R. 111, stated that "the first draft of this resolution was prepared for me by representatives of the National Oceanographic (sic) Association."[11] This raises an interesting question. Did the National Oceanography Association prepare the texts of H.J.R. 816 and the other similar resolutions listed in Table 3 opposing internationalization; or did the association simply borrow the text of H.J.R. 816 and give it verbatim to Senator Cotton? Whatever the case, the action suggests that the association felt strongly about the Malta proposal, and wielded considerable influence among representatives and senators on committees dealing with marine affairs.

After all of the hearings had been concluded, the House Subcommittee on International Organizations and Movements presented its conclusions in an *Interim Report on the United Nations and the Issue of Deep Ocean Resources*, recommending that the United States take no immediate action on the question of internationalization. The report gave reasons for the recommendation. It stated that not enough is known about the oceans in general, although there are private, national, and international studies underway focusing on the oceans. The report noted further that there are legal uncertainties concerning title to ocean resources, and that the proposal to vest title to the sea floor in an international group might upset the *status quo* with respect to present United States operations. The subcommittee recommended that more research be conducted, and that, pending the results of this research, the United States Government actively discourage any efforts at internationalization of the sea floor. It also recommended that the United States should be extremely circumspect about any related suggestions for internationalization; while, at the same time, "constructive international cooperation" should be encouraged. Finally, the subcommittee concluded that: "We are strongly of the opinion

[10] House, Committee on Foreign Affairs, *Interim Report*, p. 83.
[11] Senate, Committee on Foreign Relations, *Governing the Use of Ocean Space*, p. 16. Senator Cotton stated that, while he did not necessarily agree with the exact wording of the resolution, he did support its intent.

that hasty action in this field can create more problems than it will solve or avert." [12] Only two members of the subcommittee disagreed, and they only mildly, with the negative tone of the *Interim Report*. Following publication of the report, no further action on any of the resolutions occurred in either house during the remainder of the first session of the Ninetieth Congress.

The second session of the Ninetieth saw some further action. In the Senate, S.R. 263 was introduced by Senator Pell on March 5, 1968. Where S.R. 186 relied exclusively on the United Nations as the agent to give life to its proposals, S.R. 263 made provision for the United Nations or any other agency considered appropriate to be the organizing body. The treaty provisions of S.R. 263 also differed somewhat from those of S.R. 186 in its provisions for the disposal of radioactive wastes and a more detailed definition of the term "peaceful use." S.R. 263 was referred to the Committee on Foreign Relations, which took no further action.

In the House, further hearings occurred on June 12 and July 25, 1968. These were not full-scale hearings, but rather "executive branch briefings" held again before the House Subcommittee on International Organizations and Movements, meeting in joint session with the Subcommittee on Oceanography of the House Committee on Merchant Marine and Fisheries. These hearings were addressed by representatives from State, Defense, and Interior, and were concerned largely with the reporting of developments at the meetings of the United Nations *ad hoc* committee on the Malta proposal, which held sessions in March, June, and July, 1968, as well as in August, after the executive branch briefings had been concluded. The Subcommittee on International Organizations and Movements issued a final report, *The Oceans: A Challenging New Frontier,* which marked the conclusion of House action on the issue.[13]

The final report of the subcommittee is noteworthy. Most significant is the softening to a very apparent degree of the subcommittee's attitude on the issue of internationalization. While it did not go so far as outright endorsement of the objective of internationalization of the sea floor, it did conclude that use of the sea floor for peaceful purposes

---

[12] House, Committee on Foreign Affairs, *Interim Report,* p. 5R.
[13] U.S., Congress, House, Committee on Foreign Affairs, Subcommittee on International Organizations and Movements, *The Oceans: A Challenging New Frontier,* H. Rept. 1957, 90th Cong., 2d sess., 1968.

warranted universal support (with some reservations about the real meaning of the words "peaceful purposes"). Contrary to its earlier findings, the subcommittee also concluded that establishment of an international regime deserved careful study and that the idea could not be rejected forthwith.[14] The subcommittee's final recommendation was that there should be prompt action to clarify the definition of the continental shelf through some kind of international agreement that would meet with Senate approval.[15] Although there was still a tendency on the part of some congressmen to view the Maltese Proposal as a "threat" to United States interests in ocean space, the final report made it clear that the subcommittee as a whole recognized the importance of the issue and that, like it or not, the question of sea-floor sovereignty would have to be solved by some kind of international arrangement. The swing of attitude from one of negativeness to one of moderation does not appear to be of a basic nature, but more an initial overreaction to a surprising development of unknown dimensions, followed by some reconsideration and the reappearance of level-headed leadership.

The issuance of the final report by the subcommittee signaled the end of House action for the time being. No further action occurred during the Ninetieth Congress and none seems imminent in the Ninety-first. The Senate continues to be prodded by Senator Pell, but no action has occurred since the publication of the hearings.[16]

III

The hearings in both houses of Congress raise many questions. The Senate, while apparently sympathetic to the motives behind the Malta proposal, was not convinced that the matter was one of such urgency as to require positive action on its part in spite of the strong positive leadership offered by Senator Pell.[17] The House was initially strongly

---

[14] *Ibid.*, p. 2R.

[15] *Ibid.*, p. 3R.

[16] Into the first session of the Ninety-first Congress, Senator Pell introduced two resolutions: S.R. 33 (January 21, 1969), a statement of principles addressed for consideration by the new permanent U.N. Committee on Peaceful Use of the Ocean Floor, and S.R. 92 (February 4, 1969), identical in most respects to his earlier S.R. 263. The statements of principle in S.R. 33 are incorporated in the draft treaty in S.R. 92.

[17] In all fairness, it should be noted that at the time the Senate Foreign Relations Committee was concerned with the ocean floor issue, it was also in the midst of another, more heated, controversy: that of getting Secretary

committed to preservation of the *status quo,* using the well-worn plea that more research was required before the question could be adequately addressed. This position was seen to have softened after a ten-month period.

Three general sources of opposition appeared evident after the initial flurry of activity generated in Congress by the Malta resolution. If there are other sources, they were not obvious at the hearings. First is the combined opposition of the military establishment and the marine-research-orientated industry, the latter being dependent to a significant degree on government contract work for its existence.[18] These groups have similar reasons for avoiding any circumscription of their spheres of action. The opposition of the offshore oil and mining interests is similar in rationale. They want complete freedom of access to as much of the ocean as possible. The second source of opposition is less well defined in terms of the organizations behind it and is more difficult to evaluate because of its emotional content, but the general flavor is one of simple anti-internationalist sentiment. This ranges from outright xenophobia on the one hand to the somewhat more moderate approach of the American Legion on the other. The American Legion, along with other groups, is on record opposing the turning over of the sea floor to the United Nations because parts of the Malta proposal implied that the United Nations would gain monetarily from the exploitation of the sea floor resources. These groups are opposed to the concept that the United Nations should have any source of income independent of the contributions of its member states.[19]

The third source of opposition is ignorance. The feeling of Congress and of the executive branch as expressed through the State Department is that not enough is known of the sea floor and its resource base

of State Dean Rusk to testify before it on Vietnam. Senator Pell's resolutions might have received more attention had this not been the case.

[18] The Navy contributes between 50 and 60 per cent of total Federal expenditure in marine research. See Senate, Committee on Foreign Relations, *Governing the Use of Ocean Space,* p. 39. But see also William T. Burke, *Ocean Sciences, Technology, and the Future International Law of the Sea* (Columbus: Ohio State University Press, 1966), pp. 15–17.

[19] Independent income for the United Nations is a touchy issue beyond the scope of this discussion; such income would appear to be contrary to the U.N. charter. It should be noted, however, that most internationalization proposals suggest an agency other than the U.N. itself to handle the financial aspects of leasing, licensing, and income distribution.

to make the Malta approach a valid one at this time. Wait and see—cope with the problems one at a time as they arise—is the philosophy here. This may be a valid approach. Congress has used it frequently and sometimes successfully. But the question is whether it is the best approach in this particular instance. The wait-and-see stance does give the State Department a great deal of flexibility for future maneuvering, but this can easily turn out to be the frantic, last-minute sort of maneuvering which results in solutions satisfactory to no one.

The crux of the problem raised by the Malta proposal is what exactly defines the limits of present national jurisdiction. The Geneva Conventions of 1958 contain a Convention on the Continental Shelf, which entered into force on June 10, 1964. It defines the continental shelf as being generally the sea floor adjacent to the coast out to either a depth of 200 meters (656 feet) or "beyond that limit, to where the superadjacent waters admits of the exploitation of the said areas." A second provision in the Convention states that "the coastal state exercises over the continental shelf sovereign rights for the purposes of exploring it and exploiting its natural resources." [20] In other words, as far as jurisdiction over adjacent sea floor is concerned, a coastal state maintains sovereignty as far offshore as technology will take it. The requisite technology apparently need not be in the actual possession of the coastal state. The 200-meter limit is thus virtually meaningless.

Forty-six nations signed the Continental Shelf Convention following the 1958 conference, and thirty-seven have since ratified it. However ambiguous it may now be, the convention is the present basis for all claims of sea floor sovereignty. In the technologically advanced countries with maritime interests, the ability to explore and exploit the ocean floor is increasing rapidly. Concern over this; concern over who owns what; and concern over the fact that there might be resources present which could be turned to the use of mankind as a whole instead of the already rich countries—these were the basis for the Malta proposal.

The Malta proposal provided the basis for discussion in the United States Congress, but, as we have seen, Congress chose not to act and instead tabled the matter because "more research was needed." Considerable research is, in fact, under way. The work of the United Nations Permanent Committee on Peaceful Use of the Ocean Floor

[20] House, Committee on Foreign Affairs, *Interim Report*, p. 217.

has already been mentioned. UNESCO and its Intergovernmental Oceanographic Commission have been involved in oceanographic matters for a number of years, while the Food and Agriculture Organization has sponsored work in marine fisheries. In the United States considerable relevant research is currently being pursued, perhaps most significantly that carried out under the provisions of the Marine Resources and Engineering Act of 1966 by the Commission on Marine Science, Engineering, and Resources. A member of the commission has recently described a proposal being considered which would set up an international registry agency for governing access to deep sea minerals.[21] There are other groups in the United States doing similar policy research. In light of the considerable work already accomplished, it would seem that some of the information needed to make decisions about an international regime is probably at hand, and that Congress' claim that more work is needed before progress can be made is not wholly defensible.

What can be expected if the present *status quo* policies continue? Submarine anarchy? Submarine colonialism? These charges have been made, and either could well come to pass. There are but few indications that such a gloomy prospect might be avoided by existing diplomatic machinery. One ray of hope is that the United Nations Conference on the Law of the Sea may be reconvened in 1969 or 1970. After June 10, 1969, any ratifying nation may propose revision of the Convention on the Continental Shelf by so suggesting in writing to the Secretary-General of the United Nations, after which the General Assembly will decide what, if anything, will be done with respect to such proposed revision. Should the conference be reconvened, something positive in the way of redefining the continental shelf might result. This could help to remove the present ambiguity over the limits of national jurisdiction, but by itself it would do little to resolve the question of deep ocean jurisdiction. It is also conceivable that some sort of working agreement independent of the United Nations might be worked out among the parties involved in deep sea exploitation, but if history is a guide, such an approach to ocean floor jurisdictional questions is not one to inspire confidence.

[21] Carl A. Auerbach, lecture to the Third Annual Conference of the Law of the Sea Institute, Kingston, R.I., June 24, 1968. The proposal described by Auerbach subsequently appeared as a part of *Our Nation and the Sea* (see note 6, above).

If an international regime is not arrived at fairly soon, it may be too late for such an agreement to be effective, because, lacking any reason not to do so, coastal states may be expected to extend seaward their claims to the ocean floor at every opportunity. The most recent example of this in the United States is the announced intention of a group on the West Coast to lay claim to Cobb Seamount, an extinct volcanic cone rising from about 9,000 feet below sea level to a depth of only about 120 feet below the surface, some 270 miles west of Grays Harbor on the coast of Washington. According to *Science* magazine: "Although the project is described as basically scientific in intent, one of the arguments advanced by the consortium is that the legal claim should be firmly established in anticipation of efforts at the United Nations to internationalize the sea bottom." [22] The sponsors of the project, christened Project SEA USE, believe it possible that the occupation of the Seamount for a limited time using ships, scuba divers, and a submerged habitat "may at some point be considered sufficient to establish a limited claim of exclusive rights. At least, it would seem to be sufficient to stop other nations from claiming such exclusive rights." [23] Washington's Senator Warren Magnuson has said that it would "be a healthy precedent for the United States to occupy Cobb Seamount." [24] The Cobb Seamount situation is only one example of announced intent to extend national jurisdiction far beyond the continental shelf, but in all probability it will not be the last.[25] This is

[22] Marti Mueller, "Who Will Control Cobb Seamount?" *Science*, CLXI (July 19, 1968), 252–53.

[23] Battelle Memorial Institute, Honeywell, Oceanic Foundation of Hawaii, and University of Washington, *Project SEA USE: Proposed Exploration of Cobb Seamount* (research proposal submitted to the Washington State Oceanographic Commission), 1968, p. III–11.

[24] *Seattle Times*, May 22, 1968, p. 65.

[25] A second edition of the SEA USE proposal (Oceanographic Institute of Washington, *General Plan for the SEA USE Program and Operations Guide for Project SEA USE I* [Seattle: Oceanographic Commission of Washington, 1968]) was issued September 20, 1968. This edition makes no reference whatsoever to the national-claim implications raised in the earlier edition; the project sponsors apparently decided that the time was not appropriate to make such a pitch in view of the fast-breaking developments at the United Nations. SEA USE has considerably broadened its base of support to include institutions in Oregon, Alaska, and British Columbia. The importance of Canadian participation is evident from the fact that Cobb appears to be closer to Vancouver Island than to the Washington coast: calculations based on the cosine law of spherical trigonometry using coordinates taken from U.S. Coast and Geodetic Survey chart 5052 indicate distances from Cobb to

the kind of unilateral action that the wait-and-see approach of Congress not only fails to cope with but actually encourages.

Unfortunately, undirected unilateral action leaves open the more basic questions concerning mankind's stake in deep ocean resources, as opposed to the stake of limited economic interests in certain powerful nations. Arms control, radioactive waste disposal, redistribution of wealth, precise definition of responsibilities—these are the kinds of questions that require attention. The question of treating the resources of the ocean floor as the common property of mankind to the extent of apportioning the rewards from exploitation is difficult to address. It is apparently contrary to the traditional American concept of "free enterprise," and there should be perhaps no surprise at the lack of congressional enthusiasm for proposals tending to point in that direction. Redistribution of sea floor wealth is, indeed, an idealistic proposal. It is humanitarian in the highest sense of that word. It is also quite improbable in the world of today where nationalism is still a potent force.

IV

Action on a problem of this kind is seldom immediate. It may be, however, that what we are witnessing is the beginning of a long but ultimately fruitful process in the case of ocean space similar to that which preceded the highly acclaimed outer space treaty. Hopefully, action will not be too late to prevent haphazard exploitation, arms games, and exotic pollutions. But if action is not to be of the too-little-too-late variety, encouragement of constructive ideas is imperative.

The proposal to internationalize the ocean floor is a major challenge to the United Nations. The Malta proposal was by no means unanimously supported by the member states of the United Nations, nor have the sea floor resources been proved to exist in the variety or quantity sometimes assumed by those proposing vigorous international development. However, against the possibility that the resources do exist in commercial quantities, any opportunity for international cooperation in the development of the sea floor should be followed up. It is a challenge to all nations the like of which may never again be found on earth, and it behooves all concerned to advance, not impede, progress in that direction.

Estevan Point, B.C., and to Cape Johnson, Wash., of 230 and 262 nautical miles, respectively.

On a level closer to home, the proposal to internationalize the ocean floor is also a challenge to Congress. There is an increasing awareness that many important environmental issues extend across national boundaries and that international agreements are required to cope with these issues. There is some evidence that Congress can respond to international resource problems. Successful agreements have been concluded, for example, for the development of the water resources of the Columbia River basin and with respect to migratory waterfowl. It is true that these agreements have benefited only two or three nations, and that the Malta proposal has much more extensive implications. It is tempting to suggest that Congress is unwilling to support a proposal that would result in slight material advantage to the United States, and to selected congressional constituents in particular. It is interesting, and perhaps not entirely coincidental, that the sponsors of the House Joint Resolutions opposing the Malta proposal are predominantly from coastal states. It is not unreasonable for those who see in the Malta proposal a threat to their own interests in the ocean floor to object through their representatives in the House.

The fact remains that it was difficult for Congress to give expression to the commendable but ill-defined values attached to the idea of developing the ocean floor for the benefit of mankind in general. The tendency for Congress to respond to immediate and concrete proposals that promise immediate material advantage from the environment is well known. The nature of the Malta proposal is such that it confronted Congress with values and policy choices that are unfamiliar. The response of Congress up to the present time, especially in the House, has been lukewarm if not hostile. There is a suggestion that Congress, rather than act on its own initiative, is willing to follow the lead of the State Department. The possibility that this course of action is one of delaying or buying time cannot be excluded.

Can congressmen be made aware of values and policy alternatives that go beyond the narrow confines of their own districts or the boundaries of the United States? In a very real sense, the attempt to internationalize the ocean floor affords Congress the opportunity to enrich the experience of people in nations less affluent and less technologically advanced than the United States. As the greatest user of resources and the most significant environmental manipulator, the United States has a definite interest in the sound management of the environment on a world-wide basis. It ought to be difficult for Congress to claim that effective international control of the ocean floor is not in the best long-term interests of the nation. Somehow, Congress must be made conscious of the desirability, indeed, the necessity, of positive action on the question of internationalization, without waiting for "all" the data to be available. As Senator Pell has observed:

. . . knowledge cannot be substituted for the will to develop this frontier region in a peaceful and orderly manner—one which will take account of the responsibilities, the needs, the aspirations, and the limitations of all the nations of the world. . . . Unless our will is commensurate with our knowledge, international cooperation and understanding shall continue to be burdened with suspicion and mistrust.[26]

[26] Claiborne Pell, "Statement by Senator Claiborne Pell on Introducing a Draft Treaty to Govern the Activities of Nations in Ocean Space" (mimeographed press release from Senator Pell's office, February 4, 1969).

14. National Policy for the Environment:
Politics and the Concept of Stewardship

GEOFFREY WANDESFORDE-SMITH

THE debate over a national policy for the environment posed the greatest challenge of all the environmental issues brought before Congress in the past decade. It offered Congress the opportunity to legislate a fundamental change in the institutional arrangements that have supported the steady degradation of the American environment begun in the early years of the Republic. Rejecting the advice of Washington, Hamilton, and Gallatin, the newly independent United States embarked upon the task of civilizing the American continent in a spirit of laissez-faire and unfettered individual initiative which has remained a basic ingredient of the American character.[1] The notion of government as the conservator or steward of the natural environment, or as a conservative guiding force in the physical development of the nation, has never gained ascendancy over a virtually unshakeable belief on the part of most Americans in individual ingenuity and an ever more potent technology as the keys to improvement of the human condition. Recognition that man himself is a part of the total environment and that his interference with the natural world might destroy values and objects important in giving meaning to life came belatedly. At about the end of the nineteenth century a few thoughtful men

GEOFFREY WANDESFORDE-SMITH is a J. Allen Smith research fellow in political science at the University of Washington. He is co-author of *Federal-State Development Planning: The Federal Field Committee for Development Planning in Alaska* and is currently completing a doctoral thesis on regional water policy formation in the Pacific Northwest.

[1] Lynton K. Caldwell, "Administrative Possibilities for Environmental Control," in F. Fraser Darling and John P. Milton, eds., *Future Environments of North America* (New York: Natural History Press, 1966), p. 655.

began to question the capacity of the nation to sustain continued development through the unrestrained depletion of its natural resources. The first conservation conference convened in 1908 by President Theodore Roosevelt resulted in the creation of twenty-three state departments of conservation. Henceforth, conservation became an established public responsibility at both the Federal and state levels.

The focus of this responsibility was a vague and essentially economic concept. Conservation was used to mean the management of particular resources in a manner designed to achieve wise use. Precisely what constituted wise use and who was competent to determine those uses that were wise were questions not admitting any simple or straightforward answers. Clearly, however, the concept of conservation did not encompass the management of environments, as opposed to discrete resources, nor was it intended to preserve those qualities of the biophysical environment regarded by George Perkins Marsh and others as sources of spiritual satisfaction and creatvity. In his classic work, *Man and Nature,* Marsh had elaborated a concept of environmental stewardship akin to that held by the American Indians. Central to this concept was the moral obligation of each generation to use the environment in a way that did not impair the natural endowment of future generations. The publication of *Man and Nature* in 1864 has been described by former Interior Secretary Stewart L. Udall as "the beginning of land wisdom in this country,"[2] but to Marsh's own generation, the concept of stewardship seemed farfetched.

Indeed, it is not until very recently that the concept of stewardship has been advocated as a focus for public policy by a significant segment of the conservation movement. It is true that the conservation movement always has included groups and individuals whose interest in preserving fish and wildlife, parks, wilderness, or forests has been informed by an understanding of ecology and a concern for the total environment. But it is also true that institutional arrangements in the United States have been adapted better to exploitation of the environment than to its protection and have reflected the interests or needs of user groups associated with particular resources. Consequently, argues Professor Lynton K. Caldwell of Indiana University:

Public action on behalf of natural environments has almost uniformly been defensive—until recently there has been no positive public policy to place

[2] Stewart L. Udall, *The Quiet Crisis* (New York: Avon Books, 1963), p. 94.

any but the most spectacular of them under the protective custody of government, or to formulate guidelines and standards for their management. Government has indeed too often been an agent of those who were prepared to sacrifice environmental values to economic, military, or political advantage.[3]

By the beginning of this decade tremendous achievements in science and technology had produced a level of material affluence in the United States that was the envy of the world. These achievements had extracted a severe price in destruction of the biophysical environment. Even though this could be rationalized by a belief that science and technology could fix everything tomorrow—the myth of Scientific Supremacy in Udall's words—a variety of concerned citizens were asking whether the idea of man living in balance with the natural world offered a more desirable course of action than an unquestioning faith in technological progress.

I

The main objective of a national policy for the environment is to create within the Federal government a point at which responsibility for the total environment can be fixed. Much has been accomplished since about 1960 by Congress and the executive agencies in water resources planning, air and water pollution control, provision of outdoor recreation areas, and so on. The fact remains that, despite an array of informal coordinating mechanisms, the Federal government is presently committed to a problem-by-problem approach to environmental policy. The relationships between particular environmental problems are left to take care of themselves, and there is no person or office concerned full-time with policy questions relating to the management of the natural and man-made ecosystems upon which people are dependent for their health, happiness, economic welfare, and physical survival. Decisions as to the purposes environmental policy should seek to realize must remain the responsibility of the people and their representatives, but as Caldwell, a leading student of environmental administration, has emphasized:

Our present governmental organization has not been designed to deal with environmental policy in any basic or coherent manner. The extent to which governmental reorganization may be necessary cannot be determined absolutely in advance of experience. But it does seem probable that some new facility will be needed to provide a point at which environmental policy is-

[3] Caldwell, "Administrative Possibilities," pp. 665–66.

sues cutting across jurisdictional lines of existing agencies can be identified and analyzed, and at which the complex problems involved in man's relationships with his environment can be reduced to questions and issues capable of being studied, debated, and acted upon by the President, the Congress, and the American people.[4]

The case for establishing a national policy for the environment rests upon two basic premises. The first is that the environment and man's relationship to it cannot be adequately understood and therefore cannot be adequately or effectively managed except as a highly complex, seamless web of ecological relationships. This is not to say that the science of ecology, a relatively young and undeveloped science focusing upon the biophysical environment, can provide all of the knowledge needed to create a sound environmental policy. The science of ecology does provide, however, the intellectual basis for lifting environmental policy out of the compartmentalized and largely economic framework now used by Congress and the Federal agencies. Second, there is a definite ethical basis to a national policy for the environment. This centers upon the responsibility of government as the agent of the people to manage the environment in the role of steward or protective custodian for posterity. It requires the abandonment of government's role as umpire among conflicting and competing resource interests and the adoption of the total environment as a focus for public policy.

Upon these premises the purpose of national environmental policy would be to enable the Federal government to create conditions conducive to the fullest possible measures of personal freedom, health, and spiritual satisfaction for all Americans. Thus, a national policy for the environment amounts to much more than the preservation of natural environments or the management and use of natural resources according to a method that is economically or ecologically optimal and it goes beyond the most effective use by man as the ecological dominant of applied science and technology. An effective and meaningful public policy for the environment encompasses a set of considerations and values as extensive and as various as the considerations and values people seek in the environment. In a democracy, decisions as to which set of values are best or most worth pursuing and which

[4] U.S., Congress, Senate, Committee on Interior and Insular Affairs, *A National Policy for the Environment*, 90th Cong., 2d sess., 1968 (Committee Print), p. 19. Professor Caldwell is the author of this document.

needs are to receive priority are not made by a single individual, interest group, or agency of government. For this reason, a national policy for the environment is intended to provide both the people and their government with the information needed to evaluate alternative policy choices and in so doing it would bring about a fundamental change in the process of environmental policy formation.

It is often assumed that democratic policy choices are made with information that is reliable, objective, and complete, but what is known about the political process in practice makes this assumption naïve and dangerous. Existing knowledge about the formation of environmental policy in the United States, including the preceeding chapters of this book, suggests that we should expect policy choices to favor one set of interests over another. Furthermore, those interests which emerge as "winners" do so not because their environmental and political values are better than those of others nor because they form a majority according to democratic rules of decision making. Environmental policy choices are made in practice by those interests able to manipulate the policy-making process successfully. It is a practical political matter that people disagree over which environmental qualities and values are meaningful. The cost of pursuing a policy supportive of one set of values is in denying support to another set of values, given that available resources are finite. Commenting on the passage of the Full Employment Act of 1946, political scientist Stephen K. Bailey observed that the nature of the political process makes it extremely difficult to know how and against whom political costs are exacted, or how a successful manipulation of the process is achieved. Said Bailey:

. . . majority sentiment expressed in popular elections for a particular economic policy can be, and frequently is, almost hopelessly splintered by the power struggles of competing political, adminstrative, and private interests, and is finally pieced together, if at all, only by the most laborious, complicated, and frequently covert coalition strategies.[5]

The implication of Bailey's observation is that economic policy choices are made frequently at the expense of the public interest. The same may be said of environmental policy, and from an analytical point of view the crucial question is what kind of difference it will

[5] Stephen K. Bailey, *Congress Makes A Law* (New York: Vintage Books, 1967), p. 237.

make, and to whom, that the organizational arrangements accompanying a national policy for the environment are structured in one way or another. In this context the persistent reluctance of Congressmen, administrators, and eminent scientists to engage in a careful public discussion of the politics of organizational change is a major source of difficulty. There is ample evidence of the positively harmful effects of the policies produced by existing governmental arrangements. The evidence is not all recent, although the indications that many congressmen propose to do something are very recent indeed. By late 1968 at the end of the Ninetieth Congress two approaches to instituting a national policy for the environment appeared to be politically viable, and the choice between them was delayed pending the outcome of the 1968 general election. It is important to understand the variety of proposals considered prior to the end of the Ninetieth Congress before discussing subsequent events.

II

In one form or another the idea of changing the capacity of the Federal government to handle natural resource issues has been advocated since the early 1920's, and before them during the presidency of Theodore Roosevelt. A number of suggestions have been made to reorganize the Department of the Interior, for example. Perhaps the most notable of these was the minority report of the first Hoover Commission in 1949. The Department of the Interior has been unofficially recognized for many years as America's department of natural resources. In August, 1965, Senator Frank E. Moss of Utah introduced a bill to redesignate the Department of the Interior as the Department of Natural Resources and to transfer certain agencies to and from the department. Among the benefits anticipated by Senator Moss from the reorganization would be the development of long-range, comprehensive plans for the achievement of national resource development goals. Here, as with previous reorganization proposals, it is assumed that reorganization is a necessary first step towards a more rational approach to environmental policy. The bill died in committee and was reintroduced by Senator Moss in the Ninetieth Congress.

A major obstacle to reorganization of the Interior Department has been the political strength of the Corps of Engineers. It is widely known though seldom explicitly stated that the Corps of Engineers is a major source of pork barrel projects for congressmen and of subsi-

dized water projects for widely dispersed and vociferous local interests. Over many years the corps has maintained a complex and highly
effective relationship with Congress and its local clienteles. Whatever
other questions might be asked about a department of natural resources, the likelihood of effecting a more rational environmental
policy through a reorganization such as that proposed in Senator
Moss's bill is minimal until such time as Congress and the corps are
prepared to face the political implications of this change. The brief
hearings held in the Ninetieth Congress indicate clearly that transfer
of the civil functions of the Corps of Engineers generates more opposition than any other provision of the Moss bill. They also indicate the
endless capacity of the corps to rationalize maintenance of the *status
quo.* Critical opposition to the bill also came from the Bureau of the
Budget. The bureau argued against giving to a new department of
natural resources coordination and planning functions assigned by
Congress to the Water Resources Council through the Water Resources Planning Act of 1965.[6]

The provisions of the Moss bill affect several departments and
agencies in addition to the Interior Department and the Corps of
Engineers. In general, none of these agencies is prepared to face the
uncertainty a new department of natural resources would entail. By
creating new patterns of decision making and setting new priorities
reorganization would upset the *quid pro quo* pattern of relationships
and alliances now prevalent within the executive branch and with
Congress. That there is interagency conflict and competition and that
Congress and the agencies are anxious to protect and perpetuate
existing interests are by now far from profound observations about
environmental policy making. The perplexing problem after forty
years of effort to reorganize the Interior Department is the inability of
those involved to treat conflict and competition overtly as central
political issues. It is possible that competition at least may have
beneficial as well as adverse consequences and this possibility merits
open discussion before Congress.

Interagency conflict and competition also characterize a number of
other attempts to improve environmental policy. Senator Gaylord
Nelson of Wisconsin introduced a bill into the Eighty-ninth Congress

[6] U.S., Congress, Senate, Committee on Government Operations, *Hearings, Redesignate the Department of the Interior as the Department of
Natural Resources,* 90th Cong., 1st sess., 1968, pp. 129–40 and *passim.*

in July, 1965, to authorize the Secretary of the Interior to conduct a program of research and survey into the natural environmental systems of the United States. In order for the Secretary of the Interior to conduct this program without duplicating the work of other Federal agencies, the bill proposed to give the Interior Department certain coordination and evaluation functions. The bill provided, for example, that the Interior Department maintain an inventory of resource development projects having significant impact on the natural environment. The bill also provided for the establishment of a system of natural areas for scientific purposes. The Secretary of the Interior would accomplish this through coordination with other Federal agencies.

The bill would have made the Interior Department the lead agency in the Federal establishment for ecological research and surveys. In the hearings on the bill those government agencies with significant research programs of their own showed no enthusiasm for the aggrandizement of the Interior Department. Slightly more than a year before the hearings, and about six months before Senator Nelson introduced his bill, President Johnson asked the Office of Science and Technology and the Bureau of the Budget to recommend the best way of directing Federal efforts aimed at advancing scientific understanding of natural plant and animal communities and their relationship to man. Taking refuge in the failure of the Office of Science and Technology and the Bureau of the Budget to complete their study prior to the hearings, government witnesses asked Congress to delay action on the Nelson bill. The hearings on the bill were completed in a single day. Despite support for the bill by a large number of nongovernment witnesses, no further action was taken in the Eighty-ninth Congress. Senator Nelson reintroduced his bill in the Ninetieth Congress and later incorporated its provisions into bills which would have created also a council on environmental quality in the Executive Office of the President. However, the study commissioned by President Johnson remained tied up in the office of the President for almost three years and none of the ecological research and survey bills introduced during that time made any progress. The Office of Science and Technology has a vested interest in maintaining its position as the primary source of advice to the President on scientific and technological matters, including Federal research programs and relations between government and the scientific and engineering communities. Designation of the Interior Department as the lead agency for ecological research posed a threat to the jurisdiction of the office. The further proposal to locate a council on environmental quality in the Office of the President threatened to weaken the role and influence of the Office of Science and Technology within the circle of presidential advisors.

The first bill to propose a high-level council of environmental advisors was one introduced by Senator James Murray of Montana during the Eighty-sixth Congress. Senator Murray suggested the creation of a council of resources and conservation advisors. The bill failed to pass, as did similar bills before the Eighty-seventh Congress. In February, 1965, Senator George McGovern of South Dakota introduced a bill calling for a council of resources and conservation advisors and for select committees in the House and the Senate to evaluate the reports of the council. No hearings were held on the McGovern bill. In 1960, Senator John F. Kennedy endorsed the idea of an advisory council as proposed by Senator Murray, but following his election to the presidency he proposed instead a presidential advisory committee on natural resources as a mechanism for improved coordination within the executive. He initiated a study by the National Academy of Sciences on the scope of Federal research and planning relating to natural resources and conservation. The NAS report released in December, 1962, was a major breakthrough in government thinking about environmental policy. It recommended a central natural resources group within the Federal government to act as an environmental intelligence agency. The proposed agency would be primarily concerned with research and the NAS report was not clear about the political role it would play. Nevertheless, the NAS report proposed to move away from the traditional role of government as umpire among conflicting resource interests toward the concept of environmental stewardship. In this respect it contrasted markedly with a 1963 report issued by the Federal Council for Science and Technology. The FCST recommended either an improvement of existing coordinating mechanisms or a new interdepartmental committee on natural resources.

The FCST report failed to recognize the basic weakness of *ad hoc* administrative rearrangements within the executive.[7] Such modifica-

---

[7] Attempts to improve the capacity of Federal agencies to handle environmental policy have been made by the agencies themselves in the past decade, although a separate essay would be required to discuss these changes fully. The complexity of the agency structure, including interagency coordinating

tions perpetuate a resource-by-resource approach to environmental policy and leave unchanged the formal responsibility of a large number of departments and agencies for selected aspects of the environment. In addition, they leave unchanged the capacity of the executive to exercise policy-making initiative, and one result of this is to strengthen the influence of Congress in determining who benefits from Federal programs and policies. Michael Brewer pointed out in his recent analysis of the situation that Federal resource development policies have provided a strong motivation for Congress to dominate the initiation of new programs.[8] This is because these programs mean brick-and-mortar projects with an immediate impact on local employment and prospects for tangible monuments to the beneficence of local representatives. A complex system of alliances between individual resource agencies and legislative committees has proven very profitable for both sides. In recent years, as the Federal budget for research and development has increased, Congress has attempted to control the allocation of Federal research funds in much the same way and for much the same reasons as are applicable in the case of resource development funds.

For the past several years the Subcommittee on Science, Research, and Development of the House Committee on Science and Astronautics has been examining the implications of modern technology. Under the chairmanship of Representative Emilio Q. Daddario of Connecticut the subcommittee has pulled together a tremendous amount of information with the help of witnesses from the scientific community, from industry, and from a number of government research agencies. Although the interests of the subcommittee have been wide-ranging, considerable attention has been given to the environmental impact of technology. The subcommittee was formed in August, 1963, to strengthen congressional sources of advice and information on science and technology and to recommend effective means of using science and technology to achieve broad national goals. Based on its studies the subcommittee has concluded that coping with science and tech-

---

committees, is illustrated in Senate, Interior Committee, *National Policy for the Environment*, pp. 32–34.

[8] Michael F. Brewer, "Resource Quality: New Dimensions and Problems for Public Policy," in S. V. Ciriacy-Wantrup and James J. Parsons, eds., *Natural Resources: Quality and Quantity* (Berkeley: University of California Press, 1967), p. 209.

nology demands more science and technology. In 1966, for example, it supported significant increases in Federal funding for science and engineering related to environmental quality. For waste management alone, it recommended a ten-fold increase over a five-year period of the level of funding for research, development, and demonstration projects ($30 million per year in 1966).

This "more of the same" approach applied also to governmental organization. Reporting to the full committee in 1967, Representative Daddario observed that "Congress can strengthen its ability to assess and judge technological programs without radical change" in existing government organization.[9] The activities of the subcommittee have resulted in only one legislative proposal, a bill which chairman Daddario introduced in the Ninetieth Congress. It would create a technology assessment board of five members. The members would be appointed by the President on the basis of their qualifications, but they would function independently of the executive branch. The functions of the board would include the making of a continuing assessment of current and potential technology, and the recommendation of ways to use technology without incurring major unforeseen consequences. The bill also provides for a general advisory council of twelve members appointed by the President. The advisory council members would serve for six years; board members for five. The board would be required to maintain liaison with the Office of Science and Technology and the Federal Council for Science and Technology. Congressional oversight would be provided by the House Committee on Science and Astronautics and the Senate Committee on Labor and Public Welfare. The bill was introduced mainly to promote congressional discussion of technology assessment. When the National Academy of Sciences and the National Academy of Engineering complete their studies of technology assessment a new bill undoubtedly will be prepared and additional hearings held.

These extensive efforts by the House subcommittee have no real counterpart in the Senate. However, Senator Edmund Muskie of Maine did introduce a resolution in the Eighty-ninth Congress to create a select Senate committee on technology and the human environment. Senator Muskie originally proposed a committee of fifteen members drawn from five Senate standing committees. The select

[9] U.S., Congress, House, Committee on Science and Astronautics, *Technology Assessment*, 90th Cong., 1st sess., 1967 (Committee Print), p. 12.

committee would be charged with developing the information and recommendations needed by the Senate to consider the implications of science and technology as they relate to the individual and his environment. The select committee would have a limited life, during which it would prepare a report, and no powers to influence legislation directly. It would be primarily a device to bolster the expertise of the Senate in analyzing environmental policy alternatives. After brief hearings in December, 1966, and more lengthy hearings early in the Ninetieth Congress, Senator Muskie expressed satisfaction and adjourned his subcommittee saying that his next move would be to expedite the resolution. According to *Science*, however, this move was sidetracked by colleagues fearful of their own committee jurisdictions.[10] Senator Muskie reported that initial opposition came from Senator Henry M. Jackson, of Washington, chairman of the Senate Interior Committee, and later from Senator Fred R. Harris of Oklahoma, chairman of the Senate Subcommittee on Government Research. As a result, no further action was taken on the resolution in the Ninetieth Congress and Senator Muskie reintroduced the resolution in the Ninety-first Congress with an amendment to increase the select committee by three members drawn from the Senate Government Operations Committee, on which Senator Jackson and Senator Harris both serve.

III

The variety of proposals before Congress to modify the capacity of the Federal government to handle environmental policy had been effectively reduced to one at the beginning of the second session of the Ninetieth Congress. This was the proposal to create a council of environmental advisers in the Office of the President. The alternative strategies were contained in bills which had been killed in committee or were unlikely to be scheduled for committee hearings. The bill which most closely approximated the stewardship concept was one introduced by Senator Jackson and the ranking minority member of the Senate Interior Committee, Senator Thomas Kuchel of California. The Jackson-Kuchel bill had two titles. The first would have created a program of ecological research and surveys in the Interior Department. The second would have established a five-member council on environmental quality in the Office of the President. The bill required

[10] *Science*, CLXIII (March 14, 1969), 1179.

the council to study and analyze environmental trends, to advise the President on national policies for the environment, and to collect and publicize information about the changing state of the environment in America. It also required the council to appraise Federal and federally funded programs with an impact on the environment. The council on environmental quality outlined in the bill would be composed of members professionally qualified to analyze and interpret environmental trends and responsive to the scientific, economic, social, aesthetic, and cultural needs and interests of the nation.

Bills with provisions very similar to the Jackson-Kuchel bill were introduced by Senator Nelson and Representative John Dingell of Michigan. Senator Nelson's bill contained a title which would have created a program of comprehensive waste management research in the Department of Health, Education, and Welfare. It was referred to the Senate Public Works Committee and died there. The Dingell bill was limited to the setting up of a council on environmental quality. It was initially referred to the House Interior Committee and later transmitted to the House Science and Astronautics Committee. The latter committee also received three identical House bills which would have created a council of ecological advisers in the Office of the President. A principal difference between the Jackson-Kuchel bill and these three House bills was that the latter proposed a nine-member council composed of representatives from science, industry, and other professions concerned with environmental and ecological problems.

Neither a council on environmental quality nor a council of ecological advisers as proposed in legislation before the Ninetieth Congress would have had formal authority to enforce its recommendations. In order for either council to be effective the people appointed by the President would have had to command the highest national prestige and respect, and to capitalize fully on its status in the Executive Office of the President a council would require the vigorous support of the President it advised. But what of the impact of a council on Congress? The proposals for a council of ecological advisers did not formally require the regular transmission of reports to Congress. The bills proposing a council on environmental quality did contain this requirement but did not specify what should happen to the reports once Congress received them. The Full Employment Act of 1946 created not only a Council of Economic Advisers in the Office of the President but also a joint committee of Congress to review and act on the annual economic report. The House and Senate Interior committees come closest in many ways to meeting the need for congressional review of environmental legislation, but their jurisdiction overlaps that of several other existing committees some of which might also claim a legitimate interest in the work of a council on environmental quality or council of ecological advisers. The lack of provisions to reorganize Congress was a major weakness of the council proposals before the Ninetieth Congress.

In the first three months of 1968 the Daddario subcommittee of the House Science and Astronautics Committee held hearings on the three bills to create a council of ecological advisers and on the Dingell bill to create a council on environmental quality. In almost six hundred pages of testimony concerning the environmental impact of science and technology these bills received scant attention. It was as if the subcommittee had set out to answer the wrong set of questions given the nature of the measures before it. Chairman Daddario stated that he considered the hearings a natural sequence to those held in 1966 on the adequacy of technology for pollution abatement. Two days were devoted to the technology of air pollution control, one day to water pollution control, and one day to waste disposal problems. Atomic waste disposal and the environmental side-effects of agricultural programs received less attention. On the day reserved for ecologists, attention focused on mechanisms for promoting ecological research, but the witnesses from the Ecological Society of America confessed they had given little thought to the utility of a council of ecological advisers.

The subcommittee report on the hearings declared that science and technology held the key to the future of the environment.[11] The objective, it said, should be to keep the environment in good operating condition like any other machine, because this was the best and most efficient way to run the world. The report therefore urged adoption of a national policy for environmental management based on the use of science and technology in a way that would avoid the mistakes of past management. The subcommittee concluded that only if improved interagency coordination failed to realize this policy should Congress consider a permanent council of environmental advisers in the Office of the President. This conclusion was in line with the recommenda-

[11] U.S., Congress, House, Committee on Science and Astronautics, *Managing the Environment*, 90th Cong., 2d sess., 1968 (Committee Print).

tions of the study by the Bureau of the Budget and the Office of Science and Technology ordered by President Johnson in 1965. The study was released during the Daddario subcommittee hearings. It was based in large part on the findings of a panel of experts assembled by the Office of Science and Technology and it was hardly surprising that it recommended designation of the Office of Science and Technology as the lead agency for all Federal efforts to understand the environment.

The Daddario subcommittee report was a rejection of the stewardship concept underlying the Jackson-Kuchel bill. It asserted the technological and coordinate approach recommended to President Kennedy in the 1963 report of the Federal Council for Science and Technology noted earlier. A national policy for environmental management would not require the Federal government to adopt the responsibility of environmental stewardship nor would it substitute environments as opposed to discrete resources as the focus for environmental administration. Environmental management was clearly in the tradition of economic concepts of conservation; the term itself suggested a businessman's approach. It was based on a conservative, "hair of the dog" philosophy which threatened to multiply rather than solve problems created in large measure by the unbridled application of science and technology to the natural world. In order to promote discussion of both environmental management and stewardship as bases for a national environmental policy, Senator Jackson took advantage of a recommendation by the Daddario subcommittee for periodic informal meetings of House and Senate committees concerned with environmental policy making.

In July, 1968, the Senate Interior Committee and the House Science and Astronautics Committee convened a Joint House-Senate Colloquium to discuss a national policy for the environment. The meeting was chaired by Senator Jackson and Representative George Miller of California, chairmen of the sponsoring committees, and was attended by several Cabinet members and an invited audience from the industrial, scientific, and academic communities. A panel of distinguished witnesses included Laurance Rockefeller and the Dean of the Kennedy School of Government at Harvard University, Don K. Price. The meeting was described by one of those present as the biggest social gathering during the second session of the Ninetieth Congress. The colloquium also had a symbolic significance; it was the first time that the House and Senate committees most concerned with improving environmental policy making had sat together publicly to discuss their common concerns.

The colloquium provided an opportunity for congressmen and administrators retiring at the end of 1968 to speak their minds. However, none of those present offered ideas that had not been heard previously in congressional hearings or government reports. There was some encouragement in the agreement between Senator Jackson and Representative Miller that a further meeting might be profitable. Looking at the volume of verbal testimony and written evidence already available, it can be argued that the colloquium might better have been devoted to an open discussion of the political obstacles in the way of reorganization to improve environmental policy. The congressional white paper published after the colloquium was noncommittal. It noted stewardship and management as possible bases for a national environmental policy but did not choose between them.[12] It was evident that a choice would not be made until after the 1968 general election.

Environmental issues remained in the background of the 1968 election campaign. However, the environment was selected as a topic for one of the policy task forces created by President-elect Nixon. The task force was headed by the President of the Conservation Foundation, Russell E. Train, who was subsequently appointed Under Secretary of the Interior. Its report urged improved environmental management as a principal objective of the Nixon administration. Mammoth new programs were not required, said the task force. Emphasis should be placed instead on making existing programs work. The task force recommended appointment of a special presidential assistant for environmental affairs who would also serve as executive secretary of a new President's Council on the Environment to be chaired by the Vice-President.[13] The proposed council would act as a more comprehensive interagency coordinating device than the President's Council on Recreation and Natural Beauty created by President Johnson in May, 1966. Like the Johnson council, the council recommended by the task

[12] U.S., Congress, Senate Committee on Interior and Insular Affairs and House Committee on Science and Astronautics, *Congressional White Paper on a National Policy for the Environment*, 90th Cong., 2d sess., 1968 (Committee Print).

[13] U.S., *Congressional Record*, 91st Cong., 1st sess., CXV (1969), S1794.

force would exist at the pleasure of the President and would have no statutory permanence as an agency of the Executive Office of the President.

After assuming office, President Nixon chose to refuse the advice of the task force concerning a special presidential assistant because, as his science adviser explained to the Senate Interior Committee, the number of presidential assistants was already too large. The President did favor a Cabinet-level interagency coordinating committee and in February, 1969, he began reviewing a draft executive order to create such a committee. The order was prepared by the Office of Science and Technology, which proposed to call the committee the Environmental Quality Council. Members of the council would be Cabinet officers and staff support would be provided by the Office of Science and Technology. Senator Jackson let his opposition to this proposal be known and scheduled hearings for mid-April on his bill to create an environmental advisory council as a permanent branch of the Office of the President. The Jackson bill had been reintroduced with minor amendments from the Ninetieth Congress and was cosponsored in the Ninety-first Congress by Senator Ted Stevens of Alaska, a minority member of the Senate Interior Committee. Senator Jackson observed that in the opinion of some authorities the environmental quality council proposed by the Office of Science and Technology "is a highly visible but ineffectual gesture on behalf of environmental policy; that it promises more rhetoric than action; and that it will be an unobtrusive symbol of concern." [14] In Senator Jackson's own view it was unrealistic to expect a Cabinet officer to criticize the programs of his department or those of other Cabinet members at interdepartmental committee meetings.

On the eve of the hearing on the Jackson-Stevens bill, President Nixon was persuaded to delay creation of an environmental quality council by executive order. Senator Jackson had suggested to the President's staff that the administration should not decide on a rigid format for handling environmental policy until after all the arguments had been heard at the Senate hearing. His powerful position as chairman of the Senate Interior Committee gave him control over the fate of much environmental legislation and a strong bargaining position with the administration. At the hearing, administration witnesses

[14] *Christian Science Monitor*, April 7, 1969.

toned down their opposition to Senate proposals for an environmental advisory council in the Office of the President. They argued that the President needed an action-oriented council to settle current environmental problems and that an interagency group could fill this need. Senator Jackson insisted that the most important need was for a means of establishing environmental policy goals and priorities on a long-range basis. Through Dr. Lee A. DuBridge, the President's science adviser and director of the Office of Science and Technology, the administration offered the basis for a compromise. DuBridge stated the administration's willingness to work with Senator Jackson in formulating a statutory declaration of national policy for the environment, which would go some way toward meeting Jackson's insistence that attention be given to long-range policy goals.[15]

After a month and a half of negotiations between Senator Jackson and the White House staff, President Nixon established an interdepartmental Environmental Quality Council. On the same day and with prior approval of the administration Senator Jackson released the text of a proposed national policy for the environment.[16] Until it is acted on by Congress Jackson's proposal will have no effect. However, Jackson has obtained agreement that the administration will not oppose enactment of a statement of national policy for the environment. The administration has agreed further not to oppose creation of a council on environmental quality in the Office of the President. If approved by Congress, the proposed national policy would require Federal officials to apply a four-point standard to every legislative and administrative act likely to have significant consequences for the quality of the environment: Has the impact of the act been studied? Have the adverse effects which cannot be avoided by following alter-

---

[15] *Ibid.*, June 4, 1969.

[16] *Ibid.* The Environmental Quality Council will be composed of the President (chairman), the Vice-President, and the Secretaries of Agriculture, Commerce, the Interior, Transportation, Housing and Urban Development, and Health, Education, and Welfare. The director of the Bureau of the Budget, the chairman of the Council of Economic Advisers, and the executive secretary of the Urban Affairs Council may participate in meetings, and the heads of other agencies may be invited to attend as required by the business of the council. The director of the Office of Science and Technology will be executive secretary of the Environmental Quality Council and will provide staff support. The order signed by President Nixon also created a Citizen's Advisory Committee on Environmental Quality of fifteen members, chaired by Laurance Rockefeller.

native courses of action been justified by considerations of national policy? Are local short-term uses of the environment consistent with long-term goals? Are irreversible and irretrievable commitments of resources warranted? These criteria are incorporated in an amended version of the Jackson-Stevens bill which would create a council on environmental quality.

IV

The essence of the compromise negotiated between Senator Jackson and the Nixon administration was that the advocates of environmental management and the advocates of environmental stewardship would each get a high-level advisory group. The President's Environmental Quality Council is the kind of device persistently advocated by the Daddario subcommittee, the Office of Science and Technology, and a variety of private and public interests associated with the rapidly growing research and development business. It may be expected to recommend policies which are technological and coordinative in approach and designed to settle short-term environmental issues. It is essentially a mechanism for treating the symptoms rather than the environmental quality, if approved by Congress, would have a respon-causes of environmental deterioration. On the other hand, a council on sibility for long-term policy goals aimed at the attainment of a wide range of economic, social, and aesthetic values. The advocates of this structure are liberal congressmen, a variety of conservation organizations, and several prominent individuals in government and the academic community, who have stressed the need to break away from the shackles of fragmented government responsibility for the environment.

The wisdom of the compromise pressed for by Senator Jackson rests upon the assumption that the Nixon administration will lend vigorous support to a national policy for the environment and a council on environmental quality once Congress approves these measures. But President Nixon is already on record as preferring to work through an interdepartmental committee, presumably because he expects this kind of structure to develop policy choices he can support. If a council on environmental quality is created it will have members appointed by the President and can be expected to recommend policies in tune with President Nixon's own preferences. The closest parallel to a council on environmental quality is the Council of Economic Advisers, whose advice reflects the policy commitments and political philosophy of the President. It is conservative when the President is conservative, and liberal when he is liberal. Presumably, a council on environmental quality will respond to similar political alternations. Senator Jackson's proposed national policy for the environment is also subject to differing interpretations, and the nature of the decisions it produces may vary considerably depending upon which political party exercises control over the Congress and the Presidency. Of the two major political parties, the Democratic party has traditionally upheld a strengthening of the Federal role in economic and social change. The majority of proposals to move Federal policy in the direction of stewardship have been sponsored by congressmen who are Democrats or liberals, or both.[17] Until their numbers are larger and until their position receives the enthusiastic support of the President, environmental management is likely to be the concept underlying national policy for the environment.

The concept of environmental stewardship, which seemed to offer hope of bringing a measure of sanity to environmental policy, appears to have been shelved. Even if Senator Jackson and others in Congress are successful in securing approval of a council on environmental quality and a statement of national environmental policy, the Nixon administration is committed to another concept, one which in essence legitimizes the *status quo*. There is little to be gained from forcing a council on environmental quality on President Nixon, although under a different administration the stewardship concept may stand more chance of success. For the immediate future Senator Jackson can be most effective by pressing for reforms closer to his own bailiwick.

One of these is the creation of a joint committee of Congress on the environment and the development of a working relationship between this committee and the other committees of Congress. A second needed improvement is in congressional staffing. Existing levels of staffing for both majority and minority members is inadequate to permit thorough consideration of environmental legislation. Congressional response to environmental problems could also be improved by

[17] The number of bills before Congress to modify the capacity of the Federal government to handle environmental policy increased markedly in the Ninety-first Congress. A brief explanation of most of the bills will be found in *Conservation Report*, a weekly publication of the National Wildlife Federation, Washington, D.C.

a number of reforms which would generally improve congressional procedures and which have already been placed before Congress in reform bills introduced in the Ninety-first Congress. These include allowing committees to hold hearings in the fall, when Congress is not in session, in order to prepare legislation for the first few months of Congress, and the provision of electronic data-processing equipment to enable Congress to come to grips with a Federal budget of nearly $200 billion.

Another alternative that could yield constructive results would be to press for a constitutional amendment to provide the American people with a "conservation bill of rights." This approach has been embodied in legislation sponsored in the Ninetieth and Ninety-first Congresses. Briefly, it would guarantee to the people the right to clean air, pure water, freedom from unnecessary noise, and other natural, scenic, historic, and aesthetic qualities. It would also require Congress to conduct periodic inventories of the nation's natural environments and would prohibit government agencies at all levels from taking actions likely to have adverse environmental impact without first conducting a public hearing. The wording of Senator Jackson's proposed national policy follows the intent of the constitutional amendment. It would declare as an objective of national policy protection of the fundamental and inalienable right of each person to a healthful environment. An amendment to the Constitution would be more binding than a congressional declaration of intent and, although it would take a long time, it would have the effect of involving the courts much more directly in environmental issues than has so far been the case.

It would be an exaggeration to suggest that if Congress would put its own house in order, or would enact a constitutional amendment, the conflicts now characteristic of environmental policy making would disappear. But the history of efforts to establish a national policy for the environment indicates that when the President is unable or unwilling to act, Congress must take the lead in determining whether the ends to be served by environmental policy will improve human well-being and enrich the meaning of life for the people of the United States. This task requires institutional arrangements that can reach out to larger and more inclusive ends than those which can be accommodated to the seniority system, the established committee structure, and the wishes of the wealthiest constituents. Severe environmental problems created in large part by science and technology have forced into the open questions about the kind of environment that will allow fruition of the human spirit. No amount of environmental management will answer these questions because science and technology have no built-in social purpose. Congress must equip itself to remedy this deficiency.

15. Conclusions:

Congress and the Environment of the Future

RICHARD A. COOLEY and GEOFFREY WANDESFORDE-SMITH

THE central problem raised by the essays in this book is whether or not the American political system, and especially Congress, can deal effectively with both a wide range of specific environmental issues and with the larger challenge of providing the nation with a meaningful public policy for the environment as a whole. The major conclusion is inescapable and bitterly disappointing to those aware of the environmental crisis facing the nation. It is that Congress has failed to do more than make halting progress through a series of incremental adjustments. Every chapter in this book points to serious flaws in the response of Congress to the basic moral and political issues posed by the quiet crisis identified by Stewart Udall in 1963. These issues have been subordinated to a set of narrow and short-term interests largely irrelevant to the nature of the problem at hand.

Congress has been criticized severely in a well-known and recent book by Drew Pearson and Jack Anderson, *The Case Against Congress*, as an institution riddled with corruption and closely linked with the larger and more influential economic special interests. But it is not the corruption of a few congressmen that should cause deep concern. The more telling case against Congress is its frequent unresponsiveness, paralysis, negativism, and irrelevance in the face of the pressing political issues of our times. As the political analyst, Ronald Steel, put it recently:

Congress cannot deal with these problems because it can scarcely admit that they exist without throwing into question the beliefs held by individual congressmen. . . . Incapable of leading the process of social reform, unwilling to offer a responsible challenge to the arbitrary power of the executive branch, responsive to the demands of economic interest groups at the expense of the public welfare, Congress has fallen into disrepute without even realizing that anything is wrong.[1]

This statement should not be allowed to obscure the highly commendable efforts of some members of Congress whose names have appeared repeatedly in this book as advocates of a more sane and sensible congressional response to environmental problems. They are from both major political parties, although most of them tend to adopt positions which can be described as liberal as opposed to conservative. They seek an active role for government, especially the Federal government, in changing the nature of American society; they are frequently critical of the structure of Congress and tend not to have sufficient seniority to change it; and they are in a minority. Since Congress prides itself on being responsive to the wishes of the people, can it be assumed that a majority of voters favor a backward approach to the resolution of environmental issues? And if not, what circumstances may be expected to produce a more adequate congressional response?

I

There is evidence that the people of the United States are acutely aware of the degraded state of their environment and favor positive government action to improve and enhance the quality of their surroundings. In August, 1968, journalist Robert Cahn of the *Christian Science Monitor* concluded a landmark study of the National Park System.[2] The more than two thousand responses he received to a questionnaire constituted the largest public survey conducted on national park policy. Cahn reported responses from a wide variety of park users and potential users. He concluded that the vast majority of those responding want the national parks preserved, even at the expense of personal sacrifice or limitations on park use. Strong support was expressed for several specific measures including drastic limitations on stays in park campgrounds, park entrance fees and campground user fees, restrictions on automobile access to parks, and the use of public transportation rather than private use of cars within

[1] Ronald Steel, "Inside Dope," *New York Review of Books,* XII, No. 3 (February 13, 1969), 10.

[2] Robert Cahn, *Will Success Spoil the National Parks?* (Boston: Christian Science Publishing Society, 1968).

parks. National parks represent only one aspect of environmental policy; also the sample of views reported by Cahn may be biased because the readers of the *Christian Science Monitor* that Cahn sampled are not necessarily a representative cross section of the general public, and possibly an overly large percentage of responses came from those already committed to park preservation. Nevertheless, the Cahn study demonstrated a deep concern over the future of the American outdoor environment that extended to suggestions of finding ways to aid minority groups, particularly those without the financial means or transportation, to visit national parks.

A more detailed survey of public opinion was recently conducted by the Gallup poll and reported by the National Wildlife Federation. This survey explored public reaction to a broad range of environmental problems. At hearings before the Senate Interior Committee in April, 1969, a spokesman for the federation stated emphatically: "We concluded that the American public appreciates quality in the environment, deplores what is happening to it, and stands ready to support corrective measures, even to the extent of paying for it."[3] Also in April, 1969, Senator Henry M. Jackson of Washington told the National Audubon Society that in his view "the public sense of priorities and those of the government are poles apart with respect to the importance of environmental matters." And he made it clear it was the public rather than government who were convinced real progress lay in the direction of adapting "our lives to the natural conditions, to the environment and to the ecological principles which govern life on this earth."[4]

One of the reasons why Congress has lagged behind public opinion was pointed out by Senator Jackson in a paper published in the July-August, 1968, issue of *Public Administration Review*. The committee system of Congress, he said, was designed to achieve many specific objectives but was not readily adaptable to the needs of an over-all environmental policy. Since no one committee jurisdiction encompasses all environmental legislation, he felt that Congress must

---

[3] Louis S. Clapper, "Ecological Systems and Environmental Quality," statement on behalf of the National Wildlife Federation before the Senate Committee on Interior and Insular Affairs, April 16, 1969 (mimeographed).

[4] Senator Henry M. Jackson, "A National Policy for the Environment," address before the National Audubon Society, St. Louis, Missouri, April 26, 1969 (mimeographed).

look toward some joint action by the committees principally involved.[5] A more straightforward way for Congress to modify its structure would be to reorganize the committee system itself by creating, for example, a committee on environmental quality in each house, or a joint committee. This has been proposed in connection with efforts to create a council on environmental quality in the Executive Office of the President, noted in the preceding chapter. A precedent exists in the Full Employment Act of 1946 which created the Council of Economic Advisors and a Joint Economic Committee of Congress.

The papers in this book reaffirm the conclusion that the congressional committee system hinders rather than assists the careful evaluation of environmental legislation. Congress is particularly prone to treat environmental issues according to its own internally defined values rather than in relation to values appropriate to the issues themselves. The congressional committee system, for example, usually requires the referral of environmental policy bills to several committees. There is no committee in either the House or the Senate with responsibility broad enough to encompass proposals as diverse as the protection of endangered species and the elimination of automobile junk yards in urban areas, although both proposals require systematic consideration from the viewpoint of the total environment. As a consequence, bills dealing with environmental issues often are given inadequate consideration. The case of the junked auto disposal bill is an excellent illustration of the limitations inherent in present committee jurisdictions. No committee system would be perfect in the sense that, to use an economist's phrase, no one committee could successfully internalize the environmental externalities attaching to all the bills brought before Congress. For this reason a joint committee, or House and Senate environmental quality committees, should be supplemented by both formal and informal arrangements permitting more frequent joint meetings of committees in both houses on an *ad hoc* basis. There is a precedent here in the July, 1968, colloquium convened by the Senate Interior Committee and the House Science and Astronautics Committee to discuss a national policy for the environment. Joint meetings of committees within each house also have precedents and should be encouraged.

A number of other conclusions about Congress are evident from this

[5] Senator Henry M. Jackson, "Environmental Policy and the Congress," *Public Administration Review*, XXVIII, No. 4 (July/August, 1968), 303–5.

book. One is that the present, highly fragmented committee system favors special, frequently economic, interests at the expense of giving adequate recognition to the full range of values and interests to be served by environmental policy. Repeatedly, the case studies demonstrate a symbiotic relationship between congressmen and interest groups with a material stake in government programs: the research and development interests with the House Subcommittee on Science, Research, and Development; the construction, flood control, navigation, and mass recreation interests with the Committees on Public Works; the air transportation groups with the Commerce Committees; the mining interests with Subcommittees on Mining and Minerals. This pattern is well known, even widely accepted. But its costs are less well known largely because they accrue to the public at large and are charged against its interest in a quality environment. Economic interests have a major stake in a fragmented committee structure dominated by a few powerful committee chairmen and they are firmly entrenched. Asking the House Subcommittee on Science, Research, and Development to evaluate the environmental consequences of science and technology is akin to asking the Bureau of Reclamation or the Corps of Engineers about the feasibility of diverting the Columbia River to the Southwest. When enthusiasts undertake a feasibility study or a program evaluation, they invariably find that it is feasible. It is little wonder that those concerned about the environment almost always find themselves fighting a rear guard action.

The failure of senior congressmen to press for reorganization of committees with jurisdiction over environmental legislation is a further indictment of a seniority system already subjected to extensive criticism. Seniority carries with it a capacity to influence the referral of bills to committee. This book reveals no logical pattern of referrals. Many committees are involved and this has the effect of dissipating the energy of congressmen in reviewing legislation. This effect is magnified by inadequate staff support to enable legislators to master the welter of technical details frequently involved in environmental legislation. Senator Douglas' testimony on the Junked Auto Disposal Act, for example, contained many statistical discrepancies and caused some embarrassment during the hearings when his position was successfully attacked by scrap iron and junk-yard dealers. More careful staff support and preparation for the hearings might have helped save the Junked Auto Disposal Act from being itself junked. Personal staff, committee staff, and the staff of the Legislative Reference Service are not sufficient to keep congressmen well informed and to save them from embarrassment before expert witnesses. It is partly because of this weakness that some congressmen are led to uncritical acceptance of the advice of the interests they are supposed to regulate and oversee. Not all congressmen have a primary interest in environmental policy. Some have access to informal sources of advice in universities, foundations, and private firms. In general, however, the level of understanding of environmental problems among congressmen appears to be low and serious attention should be given to strengthening, probably through the Legislative Reference Service, congressional sources of information and advice on the volume and complexity of environmental legislation.

That the committee structure tends to place tremendous power in the hands of a few individual congressmen is well illustrated by these case studies. As chairman of the House Interior and Insular Affairs Committee, Representative Wayne Aspinall has demonstrated time and again the power of his position to influence the timing, character, and outcome of almost all environmental legislation, and because of his particular philosophy and outlook, as well as his close alignments with various economic interests, that power has been used almost exclusively in a negative way. Perhaps the most striking example revealed in these pages was his ability to delay passage of the wilderness bill for nearly a decade despite intensive public pressure for the legislation.

While Wayne Aspinall has been an anathema to conservation interests, his counterpart in the upper chamber has been an enigma. As chairman of the Senate Interior and Insular Affairs Committee, Senator Henry M. Jackson has pressed vigorously for environmental legislation and is considered by many as one of the most ardent and influential leaders of the "third wave" of the conservation movement. To others, however, his support of environmental legislation is viewed more as an attempt to offset the adverse electoral consequences of his hard-line policies on national defense and foreign relations. For a senator from a state that contains some of America's most beautiful natural environments and most ardent outdoor recreation enthusiasts as well as one of the nation's principal defense and aerospace contractors, the mix of policies espoused by Senator Jackson may be most defensible in practical political terms. However, a remarkable feature of the modern conservation movement is its impatience with the demands of practical politics. It is a movement pressing for policies principled by strong moral and ethical convictions. Ironically, conservationists have been forced into a political alliance with Senator Jackson, almost to the point where it is considered bad form to criticize him. It may be that Senator Jackson is more deeply committed to conservation and environmental quality than some of his critics are prepared to admit. It may be also that Senator Jackson himself finds no contradictions among the set of foreign and domestic policies he advocates. Whatever his personal motives may be, it is certain that Senator Jackson is powerful and that he has done much for the conservation movement.

As Stewart Udall pointed out in his recent book, *1976: Agenda for Tomorrow*, Congress has been the least adaptable, least dynamic entity of our constitutional triad: "Only when its committees and individual members think and speak for the nation as a whole—and not as standpat defenders of special interests or the narrow aims of the several states—is the Congress worthy of its highest mission. . . . The time has come for Congress to play a more positive role in the life of the nation." [6]

II

A further consequence of the poor organization of Congress for handling environmental issues is that Congress is placed at a disadvantage vis-à-vis the executive. In a recent article in *Harpers*, Arthur Blaustein asserted that "it is a simple fact that for the past thirty-six years [Congress] has become almost exclusively dependent on the Executive Branch for any forward motion." One is hard pressed, he said, to think of any important legislation in the last three decades that can be attributed solely to Congress. [7] Presidential leadership and initiative was a factor of prime importance in nearly all the environmental legislation considered or enacted during the 1960's. In the passage of the Highway Beautificaction Act of 1965, for example, the President and his First Lady were able to mobilize support on a national basis because the goals of the legislation promised to benefit

[6] Stewart L. Udall, *1976: Agenda for Tomorrow* (New York: Harcourt, Brace and World, 1968), pp. 147–48.
[7] Arthur Blaustein, "536 Characters in Search of a Legislative Program," *Harper's Magazine*, CCXXXVIII, No. 1426 (March, 1969), 31.

citizens regardless of their location in one or another congressional district. The influence of the highway advertising lobby was much less powerful in relation to the country as a whole than it was within the boundaries of individual states and districts. Despite the opposition of many congressmen, President Johnson was able to secure passage of the act. But presidential leadership and initiative proved insufficient to overcome obstructions Congress can, and frequently does, place in the way of proposals it feels are too far-reaching, and the act as finally passed was little more than a cosmetic approach to the problem of cleaning up the landscape along the nation's highways. In pursuit of limited and constituency-oriented objectives Congress is able to use a variety of tactics, some of the most effective of which are negative.

Congress has also steadfastly refused to face up to the need for governmental reorganization in the executive branch to reduce the highly diffuse and fragmental system of decision making on environmental issues that makes bargaining among agencies and levels of government a rewarding and even necessary pastime. Numerous proposals have been made in the past to eliminate the bargaining and competition between Federal agencies, especially those charged with water resources development. But the heated conflicts between the Corps of Engineers and the Bureau of Reclamation in several of the nation's major river basins have produced little more than policy agreements that are essentially interagency bargains concluded without reference to the larger and more lasting values that fall outside the scope of narrow bureaucratic goals. Such decisions have little relationship to the national interest. In spite of this, Congress has evinced little enthusiasm for modifying a method of water resources decision making that in the process of negotiating provides payoffs to constituents in the form of construction payrolls and power and irrigation benefits.

A finger in the dike is *not* enough. The methods of pork-barrel decision making may have served a purpose in the past but are not adequate to the task of promoting and enhancing environmental quality in the United States today. The Water Resources Planning Act of 1965 requires Federal agencies and states to produce river basin plans that are comprehensive, coordinated, and designed to reflect a variety of values, including environmental quality. Yet Congress is under no obligation to implement water resources development plans in a way that places widely shared and highly valued environmental goals beyond the realm of the possible bargain, or even in a way that gives the environmental quality aspects of water development priority over the seemingly endless urge to maximize economic returns from resource exploitation. Nor is there any requirement placed on these agencies to force them to consider alternatives other than construction of dams to meet regional and national water needs. This is well illustrated in the Federal Water Projects Recreation Act of 1965. The act intended to give greater recognition and protection to recreation and fish and wildlife values in the calculation of benefit-cost ratios, but in many cases the corps and the Bureau of Reclamation have subverted the intent of the act so that these additional values are used to produce favorable benefit-cost ratios in otherwise economically unfeasible water projects. Without institutional change, such legislation only compounds the original problem.

Little is known about the policy consequences of alternative institutional arrangements for achieving environmental policy goals in either the executive or legislative branches. A variety of devices has been used in the past to tackle specific resource policy issues such as the oft-used Federal interagency committees, but these have been only partially successful and frequently have led to "least common denominator" decisions in which no action is taken unless all agree. It is clear, however, that the present highly fragmented system of decision making in both Congress and the executive gives inadequate representation to important environmental values.

Another problem that gets at the root causes of environmental decay is the power of Congress to deny appropriations. It is a simple matter for Congress to create the appearance of action without actually providing the money needed to do an effective job. The effort to restore the nation's estuaries provides a telling example. During the Ninetieth Congress a bill was considered which would have forbidden any dredging, filling, or excavation within an estuary without a permit from the Interior Department. As finally passed, however, the act provided only for the study and inventory of estuaries, and authorized $250,000 for fiscal years 1969 and 1970 for this purpose. But no funds were appropriated. Congress went even a step further by reducing other funds authorized for a study of estuarine pollution by the Federal Water Pollution Control Administration by more than 25 per cent in fiscal year 1969. This money-gap between authorization and actual appropriation was evident also when Congress approved the

Land and Water Conservation Fund in 1965 but failed to take adequate steps to implement the concept. As indicated in an earlier chapter, revenues to the fund fell far below expectations and land acquisition did not proceed as planned. The Ninety-first Congress amended the Land and Water Conservation Fund Act by guaranteeing annual increments to the fund of $200 million, using revenues from outer continental shelf oil and gas leases to supplement existing revenue collections. However, the guarantee extends for only five years and provides the fund with only one third of the amount originally recommended. It also requires specific congressional approval before any monies from the fund can be used. Similarly, earlier chapters have shown that appropriations for water pollution control and land acquisition for national parks have lagged far behind the amounts Congress originally authorized as necessary.

The money-gap is partially attributable to the financial burden of the Viet Nam War. However, the root of the problem goes much deeper. Budgetary priorities as expressed by the President tend to be reinterpreted by appropriations committees with much narrower bases of political support, and many congressmen are reluctant to give high priority to environmental problems when other programs and policies appear to have more concrete and immediate pay-offs for their constituents. Cosmetic and inadequately funded programs fail to provide more than a superficial response to environmental problems, and too much of the legislation enacted since 1960 has been of this variety. A quality environment is not available at zero cost, whether costs be measured in economic, social, or political terms. The money-gap must be closed, the conflict between private and public property rights must be faced, and a countervailing power to the influence of economic interests must be given a firm institutional basis. Perhaps Congress is responding to these and other economic, social, and political issues in its own ponderous way. But it may be a matter of too little, too late.

Congress has taken a few haltering steps to improve its ability to deal more effectively with complex environmental issues. Of particular significance is the recent formation of an Ad Hoc Committee on the Environment, composed of some ninety members of Congress from both the House and the Senate, who have joined forces on an informal basis to discuss and exchange information and ideas about pressing environmental problems. The group has also formed an advisory board made up of over one hundred distinguished scientists and other persons knowledgeable about these matters. In addition, two new congressional subcommittees were created in March, 1969, in an apparent effort to avoid the pitfalls that result when too many separate committees are involved in the piecemeal consideration of environmental legislation. In the House of Representatives a Subcommittee on Conservation and National Resources was established within the Committee on Government Operations with jurisdiction over "the continued deterioration of the land, water, air, fish and wildlife, growing things, esthetics, and other important features of the nation's environment." Congressman Henry Reuss of Wisconsin is chairman. In the Senate, a Subcommittee on Energy, Natural Resources, and the Environment was formed in the Committee on Commerce "to put new emphasis on problems relating to radiation; the impact of wastes on fish and wildlife, despoliation of the environment and other facets of natural resource conservation." Senator Philip Hart of Michigan is chairman. Whether these new organizational mechanisms will result in greater cohesiveness or greater divisiveness within the congressional committee structure is yet to be seen.

Congress can respond when a crisis is demonstrated beyond all reasonable doubt. But is this an acceptable way of conducting the nation's business? Must the development of the SST proceed to the point at which the daily occurrence of sonic booms is inevitable and the resultant noise pollution demonstrated by commercial flights? How many Santa Barbara fiascos or Torrey Canyon episodes must occur before adequate protection and regulation are provided to prevent damaging oil spills and seepages? How serious will thermal pollution from nuclear power plants become before Congress decides to recognize the problem and act? How many more parks and neighborhoods must be sliced into unbridgeable segments by new freeways before alternative approaches are sought to the nation's transportation problems? How many more delicate estuarine areas will be turned into biological deserts while Congress studies the problem?

Governmental institutions must be modified to provide both Congress and the executive branch with the capacity to do more than simply respond to a series of environmental crises in a piecemeal fashion. There is now no agency of the Federal government with the sole, specific, and full-time responsibility of assessing and continuously maintaining an overview of the condition and rate of change of the natural environmental systems in the United States. There is no one committee in Congress with jurisdiction that extends beyond more than a small segment of the entire range of environmental issues. Decision making by the various Federal departments, bureaus, and agencies occurs without any significant attempt to take account of ecological and environmental consequences. There are no institutions and procedures designed to anticipate environmental problems *before* they reach the crisis stage. There is no national policy for the environment.

III

Events in recent years have dramatized the price that must be paid for unabated environmental pollution. They have given rise to the third wave of the conservation movement, a movement which McConnell argues in the first chapter of this book "has come of age." What can be said of McConnell's thesis about the strength of the modern conservation movement and its capacity to grow and succeed so long as it stands by its principles? These case studies indicate that public sentiment in the 1960's began shifting in favor of positive government action to preserve and protect the balance of nature on which persistence of life on this planet depends. Conservation organizations have grown in membership and influence and have succeeded in stating the ethical and ecological principles necessary to a more sound environmental policy. Their firm stand on principle has been paralleled by equally firm stands on other vital national issues—the Viet Nam war, civil rights, poverty, defense spending, urban blight, hunger. Since the end of the Eisenhower administration the executive branch of the national government has pushed in the direction of realizing the moral and aesthetic ideals identified by McConnell as being increasingly the fundamental material of politics and common life.

But Congress has resisted this push, claiming that public opinion would not uphold radical change. By an accident of history many of the most powerful voices in Congress represent traditionally conservative districts and states, many of them in the southern United States. The 1968 general election revealed support for the forces of conservatism and reaction that spread beyond the South. Both Congress and the administration acquired a more conservative complexion and to some extent the cautiousness of Congress was vindicated by the election returns. If the third wave of the conservation movement crested during the Ninetieth Congress, it was not because the changes it sought had been accomplished but because it was overtaken by this larger wave of conservatism.

Thus for the next four years, possibly for longer, the conservation movement faces a period of testing likely to be most severe. Standing on principle may prove to be very much more difficult than the making of deals and compromises in the spirit of what McConnell calls economic politics. For it is still true that conservative politics is the politics of business; and deals and compromises are what big business understands. The strength of the movement and the deep conviction of its members rules out any return for a protracted time to widespread complacency about the environmental crisis. People no longer need experts with crystal balls to predict the consequence of inaction. As Lord Ritchie-Calder of Edinburgh University has put it, "We can see [the crisis] through smog-colored spectacles; we can smell it seventy years away because it is in our nostrils today; a blind man can see what is coming." [8]

The change in emphasis following the 1968 general election has been dramatic. It was clearly stated by President Nixon's task force on natural resources and the environment, although the full extent of the change remains to be seen. The task force said it was not suggesting any large new programs but emphasizing instead performance, making existing programs work. As noted earlier, this theme was echoed by Secretary of the Interior Walter Hickel at his Senate confirmation hearing when he called for a period of time to consolidate gains and reassess objectives. [9] The message has been handed down to the Federal bureaucracy to be repeated and elaborated. Addressing a conference in Seattle on Issues and Priorities for the Development of Northwest America in June, 1969, Dr. Donald King, an adviser to the President in life sciences and a staff member of the Office of Science and Technology attached to the President's interagency Environmental Quality Council, complained that total environment and human ecology are extremely abstract concepts. He doubted that anyone really wanted to return to nature but conceded that man's interference with the environment has reached great enough proportions to cause

[8] Lord Ritchie-Calder, "Polluting the Environment," *Center Magazine,* II, No. 3 (May, 1969), 7.

[9] U.S., Congress, Senate, Committee on Interior and Insular Affairs, *Hearings, Interior Nomination,* 91st Cong., 1st sess., 1969, p. 7. See pp. xvi–xvii of this book for full quotation.

some concern. He saw no reason to conclude, however, that science and technology were the villains of the piece. His own judgment was that people prefer homes and labor-saving devices to caves and shovels, and that the real need was to balance decisions as to whether economic improvements were more or less important to society than preservation of the environment.

This is fallacious reasoning, and coming from an adviser to the President, it is alarming. The fallacy lies in assuming that the only choice is between preservation of the environment or environmental exploitation through science and technology to produce economic improvements. In the first place, no amount of science and technology can escape the ecological fact that every living thing is related to the total environment, which is far from being an abstract concept even though all of the relationships cannot be identified and measured. Man's spiritual and emotional attachment to natural beauty and wilderness is just one relationship, albeit a vitally important one. Second, it is just not true, as King implies, that preservation of the environment amounts to a return to nature, a reversion to caves and shovels, and an end to industrial progress. Third, neither is it true that science and technology can produce an environment guaranteed to improve the human condition. The evidence to the contrary is littered across the American landscape. Finally, simple observation reveals that the coexistence of economic improvements with preservation of some parts of the environment is possible; and the science of human ecology warns us that there is no practicable alternative if life as we know it to be good is to persist.

If the argument advanced by Dr. King is indicative of the reassessment of long-range objectives conducted by President Nixon and Secretary Hickel, the conservation movement faces some very serious battles. The opening shots have been fired by recent administration appointments placing businessmen and industrialists in key positions. Legislation before the Ninety-first Congress includes measures which, if enacted, would undo much of the progress made during this decade. The proposed National Timber Supply Act, for example, would declare that national forests are to be dedicated primarily to timber production, a priority that would give second class status to other National Forest purposes—wildlife, fish, range, outdoor recreation, wilderness, and watershed management—spelled out by Congress in the National Forest Multiple Use Act of 1960. This proposal would place no restrictions on the lucrative log export business engaged in by a number of the same forest industries calling for greater cuts on national forests. In true robber-baron style, a national timber trade association has hired a public relations firm to promote the industry's cause and to seek to convince the public that the proposed National Timber Supply Act is in the public interest. Problems stemming from the Santa Barbara oil spill and the planned development of oil in the Alaskan Arctic promise severe confrontations with the king of special interests—the oil industry.

These developments portend the challenge ahead. The economic and political forces producing environmental deterioration are deeply entrenched and are likely to yield only to concerted and persistent public pressures to force public policy in the direction of protecting and enhancing the ecological systems that sustain life on this planet. The overwhelming need is to arrange an overdue marriage between economics and ecology; to bring the corporate system to realize that the earth is not only a vast storehouse of natural wealth to be drawn upon freely for our material well-being but is also our abode, the place we live and bring up our children and seek psychic sustenance. Business leaders must be challenged as never before to become mindful of ecology; to be shown that we can construct factories that will assure abundance without befouling the air, contaminating the water, blighting the land; that in this new age it is in their own selfish interest, even in Adam Smith's terms, to go beyond the old criteria of profit and unbridled growth to become wealth-protecting guardians of the nation's environment. Likewise, conservative politicians must not merely be railed at but shown conclusively that conservatism and conservation are not antithetical; that the concept of stewardship over the real capital of the nation is essentially a conservative philosophy but can be attained only through innovative politics and the wholesale modernization of our basic institutions of government. If the conservative can be "turned on" in this way, to use the lingo of today, he will likely become a much more ardent supporter of the conservation ethic than the liberal because of his particular psychology. The strategy of the conservation movement must lie in this direction, to meld the liberal and conservative philosophies in such a way as to produce a new and deep-seated awareness of the tenuous interrelationships that now exist between man and his total environment within which we are indivisible.

Beyond this are major political struggles that have only begun to emerge over international conservation issues. The inept congressional response to the issue of international control of the ocean floor, raised earlier in this volume, is a sad omen. Modern means of communication have reduced the world to a neighborhood and made imperative a clearer understanding of the nature and significance of the biosphere, the atmosphere, the hydrosphere, and the lithosphere on a global basis. The environmental consequences of international development programs and of engineering schemes which contemplate the transformation of continents are mine-fields of undetected ignorance. Yet Congress stumbles blindly ahead, seemingly unaware of serious environmental problems which do not respect the boundaries of the United States and have consequences for millions of people in other countries. Despite assurances from men of science, the testing of the H-bomb produced fallout in the form of radio-strontium particulate heretofore unknown in nature, and this matter is in the bones of every child who was growing up during the period of bomb testing—every young person, everywhere in the world. Recent studies indicate, for example, that nuclear fallout may have played a significant role in increasing infant mortality rates all over the globe.[10] The SST threatens to crisscross the earth with carpets of sonic boom affecting hundreds of millions of people everyday, several times a day. The increasing carbon dioxide content of the upper atmosphere which results from the burning of fossil fuels over the last fifty years has begun to alarm scientists because of the potential "green house effect" it may have in increasing the temperature of the earth's surface. DDT has now been found to occur even in the penguins in the Antarctic. As Kenneth Boulding pointed out so clearly in a paper perceptively entitled "The Economics of the Coming Spaceship Earth," the shadow of the future spaceship, indeed, is already falling over our spendthrift merriment, but oddly enough it seems to be in pollution rather than in exhaustion that the problem is first becoming salient. The fouling of the nest which has been typical of man's activities in the past on a local scale now seems to be extended to the whole world society; and one certainly cannot view with equanimity the present rate of pollution of any of the natural reservoirs, whether the atmosphere, the

[10] Ernest J. Sternglass, "Infant Mortality and Nuclear Tests," *Bulletin of the Atomic Scientists*, XXV, No. 4 (April, 1969), 18–20.

lakes, or even the oceans.[11] It is frightening to think how poorly Congress is prepared to meet these larger problems, let alone the more immediate ones discussed in this volume. But it is obvious that the new conservation must become global in scope if it is to be ultimately successful, and this will put new and unimaginable burdens on our already rickety and unwieldy political institutions. Of all the dangerous games people play, could it be that the ultimate is environmental Russian roulette?

It would be an obvious overstatement to say that if Congress would put its own house in order these problems could be solved; but it is not at all an exaggeration to say, as one student of politics recently noted, that Congress is weakest in carrying out what should be its most vital function: the synthesis, shaping, and supervising of the nation's paramount goals and priorities. "Congress has been content to be a passive audience when it could readily become a vast sounding board to arouse and educate the Nation." [12] This points up the responsibility of Congress, but the onus extends to all levels of government and to every individual citizen. This book does not conclude with the traditional plea for more research. The merit of that plea is self-evident and the authors are committed to the task along with many others. Rather, every reader is urged to declare himself for what he believes in and to act upon whatever reflection these pages may have prompted. A letter to a congressman would be an excellent beginning.

[11] Henry Jarrett, ed., *Environmental Quality in a Growing Economy* (Baltimore, Md.: Johns Hopkins Press, 1966), p. 13.
[12] Udall, *1976: Agenda for Tomorrow*, p. 150.

16. Epilogue:

Environment and the Shaping of Civilization

LYNTON K. CALDWELL

WITH the insight of the poet, Matthew Arnold spoke for his time but not for ours when he wrote of "wandering between two worlds, one dead, the other powerless to be born."[1] In Arnold's time the loss of tradition could be regretted, but the shape of the new world yet unborn was hidden. Neither poet nor man of science could know how to relate to it. But the world in gestation in the nineteenth century is now emerging. Its initial outline and its character are beginning to appear and it is a task of our generation to consider what it may become. Will it be a better world or will its already evident tendencies toward the monstrous prevail? Is this new world ours to shape or is it, and are we, analogous to digits in a computer unable to perceive or to control the cosmic program?

We begin with these questions, not to consider if or how they may be answered, but as reminders that our practical way of dealing with this imponderable aspect of the real world poses for us a moral

LYNTON K. CALDWELL is professor of government at Indiana University (Bloomington). He has been editor of *State Government* and the *Book of the States* for the Council of State Governments and Director of the Maxwell School of Public Administration at Syracuse University. Following a distinguished career in public administration, which included service with the United Nations, he has recently devoted attention to environmental policy. He is the author of *Administrative Theories of Hamilton and Jefferson* and editor of *Environmental Studies: Papers in the Politics and Public Administration of Man-Environment Relationships*.

[1] "Stanzas from the Grande Chartreuse" (lines 85–86), *The Poetical Works of Matthew Arnold*, ed. C. B. Tinker and H. F. Lowry (London: Oxford University Press, 1950), p. 302.

obligation to act as if we could shape our future. We resolve the questions by assumptions of our autonomy and our competence. But we evade the teleological question of predetermined ends only to confront the ontological question of future development.

Our new world emerges with an implicit assumption of our self-actualizing power. The logic of this position implies a corollary responsibility to consider and evaluate the purposes for which resources are used. We are not compelled by logic to determine the ends of our efforts or even to forecast their unplanned outcomes. But it seems irrational to concern ourselves with means to the neglect of ends. For we have already seen the harm that can come from unprecedented and inadequately considered use of power. If there is meaning in the word "wisdom," it surely implies the attempt to use the resources of science not only for immediate purposes, but to shape a future in which human happiness and welfare will be possible.

I

The shaping of man's future implies the shaping of his future environment. His ability to plan his future depends largely upon his capacity for reason. Disagreement over whether planning of the environment should be comprehensive or incremental reflects differing assessments of human capacity for rational conduct. The difference is one of degree, for no one contends that rationality is unlimited, and few would argue that human behavior is totally irrational. Rationality is always bounded, but incrementalists doubt man's capacity to deal effectively with comprehensive, complex, and long-term developments. They contend that because individual man cannot foresee his future, and societies of men differ among themselves as to what the future ought to be, man as a species is doing the best that he can. He cannot purposefully shape the course of environmental change and should not attempt to do so. His environmental correctives should be confined to specific, immediate, and manifestly harmful effects.

This attitude tends to the conclusion that, whatever its failures, ours is the best possible world. It may not be the best of all possible worlds, but it is the best that is possible for us. We are what we are as a consequence of an evolution over which human rationality has had little or no control. Our expectations of shaping our future, if realistic, must be modest. One may regret that in pursuit of his perceived self-interest man so often degrades the environment that sustains his life—but then, *ecce homo*, this is the kind of creature that the human animal is.

The empirical evidence in support of this conclusion is formidable. We see it on all sides. Continuing disregard of the known causes and consequenses of man's misuse of his environment is discouraging. But any conclusion regarding the potentialities of man is tentative. It is a current thesis that man has taken over direction of his evolution. This opinion appears to be shared more widely among physical scientists and geneticists than among social and behavioral scientists. Those who should know man best seem least optimistic about his capacity for collective self-control. Nevertheless, history indicates that human behavior does change and that human societies are capable of planning and sustaining massive, complex, and relatively long-term efforts. Were this not so world wars and space exploration would never have proved feasible. There appears no limit to opinions regarding man's rational capacities. Yet the fact is that we have no verified knowledge regarding man's potential intellect, and no adequate scientific explanation for the evolution of human values.

We are as yet unable to explain the process by which the human brain evolved, separating man from his primate relatives; and we have no basis for assuming that man's evolution is complete. Our knowledge of human evolution is so fragmentary and covers so brief a period of geologic time that we cannot plot a reliable trajectory of man's development. But our knowledge of the forces of evolutionary change is growing, and our technical understanding of man's mental processes, although still rudimentary, is much greater than that of our forebears. If self-understanding is a key to self-control then progress is being made toward a point in human development when man may be able voluntarily to push outward the bounds of his rationality. In brief, as one looks to the future, the limitations of bounded rationality on shaping the environment would seem to be conjectural rather than certain.

In order to improve the quality of man's environment the quality of man himself must also be improved. The upgrading of man and his environment are aspects of a single great and complex process: advancement of the quality of civilization. And it may be argued that neither aspect of the process can occur to a significant degree without the other. The phenomenon of man occurs only in context, and whether one looks outward from man toward his environment or inward from environment toward the nature of man, the *field* in which inquiry takes place is the same. The viewpoint or perspective changes, and the focus of attention shifts, but the man-environment universe, although infinitely extended and complex, is integral and holistic. The amenability of the human factor to purposive self-control is discovered through tests of action. Environment-shaping action is one of these tests and one of the most significant of them because of its contextual relationship to the human condition. Forethought, restraint, and a considered appraisal of alternative means to socially desirable ends are characteristics of the civilized aspects of man. They are qualities of mind and personality that will be emphasized in education of any people who seriously attempt to shape their civilization.

II

Civilizing is the process of achieving civilness or civility. The form and substance of civility are not things upon which all men agree. But the essential or basic meaning of civilization is the attainment of relationships under which men are able to live together in communities. Animal and plant communities exist without the assistance of civilization. There are communities of men in which the state of civilization is rudimentary. Yet, the psychobiological distance between the most primitive living men and the most advanced nonhuman social species appears to be far greater than the distance between the most primitive and most advanced human societies. Man, unlike his fellow creatures, has an aptitude for civilization. His imagination and ambition impel him to refine and complicate his social arrangements and his technology in order to attain his objectives. Given time and an appropriate environment, primitive men have shown that they can become "more civilized," but no ape or insect has as yet demonstrated this capacity.

In the process of becoming "more civilized," man has developed elaborate technologies that are sometimes erroneously identified with civilization itself. Clearly, technology is a major aspect of civilization, and it is through technology that man undertakes to reshape the natural environment better to satisfy his wants. It is what man wants that determines the quality and direction of his civilizing efforts. Technology is the knowledge of means. In a society of self-imposed limitations on perspective, the advancement of technology may become an end in itself. The result is the technological society that Jacques Ellul describes and humanists deplore.

Civilization expresses its dominant impulses through its use of technology, and the consequences of this usage may be seen in its effects upon man-environment relationships. Throughout historic time, deterioration of the viability or self-renewing capability of an environment has presaged a decline of civilization. Evidence from Central Asia, the Middle East, the Mediterranean littoral, and Central America appear to substantiate this hypothesis; and yet, paradoxically, the spectacular advancement of technoscientific civilization in the nineteenth and twentieth centuries has also been accompanied by measurable, verifiable decline in many aspects of man-environment relationships. Skeptics are therefore moved to question the reality of an environmental crisis. Technologists now argue that the environment, in its natural evolved form, can almost if not wholly be ignored. Man can make his own environment. Under plexiglass domes he can lay out golf-courses on the Moon.

A civilization reveals the nature of its internalized goals and values in the environmental conditions that it creates. Obviously the environment of a civilization does not express all of the values and conditions implicit in a civilized society. Yet if read perceptively, the environment reveals much more than the untrained eye sees. The science of archeology is based upon the reconstruction of past environments, and upon the extrapolation from them of the activities, attitudes, and institutions of the peoples of past civilizations. We cannot be sure of the accuracy of these extrapolations and it is helpful to have written records that verify or supplement material artifacts. We cannot always tell, where natural environments have declined, how much change was caused by man and how much by nature. Did, for example, stream siltation, continental uplift, or both, destroy the harbors of Ionian cities on the Aegean Sea?

But although the physical environment may not tell all that is to be told about the quality of a civilization, neither does it lie, as written records sometimes do. Man may misinterpret, but the physical evidence does not dissemble. In many societies, and not least in the United States of America, one finds great contrasts among the varied uses of the environment. From some viewpoints, American treatment of its environment appears to be violently contradictory. Like magnificent Asian temples rising out of filth and misery, the contrast between the "best" and the "worst" of the American environment is so marked as to suggest a national schizophrenia in environmental attitudes. The analogy may not be inapt. There is ample evidence to suggest that America, as a social system, does express contradictory attitudes toward the environment, as the papers in this volume attest. But this trait is not uniquely American; and it is also true that these contradictions exist within a system that, however complex and contradictory its components, does function as a total integrated society. The contradictions are within the system; they reflect subsystems of the totality. Inconsistent as they may be with one another, such contrasts are not wholly incompatible. The system has accommodated itself to the stress of their differences. In a vernacular phrase, they are "built into the system."

It is this built-in nature of human behavior in relation to the environment that will make the effort for environmental quality in America a difficult and frustrating uphill fight. An attack upon environmental pollution, for example, is in some part an attack upon the prevailing social system. The attack is, of course, focused upon specific and from some viewpoints harmful aspects of the system. But as John Kenneth Galbraith has remarked in a satirical but all too candid essay, pollution is not a casual or spontaneous activity: "On the contrary, it has deep and penetrating roots in the body politic." [2] And in describing the environmental deterioration of present-day America, Paul Ylvisaker writes:

Call it by any name—chaos, unplanned growth, ribbon development, social anarchy, slurbs, the decline of American civilization, the resurgence of *laissez-faire*. But recognize it for what it is—a people's *laissez-faire*, which sinks its roots down past any rotting level of corrupt and cynical behavior by the few into a subsoil of widespread popular support and an abiding tradition of private property, individual freedom and "every-man's-home's-his-castle." [3]

The environment of a society as shaped by man is thus not merely an expression of social values, it is a function of the society itself. It is a part of what the society is. To shape the environment of a civilized society means nothing less than shaping the nature of the society. Those who undertake to alter or direct the process of environmental change thereby take a hand in shaping the course of civilization.

[2] "The Polipollutionists," *Atlantic Monthly*, CCXIX (January, 1967), 52.
[3] "The Villains are Greed, Indifference—and You," *Life*, LIX (December 24, 1965), 96.

There are degrees of environmental control, some of which are essentially superficial or cosmetic. But unless even relatively slight changes are integrated into the functional processes of society, the probability of their survival is not high. The flowers will wither in their planters in the downtown mall unless their presence has become a part of the value structure and operational system of the city that sought to improve its image by planting them there.

III

The anonymity and uniformity of contemporary man-made environments contrast sharply with the distinctiveness and variety of traditional cities and countryside. Contemporary style in office buildings, airports, luxury hotels, factories, motor expressways, bridges and, increasingly, in the patterns of agricultural settlement, tend to a highly similar, almost common set of qualities. Planned distinctiveness is often attempted, but the leveling logic of technique is not easily offset. It appears that technoscientific culture generates its own environmental style, freed from the assumptions or constraints of traditional cultures. Gestures contrived to provide "atmosphere" in tourist hotels or airports merely confirm the leveling effect of technoscience as man has applied it. Symbolic distinctiveness is often emphasized where loss of variety threatens business based on human interest in change and variety.

Distinctiveness and variety do appear to be human values, but one finds an apparent paradox in contemporary society. Architects, artists, and designers often go to great lengths to assert the individuality of their work. Whether the results are pleasing variety or disturbing discord are perhaps only matters of taste or preference. A result, however, is that eclecticism, rampant at the community level, creates a nondescript sameness as between communities. In traditional societies there was a much higher degree of stylistic uniformity *within* particular communities. But as *among* communities there was greater contrast. By way of example, new additions to older buildings nowadays characteristically contrast violently in style. Variety is added to the immediate environment, but its integrity and distinctiveness are often lost. Widespread, uninhibited heterogeneity results in a generalized sameness. Buffalo, Detroit, Denver, and Seattle are different primarily where nature is still visible. A once-distinctive Boston is becoming more and more like Houston. There have been some successes in accentuating civic distinctiveness. The great arch at St. Louis is one of these. But with few exceptions, all large American cities appear to be the same place.

The implications of this paradox are significant for the task of environmental planning and administration. Implicit in the differences between traditional and technoscientific environments are contrasting latitudes of choice. The constraints upon choice in traditional societies were relatively severe. Yet environmental styles were as distinctive as the images associated with Brittany and Cambodia. The choices that men made in shaping their environments were limited by religion, technology, availability of building materials, patterns of settlement, methods of transportation, agriculture, and trade. These constraints still limit choice, but the latitude of choice has expanded with unprecedented rapidity. Today, that latitude is so wide that contemporary society has hardly begun to explore seriously the range of possibilities available to it.

Traditional society was relatively stable because the choices available to it were few and frequently obvious. In contrast, the choices available to technoscientific society are vastly greater; but many of the possibilities are not perceived by the mass of people or by their leaders. Yet there is also a widespread belief that almost anything can happen. Potential conflicts of interest thus multiply. Growth in technology, in economic wealth, and in population create new opportunities for the enterprising, and new threats to established values. In shaping the environments of traditional societies man appears seldom to have been self-conscious about his choices. The limitations of circumstance, the strength of customary ways, and the relative low pressure of population enabled environment-shaping to assume an almost natural evolutionary course. In the world today, no environment is secure. There is hardly a square acre of earth anywhere that is not vulnerable to someone's plans for change.

More than any other factor, science-based technology has enlarged the scope of man's environmental choices. But more than technology is involved. The use of technology in processes that have altered environmental conditions has been highly selective. Technological feasibility is seldom the criterion by which the choice is made in the uses of technology. The real power and limitation of technology lies in its combination with other things—with economic, industrial, or military activities. Technoscience enlarges choice but does not guide it.

The effect of technological innovations in combination with other elements is determined by the interactions among the elements. The synergistic effects depend upon the nature of the combinations, seldom upon technology itself. For example, the automobile in so-called less developed countries has not had the impact upon the environment that follows when economics, industrialism, and public policy permit the operation of automobiles by the millions. It was not technologically foreordained for American society to use technology to promote transportation by privately owned automobiles instead of by public carriers. The impact of technology is a systems effect; it is seldom an isolated event.

The environmental conditions of any society, but especially of contemporary technoscientific societies, are perhaps best understood as syndromes of converging causes. This synergistic effect of technology plus economics, plus other factors in society, provides the energy that levels mountains, moves rivers, and creates smog. But this convergent power is usually organized through interrelationships and combinations that are highly resistant to competing interests. Opponents of public works policies of the United States Army Corps of Engineers or Federal Highway Administration have confronted the all but impenetrable strength of these technical-political-economic combinations and have learned how seldom their behavior can be changed by direct frontal attack. Environmental preservationists have fought battle after battle with the corps over specific decisions and policies, but the combination that is the force behind the actions of the corps remains close-knit and strong, as yet unchallenged as an environment-shaping system by any equally powerful alternative.

These technoeconomic and technopolitical combinations have evolved as the primary forces in American society in the making of environmental choices. The choices are those of interested parties, but become by institutional or political default the choices or nonchoices of the whole society. The greater freedom of choice that wealth and technology confer in theory upon contemporary man tends in fact to become illusory. Much of the frustration and anguish of the idealist who would see technoscience used to create better environments results from this paradox. The means that could shape a more healthful, aesthetically pleasing, and convenient environment are used instead in ways that achieve technical objectives, but unnecessarily destroy or impair environmental assets. The latitude of technological choice in meeting the needs of modern society is narrowed by political and economic considerations. The location of factories, dams, highways, harbors, housing developments, and airports, or the necessity for their construction in particular instances, are decided through the application of criteria that do not begin to avail themselves of the full range of possibilities. In brief, although the alibi of technical necessity is often raised in defending environment-impairing choices, the decisive factor is usually economic or political. The choice of technologies in particular instances is seldom governed by technological considerations.

It is evident that criteria for what is good, bad, tolerable, or preferable are largely functions of the total society. These criteria may be, and some have been, influenced by science. In the main they are manifestations of traditional culture and the tendency of society is to apply them uncritically to novel situations. Moreover, the fractionalization of the total culture as a consequence of the impact of technoscience has deprived society of general guidelines or standards by which the results or desirability of technoscientific innovations can be appraised. Freedom of choice thus becomes inability to make discriminating choices. Weakness of constraints on technological choices gives an open field to aggressive and purposive politicoeconomic advantage-seekers. To oversimplify for emphasis, it may be asserted that the two-culture cleavage in modern society adds to the already great difficulties of rational or coherent direction of its future. Expediency thus continues to be a prevailing characteristic of contemporary policy making at a time when available knowledge and techniques are rapidly diminishing the great historical justification for expediency—ignorance.

IV

Can we really elect to have a high-quality environment? Does the structure of American society—pluralistic, democratic, historically biased in favor of an "everyman's laissez faire"—permit the shaping of its environment in any way other than by combat and compromise? The question is not whether conflict of interests in the environment can be eliminated. There is no prospect, in a finite world, that they will be. A second practical question is how to raise the levels of information and social concern at which the process of bargaining and accommodation occurs. To improve the human environment, both man and politics must be improved. Men make politics; political institutions influence human behavior; and behavior is heavily influenced by attitudes, beliefs, and values. Purposeful shaping of the environment involves the purposeful shaping of outlooks on life. The quality of the future environment depends, therefore, upon the shaping of attitudes, beliefs, and values through present education.

Some aspects of human conduct are expressions of psychophysical nature. As a civilizing animal it is natural for man to substitute reason and culture for subrational drives, but rational behavior may serve irrational motives. It is, therefore, important to our welfare to understand the nature and effect of physiologically conditioned behavior. If man is a territorial animal, and if he displaces onto the environment aggression generated in his social relationships, knowledge concerning these circumstances could greatly assist development of feasible strategies for effective environmental policy. Yet not all men nor all societies project destructive impulses against the environment. The improvement of man can proceed through education, in the broad sense, while efforts are made also to improve the psychophysical endowment of the human species.

What are the implications for an educational process that will help to build better environmental relationships in the future? The structuring of the entire process of formal education around man-environment relationships is not necessarily indicated. Many of the attitudes, beliefs, and values that would improve prospects for better environments in the future are equally relevant to other aspects of life. Yet not all educational orientations are equally suitable to help society to set goals and establish priorities for the future. Education limited to information is of little help. The question becomes one of what attitudes, beliefs, and values the system inculcates. In the broadest sense, the issue is what kind of civilization the process of education will produce.

Within this broader context of educational policy an increased and, in some measure, new focus on environmental relationships and policies will be necessary. This basically ecological aspect of research and teaching has long been neglected to our detriment and to our increasing peril. Recent moves to establish centers or institutes for environmental studies in numbers of colleges and universities indicate intention to remedy the neglect. Through the organization of new courses of study and the reorganization of old ones, higher education is better equipping today's youths to perceive and to assess the meaning of environmental change. Only a beginning has been made and much more needs to be done. It is especially important that basic environmental concepts be built into secondary education where they have heretofore generally been lacking. Education is more than schooling, but it is through formal systematic mass education that the greatest single impact on attitudes, beliefs, and values can be made.

In a technoscientific age there is no end to the need for learning. Planned, systematic education now continues through adult life and is increasingly civic as well as vocational in character. With the displacement of traditional culture by technoscience, we are confronted with the necessity of working to obtain our civilization. We can no longer merely inherit it. To preserve the culture of the past, whether in art, in ethics, in historic sites, in landscapes, or in social institutions, requires unremitting effort. It also requires reappraisal; for not all that we inherit is necessarily good.

In the new world struggling to be born it is we who must struggle. The disintegration of traditional culture is a grim and tragic process. We see its consequences in starkest relief in catastrophes that have befallen the ancient civilization of China. Fortunately for us of the Western world, the concepts of self-actualization and of the evolution of man and society are embodied in our culture. Yet, although these internalized concepts may have helped to spare us the misfortunes of China, they have not helped us to be self-actualizing in all respects. Why have they not been more effective in guiding public effort toward better environmental decisions? The explanation lies perhaps in the complexity of our culture and in the particular ways in which these concepts are expressed in our society. More certainly, our educational system has not equipped people to make well-considered environmental choices.

We are not yet able to explain why some societies adopt ecologically valid goals and practices and others do not. Simplified explanations are likely to be wrong, but it is possible to draw certain general conclusions from the course that contrasting cultures have taken without fully understanding the causal factors. For example, although no simple explanation seems adequate to account for the decline of Chinese civilization, the inadvertent overstressing of the environment by sheer numbers of people seems to have been a critical factor. The ethos of China, less complex and more dogmatic than the ideologies of the West, was more congenial to harmony with nature. Yet neither philosophy, bureaucracy, nor science enabled China to avoid the environmental impoverishment that followed a slowly increasing but unremitting pressure of man on the land. In the West, science and technology enabled society to achieve a more productive and better balanced relationship to the natural world even though, paradoxically, the dominant attitudes toward nature tended as much toward hostility as toward harmony. Industrialization and the colonization of the Americas relieved in Europe the inordinate stress of man on his environment that accompanied the decline of Chinese civilization. But we have no assurance that the combination of culture and technology that, with obvious exceptions, has worked well for the West will continue to do so in the technoscientific society of the future.

Two obvious aspects of the historical threshold over which all society is now passing are exponential increases of people and of power. The danger in destructive or misguided attitudes toward nature has become greater today because of the greater means to translate attitudes into action. Guided ignorance in the form of dogma appears to have been a factor in the decline of the old China; unguided knowledge in the form of technocratic optimism appears to have been the characteristic danger to the West. Today, the establishment of guidelines for knowledge in the application of science and technology to the human environment is a task of urgent importance everywhere. The task is urgent because until it is accomplished there will be no adequate basis in theory or principle upon which to base public and international policies for the custody, care, and development of the human environment.

In America, we have no corpus of ecological doctrine in our public life comparable to that which now influences or governs our economic decisions. Our public life is shaped by particular interpretations, or misinterpretations, of self-actualization and freedom to change that tend to contradict the concepts that they are presumed to exemplify. These misinterpretations although deeply rooted in American society are neither uniquely nor necessarily American. They may be changed, and they must be changed, if the shaping of American civilization is to enlarge the public happiness and welfare. Among the attitudes that misinterpret the meaning of human freedom the following are especially familiar and especially harmful to the quality of civilization and its environment: first, an uncritical bias for growth; second, technoeconomic determinism; third, cultural relativism; and, fourth, self-centered individualism—the "everyman's laissez faire."

These attitudes share certain negative characteristics significant for the environment-shaping process. None of them imply or require self-restraint or control, none suggest individual or collective accountability, none concede the existence of criteria for evaluating the use of the environment that are independent of individual interest or preference. All of these attitudes suggest resistance to any general pattern of environmental development in society or to any meaningful standards of environmental quality, *per se*. They do not preclude the imposition of social control where a clear and present danger to individual well-being can be proved. But they severely retard the establishment of general principles of ecological policy upon which more specific standards can be based. More critical attention to their effects is therefore needed.

The "growthmanship" attitude is deeply embedded in American culture. Whether our national obsession with quantitative growth can be transformed into qualitative growth, or growth within a self-renewing or an internally dynamic homeostatic system is conjectural. The most problematic growth of all is that of numbers of people. In America there are grounds for cautious optimism that the national enthusiasm for numbers may someday be displaced by a concern for the quality of human life generally.

Technoeconomic determinism, or the "you can't stop progress" attitude, is still firmly ascendant in American life, despite critical attack from both science and aesthetics. Supersonic transport and airports unlimited are only current examples of a national tendency. It is curious that people vigilantly jealous of their rights in relation to government will permit their privacy, convenience, and even health to be jeopardized by costly and unnecessary technological innovation that yields little, if any, social benefit. More strange is the tendency of science-oriented, rational people to accept the metaphysical dogma of technological inevitability. It is, as we have emphasized, a contradiction to the tacit belief of Americans in the self-actualization of the human personality. It is an example of compartmentalized thinking against which education has not yet provided sufficient protection.

Cultural relativism has permeated the social sciences and has strongly influenced ethical and religious thought. The value of a demonstrably valid set of ecological principles by which public policy could be guided would be very great. It could provide a common ground for greater consensus. But it would encounter objections from those who hold that science has nothing to do with values, and that one man's values are as good as another's. Our slowness in exploring the biosocial interface in science has kept us from providing an adequate and convincing answer to arguments over relativity or priority among values in the environment. Political accommodation among conflicting interests therefore tends to occur at too low a conceptual level to give adequate weight to scientific knowledge or ecological wisdom.

The laissez-faire attitude toward the rights of individuals in relation to the environment has suffered some attrition through public action on behalf of public health and safety. Land-use planning and zoning, and emerging pollution control legislation, further constrain individual behavior in relation to the environment. We are beginning to lay a foundation for a legal doctrine of public rights in the environment as distinguished from the specific and discrete prohibitions that have hitherto characterized our environmental policy. Yet at the local level of government and throughout large areas of the country where pressure on the environment has not been felt acutely, the right to exploit the environment for personal advantage is still very broadly construed. Here again culture shapes environmental attitudes. The psychology of the frontiersman is still vigorous and when reinforced by technoscientific capability can be a very potent force, usually in ways harmful to environmental quality.

A characteristic common to all of these foregoing attitudes is that each of them is highly dysfunctional to the effective public control of applied science or technology. They derive from viewpoints formed mostly in the prescientific world, although cultural relativism reflects to some degree an inclination to be scientific. Relativistic thinking that dismisses weight of evidence and insists upon incontrovertible proof of the validity of one environmental attitude as against another has abandoned science for a philosophical fetish. In actuality these attitudes do not appear as clear-cut or consistent categories of belief or behavior. They are interwoven in the fabric of our social, political, and economic life, and this is why it becomes so difficult to change them. It is why environment shaping becomes culture shaping, and why attack upon the environmental abuses of our industrial society readily becomes an attack upon certain aspects of the structure of the society itself.

V

These remarks began with an allusion to the concept of two worlds —the familiar but no longer viable past and the future which, more than a transition from the past, appears to bring a change of state in the human condition. Related to this concept is that of two cultures, popularized by C. P. Snow. Each of these concepts is expressive of the change that science has brought into the world. Both imply discontinuities in culture: chronological, intellectual, and emotional.

The truth of these interpretations of present history is perhaps more poetic than rigorously factual, more qualitative than quantitatively demonstrable. A truth may be substantial without being universal. And it seems true that the *means* to shape the environment of civilized societies belong largely to science; whereas the purposes of men, the standards of beauty, of order, of aesthetic satisfaction, of welfare, and even of some aspects of health belong to the humanities. This separation between the custodians of means and ends in our society creates weakness and discontinuity at the point of social decision. It is in the process of public policy making that the respective contributions of the "two cultures" are needed to form a mutually comprehensible and coherent unity.

The size and complexity of modern society require specialization. In the absence of integrative forces, occupational differences tend to fractionalize society. Communication across occupational lines becomes difficult, and no common set of assumptions or values provides a meeting ground for differing interests. The openness of modern society is deceptive. Freed from barriers of class and caste, it is more subtly fragmented by technoscientific specialization and by the progressive isolation of the traditional culture from technoscience.

Here perhaps lies the answer to the question of why contemporary Western technoscientific society has not dealt more effectively with its environmental problems. Means and ends are separated. The wholeness of man and of society requires a synthesis or integration in orientation toward the world and life that conventional education has not provided. Thus, as we earlier observed, contradictory tendencies of modern American society are built into its social system. And it is this schizoid tendency that most of all makes it difficult for the United States of America to develop a guiding set of environmental policies or to employ more than a fraction of the potential power of science and technology on behalf of human welfare.

Science has placed in the hands of man knowledge and power that makes him responsible for his future; it has not given him the moral compulsion to act responsibly. The substantive values that science and technology serve are articulated in the humanities, but are seldom amenable to scientific verification. It is at this interface between science and the humanities that environmental policy, if made, is made. And it is at this interface also that higher education can contribute to resolving what some observers have called our environmental crisis.

How this task can be accomplished in the colleges and universities is yet to be discovered, and it must also be acknowledged that education alone will not solve our problems. There is no master blueprint equally applicable to all institutions or to all aspects of the educational task. But these elements in that task are universal: first, it is primarily one of synthesis—its basic data will be derived largely from the established disciplines that individually are unable to bring together knowledge relevant to environmental policy in a comprehensive or coherent system; second, its concern is not merely with the appearance of things, but with the purpose, quality, and worth of man-environment relationships; third, it reinforces rather than dilutes efforts in the separate sciences and humanities because it establishes or clarifies their relevance to life; fourth and finally, it emphasizes a truth that is too often forgotten—that through education the civilization of the future is shaped.

Past generations of Americans, and men generally, have understood education as preparation for life. It is that, but that is its smaller dimension. Its larger dimension and equally important task is to *shape* life as well as to help prepare for it. In some degree education has always done this, but often without conscious effort or intention. If man is to be the master of his own ingenuity, and not its victim, he will have to find better ways to relate means to ends, and to evaluate the ends that science makes available to him. In summation, the major task of education and politics is to shape a world in which preparation for life is worthwhile.

Bibliography

BECAUSE the literature relevant to the study of environmental policy problems is so vast and scattered, this bibliography of necessity must be highly selective. Selections have been made for their value in guiding both the student of environmental policy and the general reader to references that will provide access to the wealth of material on specific policy issues. The bibliography does not list sources according to the issues treated in each chapter of the book. References are broken down into four categories: government documents; basic books; bibliographies; and journals and miscellaneous sources. In preparing the bibliography we have kept in mind the kinds of material that proved useful to the contributors during the seminars which led to the essays in this book. The literature is not only vast but growing rapidly, and it is no respecter of established disciplinary boundaries.

It will be evident that the theme of this book, the role and performance of Congress vis-à-vis environmental policy, has received little attention in previously published work. To date discussions of this theme have been confined in large part to congressional documents issued during recent debates on a national policy for the environment. Books and articles dealing with the more general problem of governmental response to environmental policy issues have touched upon the role of Congress, but there remains a need for much more research on this subject.

Government Documents

For anyone interested in environmental policy, and for those specifically interested in tracing the history of Federal legislation, government documents are indispensable. All publications of the Federal Government are indexed in the *United States Government Publications: Monthly Catalog,* which covers everything from 1895 to the present. It contains reference to all congressional, departmental, and bureau publications which have been printed by the Government Printing Office. It is indexed by subject and agency.

For research dealing more specifically with Congress, there are two particularly helpful guides. The *Index of Congressional Committee Hearings in the Library of the U.S. House of Representatives Prior to January 3, 1943* and the *Index to Congressional Committee Hearings (not confidential)* Prior *to 1935 in the U.S. Senate Library* have both been brought up to date with supplements. The *Congressional Record* contains the proceedings and debates of Congress from 1873 to the present. It is issued daily while Congress is in session and then is revised and bound at the end of each session with a subject and author index contained in each volume. Besides congressional debates and speeches in full, it also contains presidential messages and the record of votes on all bills. The *Congressional Record* index also contains a history of all bills, arranged by bill number, with full information about a bill from its introduction to its passage and signing.

More easily obtainable than any of the government publications for checking the status of a bill at any stage from introduction to the final disposition is the *Congressional Index*. Additional information in this publication includes: all standing committees and most of the important special and joint committees; voting records of all members of Congress; bills introduced by each member of Congress; and a summary of the highlights of congressional activity.

The *Congressional Digest* also provides a good source on current legislation in Congress. It records the status of bills before the current Congress, and includes articles analyzing legislative issues, often with summaries of the arguments pro and con. The *Digest of Public General Bills* lists, for each session of Congress, bills and resolutions by number giving a brief synopsis of each and indicating any action taken. Each issue has a subject index. Three publications of the Congressional Quarterly Service are especially helpful. *Congress and the Nation, 1945–1964,* is a massive volume reviewing the activities of Congress in the postwar years. It includes a lengthy section on Natural Resources. The *Congressional Quarterly Almanac* is published annually and reviews the work of Congress on a subject by subject basis. Analyses of the major issues and background summaries of legislative history are included along with much other valuable information. This annual publication is a reorganized version of the *Congressional Quarterly Weekly Report,* which lists chronologically within a broad subject classification all major public bills introduced, their sponsors, committee hearings, and a concise summary of action taken by the House and Senate on bills that become law.

Although legal research is often so involved that it requires a specialist in this type of work, there are nevertheless a number of guides and references that can be of great help to anyone and are comparatively easy to use. After any bill is passed into law and becomes a statute it is published in the *Statutes at Large of the United States,* consisting of one volume for each session of Congress. Within each volume the statutes are arranged chronologically by date of passage of the act. Federal laws which have been passed on a given subject are listed in the *United States Code,* a series of volumes which index all the laws in force in the United States by subjects. The *United States Code Annotated* includes information on the interpretation of laws by Federal and state courts and has a broader and fuller index than the unannotated code. The *Code of Federal Regulations* codifies documents of general applicability which have been earlier published in the *Federal Register*. The *Register* itself is published daily with annual and monthly indexes. It contains all presidential proclamations, executive orders, and rules and regulations of all departments and bureaus of the Federal Government.

Among other helpful sources are the *Weekly Compilation of Presidential Documents*, the *Official Congressional Directory* published for each session of Congress, and the *United States Government Organization Manual* published annually. The last two are especially valuable for biographical information and information about the organization, activities, and current officials of Federal departments, bureaus, offices, councils, and commissions.

Since much of the research on the environment is of a scientific or technical nature, several information services are worth noting. The Clearinghouse for Federal Scientific and Technical Information sells published reports of federally sponsored research and development efforts. Its own publications include the *Government-Wide Index to Federal Research and Development Reports*, a monthly listing of reports announced in other journals of the National Bureau of Standards, the Defense Department, NASA, and the AEC; *U.S. Government Research and Development Reports*, a bibliography of documents available from the Clearinghouse; and *Technical Translations*, a bi-monthly index of translations of foreign reports. The National Referral Center for Science and Technology answers, without charge, requests for information on where to find material on a specific topic in any of the sciences or related technical areas. The Smithsonian Institution's Science Information Exchange can tell the researcher about unpublished research in his field that is planned or under way.

At the level of state government, the *Book of the States* is published biennially and contains information on state activities giving current officers, statutes passed, and other data on recent state government actions. The *Monthly Checklist of State Publications* put out by the Library of Congress attempts to index all publications of state agencies from 1910 to the present. *The United Nations Documents Index*, 1950 to the present, offers a complete listing of United Nations publications. More useful is the *Checklist of United Nations Documents*, 1949 to the present, which has a very detailed subject index. The most recent summary of United Nations activities and programs relevant to the human environment appears in United Nations Economic and Social Council, *Problems of the Human Environment*, Report of the Secretary-General (E/4667, 26 May, 1969, 66 pp.).

Basic Books

Within the last few years a number of collections of papers on environmental problems have been published. All of these volumes contain papers on policy questions and questions of government organization. *Future Environments of North America* (Garden City, N.Y.: Natural History Press,

1966), edited by F. Fraser Darling and John P. Milton, is based on the record of a conference convened by the Conservation Foundation in April, 1965. Henry Jarrett, ed., *Environmental Quality in a Growing Economy* (Baltimore, Md.: Johns Hopkins Press, 1966) presents essays from the 1966 Forum of Resources for the Future. Between 1961 and 1965 a series of papers were presented to a faculty seminar at the University of California at Berkeley as a means of circumventing the old barriers between traditional disciplines contributing to understanding of the environment and man's relationships thereto. The papers are published in S. V. Ciriacy-Wantrup and James J. Parsons, eds., *Natural Resources: Quality and Quantity* (Berkeley: University of California Press, 1967). Papers commissioned for the American Institute of Planners' Fiftieth Year Consultation formed the basis for three volumes, all edited by William R. Ewald, Jr., and published by Indiana University Press, Bloomington: *Environment for Man: The Next Fifty Years* (1967), *Environment and Change: The Next Fifty Years* (1968), and *Environment and Policy: The Next Fifty Years* (1968).

Among the leading textbooks in conservation and resource management are Shirley W. Allen and Justin W. Leonard, *Conserving Natural Resources: Principles and Practices in a Democracy* (3d ed.; New York: McGraw-Hill, 1966), Guy-Harold Smith, ed., *Conservation of Natural Resources* (3d ed.; New York: John Wiley and Sons, 1965), and Richard Highsmith *et al.*, *Conservation in the United States* (Chicago: Rand McNally, 1962). Raymond F. Dasmann, *Environmental Conservation* (2nd ed.; New York: John Wiley and Sons, 1968) shows an ecological perspective that represents an improvement over these other books, all of which discuss current environmental problems and policies and have useful bibliographies.

Particular viewpoints on environmental policy have appeared from time to time. Especially valuable as the account of a leading policy maker are Stewart L. Udall's *The Quiet Crisis* (New York: Holt, Rinehart and Winston, 1963) and *1976: Agenda for Tomorrow* (New York: Harcourt, Brace and World, 1968). Udall was Secretary of the Interior under presidents Kennedy and Johnson. *The Quiet Crisis* is available in a paperback edition. A professor of law, Earl Finbar Murphy, offers an interesting view of renewable resource regulation as the duty and not merely the ambition of man in *Governing Nature* (Chicago: Quadrangle Books, 1967). Frank E. Smith, a former congressman and director of the Tennessee Valley Authority, has provided a useful history of conservation policies from the early national period to the 1960's in *The Politics of Conservation* (New York: Pantheon Books, 1966). Gene Marine approaches environmental policy from the point of view of the muckraking journalist in *America the Raped* (New York: Simon and Schuster, 1969). A thoughtful set of papers by a group of political scientists can be found in Lynton K. Caldwell, ed., *Environmental Studies: Papers on the Politics and Public Administration of Man-Environment Relationships* (4 vols.; Bloomington, Ind.: Institute of Public Administration, Indiana University, 1967).

Although they are not books, several congressional documents deserve special mention as basic sources concerning recent debate on a national policy for the environment. Three reports issued as committee prints delineate alternative approaches to Federal involvement in environmental policy: U.S., Congress, House, Committee on Science and Astronautics, *Managing the Environment* (June, 1968); U.S., Congress, Senate, Committee on Interior and Insular Affairs, *A National Policy for the Environment* (July, 1968); and U.S., Congress, Senate Committee on Interior and Insular Affairs and House Committee on Science and Astronautics, *Congressional White Paper on a National Policy for the Environment* (October, 1968). Another Senate Interior and Insular Affairs Committee report outlines and discusses a bill to establish a national environmental policy: *National Environmental Policy Act of 1969* (Report No. 91–296, 91st Cong., 1st sess., July, 1969). Two particularly valuable hearings are U.S., Congress, Senate Committee on Interior and Insular Affairs and House Committee on Science and Astronautics, *Hearing, Joint House-Senate Colloquium to Discuss a National Policy for the Environment* (90th Cong., 2d sess., July, 1968); and U.S., Congress, Senate, Interior and Insular Affairs Committee, *Hearing, National Environmental Policy* (91st Cong., 1st sess., April, 1969).

There are a number of books on the organization of Congress, although none of them pay special attention to congressional handling of environmental issues. Drew Pearson and Jack Anderson have written a self-styled compelling indictment of corruption on Capitol Hill in *The Case Against Congress* (New York: Simon and Schuster, 1968). A critical inside view is provided by Joseph S. Clark, a former senator, in *Congress: The Sapless Branch* (rev. ed.; New York: Harper and Row, 1965). More detached commentary is available in Ralph K. Huitt and Robert L. Peabody, *Congress: Two Decades of Analysis* (New York: Harper and Row, 1969); Randall B. Ripley, *Majority Party Leadership in Congress* (Boston: Little, Brown and Company, 1969), and *Power in the Senate* (New York: St. Martin's Press, 1969); and Stephen K. Bailey's excellent case study *Congress Makes a Law* (New York: Random House, 1950).

Bibliographies

One of the most valuable bibliographies on environmental policy issues is in Lynton K. Caldwell and William B. De Ville, *Science, Technology, and Public Policy: A Syllabus for Advanced Study* (2 vols.; Bloomington, Ind.: Department of Government, Indiana University, 1968), a publication prepared with assistance from the National Science Foundation. Volume II of this work is especially valuable. The *Science Policy Bulletin* published bimonthly by the Battelle Memorial Institute contains bibliographic listings of current literature in the form of abstracts presented under a number of topical headings.

Several excellent bibliographies are available in books and government reports. Of the works already listed in this bibliography, *The Quiet Crisis* and *1976: Agenda for Tomorrow* by Stewart Udall have brief but critical bibliographies, as do *Governing Nature* by Earl Finbar Murphy and the

Senate Interior Committee report *A National Policy for the Environment.* The bibliography in Robert Arvill's *Man and Environment: Crisis and the Strategy of Choice* (Harmondsworth: Penguin Books, 1967) introduces the reader to a number of basic European references, and the book itself is well worth reading. Historical perspective on the conservation movement is emphasized in Roderick Nash, ed., *The American Environment: Readings in the History of Conservation* (Reading, Mass.: Addison-Wesley Publishing Company, 1968), and this book contains one of the most valuable bibliographies in print. Roderick Nash's earlier work *Wilderness and the American Mind* (New Haven, Conn.: Yale University Press, 1967) should be required background reading for any student of environmental policy.

The 1968 report of the President's Council on Recreation and Natural Beauty combines a listing of bibliographic sources with a listing of the Federal, state, local, and private agencies to which the citizen interested in working to save the American environment can turn for help. The report is entitled *From Sea to Shining Sea: A Report on the American Environment— Our Natural Heritage* (Washington, D.C.: Government Printing Office, 1968).

Journals and Other Sources

The established academic journals have been reluctant to publish articles dealing with environmental problems. Thus, most of the periodical literature is to be found in journals devoted to the discussion of these problems. The following are among the most helpful: *Biological Conservation, Bulletin of the Atomic Scientists, Ekistics, Journal of the American Institute of Planners, Landscape, Journal of Environmental Education, Landscape Architecture,* and *Science.* From time to time other journals publish special issues on the environment. Three recent and valuable contributions here are "America's Changing Environment" in *Daedalus,* Vol. XCVI (Fall, 1967), "Man's Response to the Physical Environment" in *Journal of Social Issues,* Vol. XXII (October, 1966), and "Environmental Policy: New Directions in Federal Action" in *Public Administration Review,* Vol. XXVIII (July/August, 1968). Comprehensive guides to periodical literature are the *Reader's Guide to Periodical Literature* and the *International Index to Periodicals.*

Sometimes it is helpful to turn to newspapers for certain lines of research. For current issues they can be very useful on questions of the day: events, policies, opinions, politics, and personalities. Back numbers can also serve the same purpose for the contemporary history of earlier periods and often contain details that are not found in books and periodicals. The most valuable newspaper is the *New York Times* because it is indexed. References are available for the date, page, and column of all articles printed in the paper since 1913. The brief synopsis of articles on a particular subject found in the index will often answer many questions without the necessity of actually referring to the paper. Among other newspapers, the *Christian Science Monitor* has the best and most reliable environmental reporting.

Many private associations publish magazines or bulletins which supply both information and opinion. The *Conservation Report* is published weekly by the National Wildlife Federation while Congress is in session. It summarizes all the environmental and resources legislation being considered by Congress and keeps a score sheet of action taken on major bills. The Federation also publishes *Conservation News*, a series of background statements and editorial opinions on current issues. The Wildlife Management Institute issues a bi-weekly *Outdoor News Bulletin* stating the institute's position on conservation issues and reporting on new developments. The Conservation Foundation publishes a monthly report on environmental issues, the *CF Letter*, which focuses on one problem each month. Some publications, such as the *Sierra Club Bulletin*, are available only to organization members.

Research Note

The sources listed above represent some of the more important tools available to the student of environmental policy. Most problems of environmental policy defy the traditional divisions of labor within the American university, which organizes knowledge into a series of subject matter areas concerned with segments of the physical, biological, and social sciences and the humanities. Environmental problems are so complex that all of these areas of investigation must be utilized in order to provide for an adequate consideration of all the variables involved. If the scholar is to provide critical analyses of contemporary environmental problems and their meanings, he must be prepared to accept the redefinition of his role and conceptual approach posed by the requirements of his problems. How to train such scholars, how to involve the various academic disciplines and professional practitioners in a more productive cross-fertilization of ideas, and at the same time facilitate the mutual criticism so necessary to the logic of scientific inquiry, poses vital and challenging questions for the modern university. Unfortunately, not much attention has been given to this problem. There are, however, a few sources that can be cited: Vincent Ostrom, "The Social Scientist and the Control and Development of Natural Resources," in *Land Economics*, May, 1953, pp. 105–16; Joseph Fisher, "Resource Policies and Administration for the Future," *Public Administration Review*, Spring, 1961, pp. 74–80; Phillip O. Foss, ed., *Education in Natural Resources* (proceedings and related papers from a seminar at Colorado State University, 1963–64, 98 pp.); A. J. W. Scheffey, ed., *Resources, the Metropolis and the Land Grant University* (proceedings of the Conference on Natural Resources, University of Massachusetts, 1963, 45 pp.); Irving K. Fox, "Natural Resources: The Outlook and Some Implications for Research and Education" (speech presented at the School of Natural Resources, University of Michigan, January, 1965, 19 pp.); and Richard A. Cooley, "Graduate Education and Research in Natural Resources Public Policy" (report prepared for the Graduate School of Public Affairs, University of Washington, August, 1966, 81 pp.). Perhaps the single important conceptual contribution in the 1960's, however, has been made by the political scientist, Lynton K. Caldwell. Among the most important of his extensive writings on this subject which have not been mentioned elsewhere in this volume are: "Environment: A New Focus for Public Policy," *Public Administration Review*, September, 1963, pp. 132–39; "The Human Environment," *Journal of Higher Education*, March, 1966, pp. 149–55; "Problems of Applied Ecology: Perceptions, Institutions, Methods and Operational Tools," *BioScience*, August, 1966, pp. 524–27; "Public Policies and Environmental Values—Toward a Sounder Basis for Decisions," *IUCN Bulletin*—International Union for Conservation of Nature and Natural Resources, April–June, 1964; "Centers of Excellence for the Study of Human Ecology," in *Proceedings of Symposium on Human Ecology*, U.S. Department of Health, Education, and Welfare, 1968, pp. 56–66. Important works on this subject by the geographer, Gilbert White, and the economist, Kenneth Boulding, are fully referenced in the published bibliographies already mentioned. Of special significance is Boulding's already-mentioned "Economics of the Coming Spaceship Earth," in *Environmental Quality in a Growing Economy*.

A forthright statement of the need for much greater emphasis on policy-oriented research in a world of contingencies is contained in an excellent report by the Brookings Institution entitled *The Study of Public Problems*, published in 1961. The report makes a clear and very important distinction between government-sponsored research (i.e., the various intelligence, staff, advisory, and program planning activities normally performed for the policy maker) and research by the independent scholar.

Index

A & C Auto Wrecking, 156
Ad Hoc Committee on the Environment, 236–37
Aeronautical Research Institute of Sweden, 184
Aerospace Industries Association, 186
Agriculture, Department of: bureau of forestry created in, 6; wild rivers study of, 164–65
Aircraft noise: congressional investigation of, 179
Aircraft Noise Abatement Act: background to, 176–77; provisions of, 177–78; opposing interests, 178; issues during debate on, 179–85; evaluation of, 185
Air Line Pilots Association, 180
Airport Operators Council, 180
Air Transport Association, 180
Allott, Gordon (Senator), 57
American Association for the Advancement of Science: 1968 annual meeting, xi; Committee on Environmental Problems, xi; statement on environmental problems, xii; memorials of 1873 and 1890, 6
American Association of State Highway Officials, 38
American Farm Bureau Federation, 103
American Forestry Association, 89
American Institute of Architects, 156
American Legion, 198
American Mining Congress, 56
American Motor Hotel Association, 39
American Pulp and Paper Association, 135, 137

American Road Builders Association, 39, 46
American Speech and Hearing Association, 183
Anderson, Clinton P. (Senator), 55, 89
Anderson, Jack, 227
Anthrop, Donald F., 185
Arnold, Matthew, 244
Arthur D. Little, Inc., 84
Aspinall, Wayne H. (Representative): and Indiana Dunes bill, 21; and wilderness bill, 54–55, 58; comments on North Cascades hearing, 78; and redwood park, 90; on free land and recreation, 110; influence on water project recreation bill, 120; on implementation of Water Project Recreation Act, 123; position on wild and scenic rivers, 172–73; role in environmental policy formation, 232; mentioned, 78, 98, 108, 165
Associated General Contractors of America, Inc., 39
Association of American Railroads, 121

Bailey, Stephen K., 209
Bayh, Birch (Senator), 21
Benefit-cost analysis, 117–18
Bentham, Jeremy, 7
Beranek, Leo L., 187
Bethlehem Steel Company: and leveling of Indiana Dunes, 20; mentioned, 19, 25, 28
Blatnik, John (Representative), 132, 139, 140
Blaustein, Arthur, 233